The Medicine Garden

By Rachel Corby

The Good Life Press LTD

Published by The Good Life Press Ltd., 2009

ISBN 978 1 90487 1583
A catalogue record for this book is available from the British Library.

Published by
The Good Life Press Ltd.
PO Box 536
Preston
PR2 9ZY

www.goodlifepress.co.uk
www.homefarmer.co.uk

Set by The Good Life Press Ltd.
Colour photography by Stephen Studd
www.stephenstuddphotography.com
Cover designed by Rachel Gledhill
Printed and bound in Great Britain
by Cromwell Press Group

Acknowledgements

I am eternally grateful to everyone who has helped me along my path, but I would especially like to thank those who have made this book possible. With deep gratitude I would like to thank my parents for bringing me safely into the world, Maddy Harland for publishing my first article in Permaculture Magazine, Ruth Tott of the Good Life Press for believing in me and providing this opportunity, Stephen Studd for his beautiful and inspirational photography, Emma Morgan and Andrew Calvert for unlimited access to their library, Stephen Harrod Buhner, Trishuwa and Julie McIntyre for the love and encouragement that created a safe space for me to grow down into my shoes and finally my nine fellow apprentices for supporting me and witnessing that change.

Disclaimer

This book is sold for information purposes only; it is not intended to diagnose any condition. It is essential to always get a professional diagnosis for any ongoing symptoms. If you are currently on medication always check with a naturally oriented healthcare professional before using plant medicines. They will be able to advise you on any possible interactions between perscribed medicines and plant medicines and any potential side effects of taking them alongside each other. Read the 'Cautions and Contraindications' for each plant before choosing to use them and exercise special caution if you are pregnant or breast feeding. If you experience any adverse reactions to a plant medicine you are using, cease use immediately and seek professional advice.

Contents

Acknowledgements - P3
Disclaimer - P3
Prologue - P5
Introduction - P7
Wild Food as Medicine - P10
Guidelines for Collecting Plants as Medicine - P13
Preparations, Dosages & Equipment List - P15

PART 1 : Close to Home
Back Doorstep – Culinary Herbs - P23
Lawn - P42
Flower Borders - P49
Veggie Garden / Allotment - P83
Borders of Property - P115
Hedgerows. - P131

PART 2 : The Far Side of the Hedgerow
In the Woods - P147
By the River - P154
Meadow - P161
Moorlands - P167
By the Coast - P170

Appendix I: Exercises to Aid in Befriending the Plant People - P175
Appendix II: Common Ailments Quick Remedy Finder - P176
Appendix III: Resources & Suppliers - P182
Glossary - P184
Bibliography - P186

Prologue

Walking in the forest, the dry brush crunching, snapping and yet comfortingly cushioning underfoot with every small advance. The smells, dry, warm and somehow smoky, dance across my senses like a brush with the softest velvet. Despite the coldness in the air the sunlight filtering through the upper canopy feels warm upon my skin. I smile inwardly, recognising a deep sense of belonging, a connection to those that have walked this way before. A little apprehensive of the task ahead I stalk my quarry. I know I am near, I can sense it. A little shiver of excitement runs down my spine as there it is before me, a strong presence in the wooded glade. As I approach there is an automatic pause and deep inhalation as the respect for my older brother fills and flows through me. I sink to my knees to pray. I sit for some moments awed by the wisdom of the beauty before me. A dapple of sunlight kisses my face and awakens me from my deep reverie; permission has been granted, it is time. I rise to my feet and gracefully, gratefully proceed from tree to tree, slowly collecting offered pieces of older brothers body. My basket now full I turn to face the glade one last time and, with a final deep inhalation, say my farewells. The journey back through the woods to the yurt seems to melt before me.

Now home in my kitchen I begin converting my forest friend into a tincture. Carefully weighing, crushing, mixing, stirring and then the waiting. Every day for three long weeks I lovingly hold the jar and gently shake it, the alchemy magically occurring inside the brown glass walls. Eventually the long awaited day dawns; I unscrew the cap and, like a genie, the presence of my wise green friend once again envelopes me. The aroma, like sparkling flecks of dust in the sunlight, twists and curls upwards filling my nostrils with strong vapours of the forest. I taste just one drop and feel the ambrosia cell by cell, like dominoes flowing through my body to the furthest extremities. It tastes deep, dark and earthy: now I have medicine. I squeeze the plant debris through muslin and pour the precious liquid into my eagerly awaiting dropper bottles. My woodland friend with me in the extract made from his flesh and spirit, dormant now, waiting for me to call upon his medicine in the swiftly approaching short, dark days of winter...

Dedicated with love, respect and gratitude to my dear friends and companions, the plants.

Introduction

This book is the product of my love affair with the natural world, which has been deepening, twisting and turning, this way and that throughout my life. Through my studies and experiences of recent years I have come to recognise that all the plants around me have a medicinal value. This book is intended as a guide to help you find your way around your local environment radiating out from your back door through your garden, along local lanes right out into the raw nature of your nearest coastline or mountain top. I encourage you to collect and forage for plants and then make medicines from them. It is enjoyable and satisfying and can involve the whole family. In fact I have found that children are delighted and intrigued by the whole process, perhaps because they are closer to the earth, to their beginnings, and can still see faeries without even trying. This is by no means an exhaustive list of the plants you will find, or their uses. It does, however, provide a useful starting point.

I am not a medicinal herbalist. I came to my knowledge of plants and their medicinal properties through following a number of golden threads which wove their way through my life and led me to this magical place. One of my early inspirations came from living in northern Guatemala in 1998, working on a project to help protect the forest. I realised the people who lived in this environment had a vast reservoir of knowledge about what each individual species was and what it could be used for. Subsequently my depth of respect and understanding of the plant world expanded and deepened. My thirst for experiencing this connection with the natural world took me around the planet, learning to use plants and their properties in a remedial sense, to heal the earth, where damage, caused by the unconscious actions of humans, had been particularly extensive. On settling back in England, I spent several years working in a herb nursery, surrounded by fragrant and health giving plants, where my interest in herbal medicines for people grew. I have spent many years studying plant medicine with a diverse range of teachers. I have learned the more scientific and practical aspects from herbalists, the spiritual and less tangible aspects from shamans and medicine men. My studies have included everything from courses in my local village and weeks living with different tribes in Africa, to a full 9 month apprenticeship in the wilds of New Mexico. Eventually, through my studies, I have reached a deeper level. I have found a true sense of belonging, where I meet with the spirits of plants and place. In all the different settings, with all the different teachers again and again, the plants so generously have offered their gifts and encouraged me to use them in a healing setting.

We have reached a critical moment in the history of human habitation on our sweet Mother Earth. We are surrounded by degraded ecosystems, polluted air & water, sick & desperately unhappy people. The paradigm within which we have evolved and exist in the west is crumbling: there are new economic, environmental and social crises reported almost daily. The realisation is growing amongst the population that despite amazing advances of modern western medicine the overall health of western nations is declining. It is time to change. It is the individual responsibility of each of us to take our own health and that of our environment into our own hands. There is so much we can do individually to re-empower ourselves, to reconnect with the wildness of the world, to hear the cries of the Earth and each, in our own modest way, to respond. The time for action is now and these pages are my response to that call. In times past, through necessity, our ancestors looked to the nature around them for their food and medicine, and often the two would overlap. Modern advances in agriculture and pharmaceutical developments have shifted the emphasis to one of wholly relying on someone else for our nutrition and healthcare. Of course there have been great improvements in our general living conditions and mortality rate as a result, but for me I believe it has gone a little too far, with a little too much reliance on someone else's knowledge. Learning how to take care of minor injuries, infections and ongoing symptoms at home with what grows in one's immediate vicinity is incredibly liberating and empowering. Incorporating plants into your diet and medicine cabinets will help fortify your entire system, keeping you from your doctor's door, creating space in the doctors surgery for the most serious cases. Incorporating wild plants into your diet and using plant medicines is as much about living a life of abundant health and illness prevention as it is about clearing symptoms once they arrive.

It is well known in folk medicine circles that a plant collected locally is 100 times stronger than one that is not. In addition it is said that a plant collected by yourself locally holds 1000 times the potency of any 'standardised' herbal medicine you can buy in a shop. Just try drinking a herbal tea brewed from a tea bag purchased from a shop. Then drink again, this time with a fresh sprig you collected yourself just moments before. You will need no further convincing. One more reason to collect and use local is the pollution factor. It's not just the carbon footprint of importing non-local products but their chemical impact when they are excreted or composted as waste. Many modern medicines have their origins in the plant world. Take Aspirin, for example; the active ingredient salicylic acid is derived from salicin, found in many plants and originally isolated from willow. Despite its natural origins there is a developing problem related to its incredibly widescale use. When it passes through the human body it is excreted into the waste water system and, despite treatment, some of the chemical residue stays in the water and cycles around again and again exposing the waterways and wider environment to this heavy chemical load. Within its natural setting salicin enhances the growth of plants in small quantities. However, when it is being excreted by so many humans in large quantities, especially concentrated around areas of high human population, it has an adverse effect on the local flora, actually inhibiting growth. The function of this in the wild is to prevent other plants from growing too close, allowing for the salicin producing plant to grow unencumbered by crowding from other vigorously growing species. Within a balanced ecosystem this is useful, but with such huge quantities being released into the environment it becomes out of control with grave potential ramifications. This is an over simplification as the effect of chemistry on plant germination and growth is incredibly complex, but is worth considering when choosing how to treat minor ailments. It is also perhaps surprising to learn that using seemingly innocuous plant remedies such as echinacea can also negatively impact the environment when used to excess in an area where they would not grow naturally. Using a natural plant medicine that grows in the locale will have much less impact. To maintain the balance within an ecosystem it is best to use compost and excrete only what already grows there as the micro-chemistry is set up to deal with it. An excess of anything literally dumped or off-loaded into the environment will act as a pollutant. So, if you can reduce your use of industrially manufactured pharmaceuticals and exotic herbal remedies, even by a small amount, through collecting, growing and using your own home remedies, you'll be doing all the inhabitants of this planet a favour, yourself included. Stephen Harrod Buhner has done a huge amount of research on the effects of pharmaceuticals in the environment. If you are interested in reading more I highly recommend reading his book 'The Lost Language of Plants.'

There are so many plants with medicinal value, some with whom I have built a wonderful relationship using them regularly from my kitchen pharmacy. However, on closer inspection, whilst researching for this book I have found some to be of a restricted nature in certain countries or earmarked as only to be used by qualified practitioners. It is for reasons of safety that certain plants have been classified in this way. Some plants contain incredibly strong medicine that, if taken in the wrong way or in the wrong doses, can be highly toxic and even fatal. It is a reminder that not all are suitable for home use: their medicine is just too strong for the inexperienced to experiment with safely.

The plants listed are categorised according to where they would be found in my garden and in the wild, but obviously we all have different microclimates, tastes and of course ideas. So perhaps you will find something in the veggie garden section of the book, for example nasturtium, where you may have it trailing from planters on your back doorstep or over the front of flower beds merging seamlessly with the green expanse of lawn. When it comes to the placing of plants there are no rules, just suggestions, and of course the individual preferences of the plants themselves.

You may want to consider adding some of the plants listed to your cultivated garden as our wild places are becoming fewer and fewer and more and more polluted as they are squeezed into narrow strips alongside roads or beside foot paths favoured by dog walkers. Always consider where plants grow naturally and choose the ones most suitable for your own unique conditions rather than simply dreaming up a wish list. Observe how plants grow in nature and which plants tend to grow alongside others. You will notice certain plants have affinities with certain others almost like families. The other consideration is that of organic gardening as many of our modern diseases and conditions may be so prolific because of the noxious cocktail of chemicals that enters our daily lives. Part of plant medicine is trusting and allowing your chosen plants to grow well and strong amongst the competition nature throws at them. With a bit of guidance through weeding and watering you can nurture your lovingly grown seedlings without the use of chemicals and they will be stronger medicines for it.

The ideas and recipes in this book are safe for a beginner to use at home, however, consuming too much of any plant will transform it from a medicine to a poison, so be gentle with yourself and your immersion into the world of plant medicines. Equally never self-diagnose. If you are suffering from an illness always get a professional diagnosis. Check with a professional before using plant medicines if you are pregnant, breast feeding, on any medication or suffering an acute, chronic or degenerative illness.

It is my hope that you enjoy this book and that you do your own research, and not just online or in books. Take it a step further to a deeper level as you integrate with other inhabitants of this wonderful planet (see Appendix 1). Feel the subtle shift as you begin to perceive the personalities of what you previously viewed simply as 'weeds.' I wish you fun, delight and great health as you embark on your journey into the wisdom of the ancients.

Wild Food as Medicine

"Let food be thy medicine and medicine be thy food"

Hippocrates

A single herb or plant alone cannot heal the body. It will, however, feed and nourish the body with what it needs, providing support while the body heals itself. All green leafy plants contain chlorophyll which builds the structure of the body. Fruits and sweet foods provide the body with fuel as, being full of glucose, they are energy rich. Whilst fats such as nuts provide lubrication, feeding the skin and oiling the joints. Good nutrition provides the basis for a well balanced healthy body that works efficiently, easily digesting food and fending off infections, whilst having the resources to heal injuries swiftly. A healthy body helps the development and maintenance of a positive mental attitude and a healthy emotional balance. Diet also affects the balance of friendly bacteria within the body, supplying the immune system with the nutrients it needs. It is generally accepted that a lack of nutrients contributes to disease, and that there is a link between diet and disease resistance.

So what is a healthy diet? The majority of the world's population are in fact malnourished, deriving the bulk of their nutrition from only 13 different types of plant: bananas, beans, beets (beet-derived sugar), cassava, coconut, corn, oranges, potatoes, rice, soy beans, sugar cane, sweet potato and wheat (Wolfe, 1999). Maybe it seems like a good variety of foods, but not when you consider that our ancestors, along with current day hunter gatherer societies, regularly eat from a range of between 100-300 different varieties of plants in a single year (Engel, 2002). This amazing statistic becomes more shocking when you realise that the majority of the 'hot 13' are heavily hybridized, which means that to make them more tasty or commercially viable they have been selectively bred to encourage certain characteristics, often at the loss of their seed. Hybrid seeds most often do not grow true to the parent, and some of these plants would die out in one generation if it were not for human intervention. It could be equated to the human race being unable to successfully reproduce without the help of fertility programmes and surely that is not the sign of a healthy, nutritious food.

The limited diversity on most peoples plates is compounded by the ongoing experiments into food processing, which have resulted in the addition of large numbers of chemicals for the purposes of lengthening shelf life and enhancing flavour amongst others. Although these chemicals and their effects are individually tested, the immense cocktail to which we are currently subjected remains effectively untestable. In our own history salt and herbs were used for these purposes, which brought different nutrients into our diets rather than chemicals that do not benefit the functioning of the human body, but instead act as toxins that the liver then needs to process and remove.

So perhaps one of the first things to consider when choosing to make one's diet more healthy would be to include a much greater variety of plants, preferably ones that have not been heavily hybridized but have survived in the wild for millenia, despite the actions of humankind. How is this done? It is actually very simple. Start looking at the wild plants, the weeds, ones that are so strong and determined to grow that they will even find a home in the crack of a paving slab. These locally derived 'weeds,' or wild greens, are full of minerals and through their consumption you will already be helping your body build its defences. These wild greens, almost without exception, contain a higher level of vitamins and nutrients than the widely available lettuces that have been selectively bred and tend to fill the shelves of the supermarkets. Incorporating, for example, nettle into the diet from when the first spring leaves start to appear in March until they become rough, grainy and unpalatable in June, in whichever form you choose, be it juice, smoothie, pesto, or infusion, will build and fortify your system, guarding against the development of, for example, hay fever symptoms. Plants like this work both ways and adding them regularly to your diet, even in small amounts, will help prevent symptoms forming. Generous as they are, if we fail to do this we can then use them as medicines instead, when symptoms do begin to appear. The only difference being that at the later point one would need a much more concentrated dose to get the establishing symptoms to shift. This example works across the board and habitually adding a little bit of all the different wild greens and herbs in their many and varied forms into your diet will prevent and lessen many nagging daily aches pains and symptoms. It's not just about waiting to get sick and being armed to deal with it, but making your body as fit and strong as possible by consuming such a wide variety of nutrients and minerals that you have the strength to stop infections and ongoing conditions in their tracks before they become a debilitating issue that needs treatment.

Raw greens are also an excellent source of fibre, and so will help clear out the intestines as they move through, providing an effective natural remedy for a constipated or sluggish bowel. The high levels of nutrients in greens help build our blood and detoxify our livers, which considering the daily bombardment of chemical pollutants modern living exposes us to, is becoming increasingly essential, even for our children. Also consider that a huge dairy cow has grown to be that size and to produce countless pints of milk from a diet of grass, and most dairy herds graze on pasture that contains only 3 species of grass. Interestingly though, both cows and sheep have been observed self-medicating with hedgerow plants if they are found growing around their pasture. These animals, despite being domesticated, still have relatively intact instincts, prompting them to vary their diet and add different leaves at certain times. For us perhaps these natural instincts have faded as our lives have become more and more urbanized and mechanised, but it is still there, somewhere deep inside but dormant. You just have to gently awaken this part of yourself and as you introduce more herbs and wild greens into your diet you will acquire a taste for them and you will soon find yourself looking forward to the taste of wild garlic or dandelion, actually preferring them to the blandness of domesticated lettuce. Wild foods seem to feed something inside that the body understands and rejoices in.

Another way to enrich your diet is to grow your own fruit and vegetables. This way you can choose a much wider variety than you would normally see at the grocer's. You can also choose to use heritage seeds (see resources). These are older seed varieties closer to their wild relatives and much less hybridized. I have introduced a few friends and family to the flavour sensations that grow from heritage seeds and most people are impressed. Equally, growing your own means that you can grow organically. Studies have repeatedly shown that organic produce contains 2-10 times the mineral content of conventionally grown crops (Wolfe, 1999). Eating the same quantity and receiving up to 10 times the nutrients sounds good to me. I'm sure that a large amount of over eating is due to the body asking for more food because it is lacking nutrients. Although I feel less full after a meal of wild greens than a big pasta dish, I feel more satisfied and am less likely to snack later.

Plants often have their most powerful effect when added as a raw ingredient. It is important to remember this and so make a habit of using fresh herbs regularly and generously in your cuisine. A powerful example of the importance of greens and other vegetables relates to the blood. Naturally healthy blood sits at a pH of around 7.4 which is slightly alkaline. The development of both arthritis and osteoporosis have been associated with high blood acidity. Once the blood has become acidic it loses its normal efficient function and minerals that are normally suspended and carried within the blood precipitate out and accumulate in muscle tissue, joints and bones. Accumulation of minerals in these places can, in time, cause arthritis, a condition which will continue to be exacerbated by diet. The acidic blood, in an attempt to regain its naturally alkaline condition, will tend to leach alkaline minerals from the bones which in time will damage the integrity of the bones and can lead to osteoporosis. One way to avoid the development of these conditions is to have a high alkaline content in your diet. Meats, dairy and cooked foods all contribute to an acidic condition whereas fresh raw leafy greens are an easily accessible and incredibly rich source of alkaline minerals such as calcium. So whatever you choose to eat, having a side salad full of different deep rich greens will help balance the pH of your meal. Consuming quantities of raw, deep greens habitually will help to protect you from these conditions. However, once either of these conditions has developed, you will need to adopt more drastic dietary measures in an attempt to control, halt the progression or hopefully even reverse it. In the case of arthritis this would involve cutting out the majority (or preferably all) of the meat and cooked foods (with an emphasis on the nightshade family which includes tomatoes, potatoes and peppers) from your diet (Wolfe, 1999). Complementing these changes by adding herbs and vegetables that help flush the deposits from your body will be of great benefit and should bring much relief. An example of eating to prevent illness or reduce symptoms is to simply eat carrot and celery regularly to avoid the development of angina or hypertension. A quick way to find which foods are beneficial for which conditions is to flick through appendix II, the quick remedy finder for common ailments and see which foods are listed alongside each ailment.

Often colds, flu and fever are side effects of the body trying to cleanse itself from a toxic overload. Once you have introduced lots of healthy plant foods into the diet you will experience less and less of these bouts of illness as your body will be cleaner, stronger and more able to fight off minor infections and viruses. Toxemia is the underlying cause of most chronic disease, and is most certainly a contributory factor. Toxemia is the build up of waste and mucous within the body and its organ systems. Taking chemicals to combat minor illness is in some senses just a further burdening of the body's already over stressed systems with yet more chemical waste that needs to be excreted in one way or another. One reason why so many people suffer with skin problems is because the skin is the body's largest organ and is sometimes the organ of choice for toxin excretion. The mucous build up and sneezing that sometimes accompany allergies can also be signs of a heavily toxic body. Mental health is also greatly affected by diet and this is becoming a huge concern as more and more people seek help for their state of mind, most often concluding in at least a short course of psychoactive drugs. According to the World Health Organisation depression is the single most common cause of disability in the world. It is my personal belief that lack of connection to the natural world and poor diet alone will account for the majority of cases. Lack of connection makes you lose your sense of purpose, of belonging, of being part of something. Watching the changes through the seasons, being out there checking when the flowers are blooming and the trees fruiting helps reestablish that connection. Making medicines, taking back a small amount of responsibility for your health, helps you reclaim some of your sense of purpose. Highly alkaline foods (fresh and raw wild greens and other vegetables) have a calming effect on the body, helping to alleviate stress and anxiety in a natural way. A healthy diet creates a healthy body which in turn creates a healthy mind, and all are intrinsically connected. There is a movement to genetically engineer foods to contain more nutrients. This is totally unnecessary. We just need to incorporate a wide variety of organic, non-hybridized fruits, vegetables and herbs habitually. Adjust your diet, include plants that you can use as remedies for your usual ailments on a regular basis and don't wait for your symptoms to arrive. If you achieve this you will find yourself getting sick less and less frequently. Try eating wild greens; you'll be amazed at what you can fill your belly with for free, whilst benefiting from high mineral content and medicinal properties. Fresh foods eaten straight from the earth or a tree are full of vibrancy, of life force and you can literally feel it flowing through your body, imparting energy and health. The only danger is that you will enjoy it so much that you may never again enjoy eating out of season supermarket foods that have flown half the way around the planet to land on your plate, and you know what? I don't think that is such a bad thing.

GUIDELINES FOR COLLECTING PLANTS AS MEDICINE

To ensure the successful continuation of species and the collection of non-contaminated specimens it is important to adhere to this short list of recommendations.

Firstly it is important to note that within the UK collecting any plant material will be subject to the Wildlife & Countryside Act (1981) which makes it an offence to pick, uproot or trade in any species listed in schedule 8. This is a detailed list which includes 7629 individual plant taxa covering everything from flowering vascular plants to lichens and algae. It can be found at www.jncc.gov.uk and checking before collecting will give you assurance that you are not adding to the endangerment of any particular species. Collecting roots of any species, even from public land, is a delicate matter and it is best to try and obtain permission first. Even when taking a tiny amount you must always replace the soil and leave the place as you found it, if possible planting a few seeds from that plant in its place. It is illegal to collect any plant or plant parts from private land without first gaining permission from the landowner.

On a practical level it is important to consider the following:

1   Always be sure to correctly identify the plant you are collecting. Take a well illustrated field guide and don't collect if you are uncertain.

2   Never take more than 10% of what is there, always leaving the oldest or 'grandfather' plant intact. If you are on a slope, collect from the bottom up so

that maturing seeds will continue to fall down the slope, efficiently repopulating the area you have just harvested. It is important to always leave the majority of the plants behind for wildlife that relies on them and for the continuation of the species in that place. This, in turn, will mean that you can return another year to harvest once more.

3 Be mindful of where you are collecting from. Roadside verges, the edges of cultivated land and popular dog walking routes are all liable to be contaminated with everything from car fumes, chemical fertilizers and pesticides to dog pee.

4 When collecting bark it is essential that you never remove it from the main trunk or larger branches. Use a clean and sharp blade or saw to remove the smallest usable branches. Make a clean cut and avoid damaging adjacent branches, in this way you will minimize chances of fungal infection or disease entering the tree. Always throughly clean your blade or saw between different shrubs/trees to avoid spreading any existing disease amongst the population.

Whenever possible carry your bounty in a wicker basket or trug as this will give the plants space so that they do not become crushed or sweat as they would in a plastic bag or container. It also means that if there are any mature seeds amongst your harvest you will sprinkle them as you go, ensuring the next generation has a chance. Once home never wash flowers or leaves, just tap them to remove any hitchhiking insects and dust. For this reason it is always good to collect a day or two after rain as this will have rinsed off any excess detritus and given them a good feed ready for the journey. Begin the drying or processing as soon as possible after collection so the plants do not lose potency or start to go mouldy. Any waste of plant material due to laziness on the part of the collector is scandalous. If you are drying for storage try to keep the plants as intact as possible as the smaller they are stored, the greater the surface area exposed to oxidization and hence deterioration. This is why buying herbs in ready made tea bags is really the lowest common denominator as they have been crushed almost to dust and lost so much of their potency in the process.

Like us, plants have feelings and like to be acknowledged and will most often give their medicine with generosity if gracefully asked. It is important to collect plants with humility, asking and thanking as you go. When I am collecting a plant for a specific use I hold it in my mind as I gather, asking that the plants will help me with the particular ailment.

Finally, remember to enjoy the experience. Make a day of it and perhaps take the family or a picnic. It is all about reconnecting to the landscape and the plants we share it with. Foraging for plants and using them for food and medicine builds a connection between you. Even if you don't physically greet the plants, something in your heart does as you begin to recognize certain individuals. Your level of respect for them will deepen as you appreciate more and more their gifts of nourishment, medicine, shade, wood, oxygen, colours, smells and, in time, the companionship they will bring into your life. Instead of seeing a sea of green plants I have come to recognize individuals with personalities of their own, and in doing so the world has become more and more alive to me.

Preparations & Dosages

The preparations mentioned in the text are detailed here with simple instructions on how to make and use them. Dosages are a little more complex as everybody is different and this does not only relate to the size of the individual but also to how sensitive one is. A general rule of thumb is that if it does not feel good, don't use that particular remedy. It may be that you have a particular sensitivity or even an allergy to something that is normally safe to consume. The easiest way of testing for this, if you are concerned, is to hold a small piece of the relevant plant in contact with your lips for a few minutes. If there is no reaction you can then progress to holding that small piece in your mouth for a few moments. Again if there is no reaction the next stage would be to chew a tiny amount and wait a few moments to check for an adverse reaction. If you do not have one at this point it is safe to proceed. The human body is incredibly complex and intelligent and, with time and after repeated use of a herb, the body will form a memory, the result being that eventually taking just a small amount will trigger a response in the body. More is not always better or necessary to generate the desired reaction.

Mirroring the individual differences between human bodies, the constituents of herbs are not uniform. Their chemical make up and strength as medicines change according to location, weather conditions and age, even varying between individual plants of the same species that are neighbours in space and time. For this very reason herbs and their dosages cannot be standardised and it is a fallacy to do so. Hence amounts suggested are not precise. Listen to your body. Does the medicine feel good? Have you taken too much or too little? As long as you don't go wildly beyond the suggested quantities you will be fine. Start to trust yourself, but if you can't do that then follow the quantities I've described accurately. If using the remedy for a youth aged 11-16 use half the described amount and use a third for a child aged 3-11. Infants are so delicate that I have mentioned in the text when a plant is gentle enough to be used for them. If your infant is in need of herbal medicine I would recommend visiting an experienced herbalist. The dosages are generalised but for some of the stronger acting plants there are very specific maximum dosages and these are detailed on the pages where the plant is mentioned. Please be aware of these cautionary notes and do not exceed them.

There is a certain artistry involved in making plant medicines. Take pleasure in creating them and be mindful of the condition you want them to help you with. Try asking the plants for their help whilst preparing them. You can even sing to them if the mood takes you! Many indigenous traditions suggest that you blow onto the herbs you are about to use whilst saying a short prayer to ask for their help. This action is undertaken with the belief that it will breathe life into the plant and make the medicine stronger, the prayer informing the plant what it is needed so it can go to the specific place where its help is required and concentrate its actions there.

It is important to always sterilize the glass jars or bottles in which you intend to store your preparations. This is a very simple process but is essential if you want to avoid all your hard work being ruined by mould growth due to a dirty storage vessel. There are several ways to sterilize and the quickest and easiest is a hot wash in a dishwasher that is clear of greasy plates and cutlery. If, like me, you don't have access to such technology you must start by giving the jars and lids a thorough wash. You then have a choice. You can put the jars in the oven and heat it up to 160°C and, when the oven achieves this heat, turn it off and leave the jars inside to cool before you use them. The lids will need to be boiled in water for 10 minutes but if you have a big enough pan you can add the jars and, by boiling them for 10 minutes, they will be sterile without having to use the oven. Leave them to cool in the water and then air dry before using.

BATHS

Place a large handful (or more precisely 30g fresh/20g dried) of the plant in a muslin or other water permeable bag either under or hanging from the taps whilst running the bath. Leave it bobbing in the water for the duration of your soak. You are basically making a huge infusion and sitting in it.

CAPSULES

Crush the dried plant material using a pestle and mortar or powder it using either a coffee grinder or a food processor. Fill the capsules (see resources to find a supplier) carefully and store in a clearly labeled glass jar, preferably a dark one, in the fridge. This will ensure the contents stay fresh for longer. The size of the capsules will determine how much powder you manage to fit in, but note how much goes in as the usual dosage will be around one teaspoon of dried herb unless otherwise directed in the text, up to 3 times daily.

CIDER VINEGAR

This is made with apples. You can easily buy it from a shop, but if you do look for cloudy ones that have strands in them. This is known as 'the mother' and is the living part which contains the health giving properties. To get a good quality vinegar it must be organic and unpasteurized. Clear brands will have been pasteurized and will not have the health benefits you are looking for. When making your own, it is important not to use any metal containers or spoons during the entire process as the vinegar will corrode the metal. Use glass, wood, plastic or enamel. Firstly you will need to crush clean ripe apples, strain off the juice and add cultivated yeast (the kind you get in wine making kits, not bread yeast). Pour into a container but only fill to ¾ capacity. Cover with muslin to allow the flow of air but prevent dust and debris falling in. You must stir the mix daily and store it away from the light at a temperature of 16-26°C; an airing cupboard would be an ideal place. Fermentation takes 3-4 weeks and you will start to notice a vinegary smell emanating from the brew. Start tasting it at this point when you give your daily stir until it has reached a strength you are happy with. If you then filter the liquid through coffee filter paper you will remove the mother and halt the fermentation process. Pour it into clean, well labeled bottles and seal with screw caps. It should store almost indefinitely.

Take 1 teaspoon 3 times daily and mix with water, a little honey or a warm drink.

COLD INFUSION

Use one teaspoon of dried plant material or two of the fresh plant per cup. Pour cold water over the herbs and leave to infuse, the longer the better and preferably overnight. Strain off the plant matter before consumption and drink up to 3 cups per day.

CRUSH

Take a small amount of the plant material, one or two leaves will often be sufficient, and either crush by hand to break the cellulose walls and release the medicinal juices and oils, or use a pestle and mortar. Rub the oils/juices directly onto the affected area, reapplying as necessary.

DECOCTION

This method is used when the active ingredients are contained within roots, bark or berries. Chop roots and bark finely, but berries can go in as they are. For every cup you make use 1 teaspoon of dried or 2 teaspoons of fresh material. If you have time leave it in cold water overnight. This can be drunk cold or gently warmed to drinking temperature the following day. Alternatively place the plant in cold water and slowly bring to the boil, allowing it to simmer for 10-20 minutes. Boiling sterilizes the brew so if you are making a quantity it can be kept in the fridge for a couple of days (after straining) and reheated a little at a time. Always strain before drinking. A therapeutic level is 3 cups a day unless otherwise stated in the text.

DOUCHE

These are like little baths for the vagina. Use the liquid to throughly douse the area, getting some inside if you can. Use a fresh infusion or decoction each time and allow it to cool to body temperature before use. Repeat three times daily for 3-7 days, but if your symptoms have not cleared up by this point see a professional.

EAT

This speaks for itself! If it is a plant you are not familiar with, try a little at first so that your body can get used to it, especially if it has a strong medicinal action. Large quantities may shock your body causing it to want to expel the plant quickly, most probably in the form of diarrhoea. Introduce new foods slowly and gradually build up the quantity to a level you are comfortable with.

EYE BATH

Make an infusion/decoction from the fresh herb and leave it to cool completely, then use it to rinse out the eyes. You may repeat this action several times a day.

FACIAL STEAM

Place a large handful of fresh plant material (slightly less if using dried) in a bowl and cover with boiling water. Cover with a towel to prevent the volatile oils from escaping and leave to cool for some moments so that the steam does not scald your skin. Put your face over the steaming bowl with a towel over your head to keep the steam in. Stay under the towel for approximately 10 minutes.

FOOT BATH

Place a large handful of the fresh plant (slightly less if using dried) in a washing-up bowl cover in boiling water, then cover the bowl with a towel. This keeps the heat in while the active ingredients infuse into the water. After 10 minutes add cold water until it is cool enough for comfort, but still pretty hot. Place your feet in the water and cover back up with the towel to keep the hot steamy vapours inside. Keep your feet in the water for 10 minutes.

GARGLE

Use a mouthful at a time of an infusion or

decoction that has cooled to body temperature. Let your head fall back and the liquid swish around the back of your throat, making it bubble and gurgle by blowing air through it for approximately 45 seconds before spitting it out. This action may be repeated as needed.

INFUSIONS

Also known as tissanes, these are made by pouring hot water over fresh or dried plant material. This method is mainly used for leaves and flowers where water can penetrate easily. Many plants contain volatile oils which are lost if left uncovered whilst brewing, so I recommend making your infusions either in a teapot, cafetière or a cup covered with a saucer. Leave to brew for 10 minutes, strain off the plant material then sip as a hot tea. Most infusions can be drunk three times a day, a cup at a time. Each cup should be made with 2 teaspoons of fresh herb or 1 teaspoon of dried. Use the quantities stated unless otherwise advised in the text. Most infusions need to be used over a period of time to have the desired effect.

JUICE

It is essential to use a freshly squeezed juice when seeking the health giving properties of the fruit or vegetable you are consuming. Use good quality ingredients and use them as freshly harvested as possible. As soon as the juice has been made it starts to oxidize, breaking down the vitamin C content and generally deteriorating, becoming acid forming and detrimental to your body. Juice purchased in bottles or cartons is often pasteurized which removes many of the health giving properties, and even 'not from concentrate' juices are not as fresh as they sound, potentially having sat in huge industrial vats protected from oxygenation solely by the pasteurization process for

up to a year. This is fine if you just want a refreshing drink but if you are looking for medicine, juice in this form cannot supply it. If the fruit/ vegetable you are juicing is organic and homegrown there is no need to peel, just give them a rinse. If it is a vegetable you can most often also juice the greens. A few specks of soil won't kill you and may in fact contain essential bacteria, the absence of which is a potential factor in so many modern conditions such as allergies and asthma.

Most juices you can use at your own discretion. Learn to listen to your body and when they no longer taste good, or you start to suffer adverse reactions such as loose bowel movements, you have had too much and should discontinue use for a while. The stronger ingredients have recommended quantities for juicing written in the text.

LIQUID EXTRACTION

Juice the fresh plant and combine in a 1:1 ratio with alcohol of a minimum strength of 40% vol. Shake to mix the liquids and store, preferably in a dark glass container, in the fridge. Try to get hold of dropper bottles for storage, then use 3 dropperfuls throughout the day as needed unless otherwise specified in the text. If you cannot get dropper bottles use 1ml 3 times daily which roughly equates to a quarter teaspoon each time. Dilute with water before consuming as the taste will be rather strong. Clearly label your storage bottle with what you have inside to avoid any confusion later.

MOUTHWASH

Use a mouthful of fresh decoction/infusion, that has cooled to body temperature and swill around the mouth for around 45 seconds before spitting out. Repeat as necessary throughout the day.

OIL

When considering which oil to infuse your plants in, it is worth remembering that the skin is the body's largest organ and is under constant bombardment from atmospheric pollution, water sanitized with chlorine and fluoride and chemical or petroleum based cosmetics. Your skin is a membrane through which anything that is laid upon it will be absorbed directly into your blood circulation through a vast network of minute capillaries. For this reason it's important to use high quality products, the same as if you were to ingest them. I always choose to use an organic base oil. If the oil is to be used mainly for massaging large areas I recommend sunflower or almond oil as these are both quite light oils and will rub in easily. Olive oil is a little more viscous, but is naturally antibacterial so it will stay fresh for longer and works better if you are planning on making a salve from it. Safflower and grapeseed oils are both slightly astringent and will help dry up excessively oily skin. Sesame oil is very nourishing to the skin and is an excellent base for inflamed skin conditions, so use it when making an oil to treat eczema or psoriasis. Avocado and wheatgerm oils are both very thick, heavy, nourishing oils and work well on dry skin. Wheatgerm has a high vitamin E content which is especially useful in healing damaged skin, however the viscosity makes both oils hard to use over a wide area, so if choosing to use either of these two oils it would be advisable to mix in with a lighter oil such as sunflower so that they go further.

Once you have decided on your oil, finely chop the quantity of fresh (you can use dried but fresh is definitely preferable) material you intend to use, place in a clean glass jar and cover with your chosen oil, sealing with a screw cap. Make sure the plant material is well covered with a layer of oil over the top; this will stop air getting to the plant matter and forming mould. Leave on a window sill in the sun and give it a gentle shake every day. After three weeks remove the plant material and store in a dark glass bottle away from sources of heat and sunlight as this will extend its shelf life. The easiest way I have found of doing this is to line a sieve with a square of muslin and place it over a jug. Pour the oil through, catching the plant material on the muslin which you can then squeeze to get the last concentrated bits of goodness out. Use the jug to pour into your chosen storage bottle, clearly label with the contents and the date and place the lid on tightly. This will be good to use for at least a year.

You can make a double or even triple infused oil by repeating the procedure one or two more times which will produce a very strong and concentrated oil. Equally you can use more than one kind of plant in an oil to make an infused oil cocktail. Either put both plants together and infuse for three weeks as per a single plant oil, or if one of the plants is unavailable until a later date make the oil infusion with the first plant and then use this oil to infuse the second plant once it becomes available. Apply as directed in the text, reapplying as needed.

PLASTER

Chop the ingredients finely, combine with a little olive oil then spread them evenly over a piece of muslin and wrap up into a little package, making sure the contents do not come into direct contact with the skin. Place onto the affected area, leaving it in position for approximately 30 minutes. Sometimes a plaster will work most effectively when heated from above with a hot water bottle. This will be indicated in the text if it is necessary.

The Medicine Garden

POULTICE

Mash the ingredients with either a mortar and pestle or by hand. If the ingredients are dried, moisten with a little water to make a paste. Place the mash/paste on the affected area and hold in place with a bandage. A moistened and warmed tea bag (of the relevant herb) will do if you have nothing else to hand. If direct contact with the skin is to be avoided, place the mash or paste between two layers of cloth, one in contact with the skin, the other on the outer surface, like a plant sandwich. Leave in place for approximately 30 minutes; less if it is causing irritation, longer if its soothing effects are so wonderful you can't bear to remove it.

POWDER

Thoroughly dry the part of the plant to be used and grind into a fine powder in a coffee grinder or high powered food processor. Store any you are not using immediately in an air tight container in a cool, dark, dry place. Use as recommended in the text.

RUB

Take the relevant part of the plant and rub it directly onto the affected area. This can be repeated as needed.

SALVE

Firstly you must make an infused oil, preferably with olive oil as the base oil. Once you have strained off the plant material you are ready to process it into a salve. Pour the infused oil into a pan and heat very gently, adding 2g of beeswax (see suppliers) for every 30ml of oil. Stir in and allow the wax to melt. Once the wax has thoroughly melted, drip some of the mix on a plate to check the consistency. It should solidify but

melt again easily with the heat of your finger tip. If it's too soft just add a little more wax, too firm add a little more oil. Take off the heat and pour into a clean screw cap jar and leave to cool before putting on the lid. If you put the lid on too soon it will suck the lid on very tightly as it continues to cool and it will be very difficult to remove. Label clearly and store out of sunlight. Apply as needed.

SLEEP PILLOWS

Sew 2 pieces of fabric, approximately 20cm x 20cm, together, placing approximately 100g of dried herbs inside before sealing them up. The pillow can then be placed by the head when sleeping. The gentle fragrance will slowly be released by the dried herbs assisting in sleep or for other medicinal properties. The fragrance will gradually fade over time but should last at least 6 months. The pillow can be opened up and refilled again and again each time the herbs inside lose their potency.

SOLAR INFUSION

Make a solar infusion and save your energy bills! Simply leave a few freshly picked sprigs of the relevant herb in a glass jar or covered glass jug full of water in a sunny place all day and drink in the afternoon or evening, either as it comes (slightly warm), or chill it with a few ice cubes. This method works especially well for fleshy but oily leaves such as peppermint and lemonbalm.

SYRUP

The sugar in a syrup will help to preserve the herb and having a bottle ready prepared in the fridge is incredibly handy. It is an easy way to get children to take medicine because of the sweetness, and is most often used for soothing and treating sore throats and coughs as it is easy to swallow even when the throat is raw and painful. Make a strong (twice the usual quantity of herbs) infusion/decoction, then for every cup of liquid add the same volume (a cup) of sugar or honey. Heat together gently until all the honey/sugar has dissolved and the mixture starts to thicken. Store in the fridge in a well labeled, dark glass bottle. It should keep for at least a year. Take two teaspoons 3 times daily. I recommend using organic, fair trade, brown sugar. White sugar has been highly processed and is not recommended. Honey is preferable to sugar. If you have the option try to source locally produced, raw, organic, honey. This will have more medicinal benefits as the bees will have been foraging the plants in your local area and these local nectars can potentially help to allay hay fever symptoms.

TINCTURE

Tincturing is a useful method of preservation. Most herbs that can be taken internally can be made into a tincture. I personally prefer to use fresh plant material if at all possible, but tinctures are certainly useful for winter and when the plants are out of season. In addition, the alcohol extracts constituents that are either insoluble or only partially soluble in water. Hence tinctures are often stronger in their actions than infusions/decoctions and in some instances can treat complaints that a water extraction alone cannot.

A simple method of making a tincture is to finely chop the plant matter and cover with alcohol, ensuring that a layer of one or two centimetres tops the plants, keeping air from reaching the plant material and ruining the brew. As always it is best to use fresh herbs in this preparation. If you only have dried herbs available cover with alcohol, being sure to check the following day that the plant is still well covered as the dried material may have expanded and soaked up some of the alcohol

and become exposed to the air. Top up at this point with more alcohol if necessary. The brew needs to be left for two weeks out of sunlight and shaken vigorously every day. Making it to coincide with a new moon and straining off the plant matter on full moon is a more traditional way of preparing a tincture and perhaps a good way to keep in touch with time. When straining give the plant matter a good squeeze to be sure you extract all the goodness into your tincture. However, be aware of any settling residue within the bottle. If this occurs the fine particles that have settled (the precipitate) will have a different strength and quality to the rest of the tincture, so it is best to filter thoroughly, for example through a coffee filter at the time of bottling. If any settling does arise it is best not to shake the bottle as this will reintroduce the precipitate and its different, unmeasured quantities back into the tincture. Store in opaque bottles and label clearly. A tincture may last for up to 5 or 6 years, but I try to make just enough for a year or two so that the strength can be assured.

Any alcohol with a strength of 40% vol. can be used. Lower strengths down to 30% vol. will extract the active ingredients but will not effectively preserve the extract. The most popular alcohols for tincturing are vodka and brandy. If using vodka any brand will suffice as its the strength that is most important, although as with everything an organic brand would be preferable. When choosing to use brandy the quality will come through in the flavour of the tincture, so although you are only having a few drops at a time it is worth using the best quality and strength brandy that you can afford.

Use 1-3ml (a dropper full is approximately 1ml) 3 times daily. First try just one or two drops on the top of your tongue, close your eyes, and really try to feel it within you. If the feeling is good then start with 1ml 3 times daily and build up slowly, listening to your body's response as you increase the dose. Do not exceed 3ml 3 times each day unless otherwise indicated in the text. If you are alcohol sensitive or administering to children, add the drops to hot water before consumption as this will cause most of the alcohol to evaporate, leaving only the medicinal properties behind.

You can make a double infused tincture by simply repeating the process. This will enhance the strength. As with infused oils, if you want to add another plant to the tincture at a later date just repeat the process with the second plant, but remember that the shelf life is only valid from the date the original tincture was made.

VINEGAR

Vinegar has a long history of use in herbal preparations and as such is one of the longest used solvents. Like alcohol it can extract the medicinal properties from plants, but it is not as strong. It is good for extracting some plant alkaloids but is not as effective in extracting some of the more acidic biochemical ingredients. It is safe to use over a long period and is often used in tonics for health maintenance. It can be especially useful for those avoiding alcohol and when administering to children.

To make a medicinal vinegar simply chop the fresh plant matter into the bottom of a jar, cover with vinegar, keep out of direct sunlight and shake daily for 3 weeks. Strain off the plant material, being sure to squeeze out the last bits of liquid goodness from the plants before composting. Label clearly and keep in the fridge in a glass jar (preferably a dark one). It should last up to 2 years.

Be careful not to use distilled vinegar. White wine vinegar has a light flavour and will go with most herbs and apple cider vinegar is always popular, having a whole host of health benefits of its own. It will, however, have a stronger flavour. The infused vinegar can be mixed with a little honey, a glass of water or a warm drink. Use one teaspoon up to 3 times daily.

RECOMMENDED EQUIPMENT

Most of the preparations can be made with the equipment in an average kitchen. Preparations such as leaf juicing require more specialist equipment. As you find yourself using plants for medicine more and more you may find some of the following items useful, and perhaps eventually indispensable.

Blender
Coffee grinder
Dark glass bottles/jars (see suppliers) You can also use old jam/mayonnaise jars with screw caps. To make them dark you can paint the outside. The aim of this is to stop light reaching the contents and causing a deterioration in their quality.
Food processor
Juicer
Leaf juicer (see suppliers)
Muslin/cheese cloth. Muslin is available from fabric shops and cheese cloth from kitchen shops. If you cannot find either just go to a fabric shop and explain that you want a thin natural fabric and they will be able to help you find something similar that will do the job just as efficiently
Pestle and mortar
Pouring jug
Tea pot & strainer or cafetière
Sieve

Back Doorstep Culinary Herbs

Those of us who have an interest in good, healthy, tasty food will probably already have a collection of culinary herbs, be they in pots on the kitchen windowsill or planted just outside the back door. All these pretty, yummy, aromatic herbs are not just great for the taste buds, but in my home act as an emergency medicine chest, especially on those soggy winter nights when my partner is laid up in bed with a serious case of man-flu.

Indeed, adding a little fresh herb to your favourite recipes may be keeping you healthier than you think; it goes further than just flavoursome delights. Knowing their healthful properties will help you make more conscious decisions about what you eat, and you will find your food literally becoming medicine.

All of the plants listed in this chapter are commonly available and relatively easy to grow, even in a small space such as a patio or balcony. Most can also be purchased fresh or as edible seed from farmers markets, health shops or garden centres. It is also possible to buy quantities of the dried herb in bulk. I have added the details of the suppliers I use in the resources section at the back of the book. Creating your own preparations will always be more satisfactory and tend to be more potent than herbal supplements, which may contain additional ingredients such as fillers or lubricants (to help ease their movement along a factory production line) and will most probably have been heat treated. Making medicines with the ailment for treatment foremost in your mind will activate the relevant property in the herb you are using.

Basil (Ocimum basilicum)

Basil, a member of the mint family, is very popular as a culinary herb and is often used in Italian dishes, most famously pesto. I like to use it to flavour salads. It is a great plant to grow if you want to deter aphids from other more precious plants and so I tend to grow it in my greenhouse. I also have it in my kitchen where it acts as a decoy for white fly who otherwise tend to coat my favourite salvia with their stickiness throughout the summer. Having it in the kitchen is also very handy when needed for a recipe or remedy and keeps it safe from slugs who also appear to enjoy its taste. Using basil is said to open the heart and mind, which is as good a reason as any to start using it.

MATERIA MEDICA

Antibacterial, anti-inflammatory, relaxes spasms, lowers fevers, sedative, digestive

The Medicine Garden

GATHERING

Gather leaves as needed throughout the growing season. If you pinch out the growing tips your basil will become more bushy and flowering will be delayed. The medicinal qualities are strongest before flowering, so it is important to do this. Basil needs to be fresh or preserved in a tincture or oil to work medicinally. Dried or frozen leaves have already lost their potency.

PREPARATIONS

- *Crush* fresh leaves and hold in mouth directly on mouth ulcer, rub directly on warts (daily), acne, insect bites and skin infections. Leaves can also be rubbed directly to temples to relieve headaches.
- *Facial Steam* to relieve headaches and colds.
- *Gargle* for inflamed throat, sore gums, mouth ulcers, oral thrush.
- *Infusion* (1-2 cups daily) for fevers, colds, flu and to clear phlegm from nose and chest. Through relaxing spasms it aids digestion, easing wind, nausea and abdominal cramps. Also for constipation, vomiting, gastroenteritis and promotion of normal bowel function. It's effective against bacterial infections and intestinal parasites. It helps lighten your spirits, easing anxiety, nervous exhaustion, insomnia, tension headaches and migraine. In addition it promotes clarity of thought, concentration and stimulates milk production in nursing mothers.
- *Tincture* can be applied either directly or as a compress to injuries and badly healing wounds. Taken internally it will have the same action as an infusion.

CAUTIONS AND CONTRAINDICATIONS

Do not use medicinally during pregnancy.

Bay (Laurus nobilis)

One of my first memories of collecting a plant to consume was being ushered into the back garden by my mother to collect a couple of Bay leaves for the meal she was preparing. It was a huge, towering, smelly and slightly scary tree to me at age four. I grow one in a pot now as they can and do get rather large when planted in the earth. Popular in soups, stews and sauces, Bay imparts a distinct and rich flavour. The leaves may be dried and burned as an incense for purification. The smoke is said to induce prophetic visions and increase psychic awareness. It is especially important to correctly identify Bay as all other Laurels are poisonous.

MATERIA MEDICA

Antibacterial, fungicidal

GATHERING

Harvest leaves throughout the year as needed

and berries as they ripen in early autumn.

PREPARATIONS

- *Infusion* (berries) for poor appetite, in total drunk a maximum of 4-5 times, (leaves) for digestion, colic, flatulence and to alleviate colds & flu. Limit to a maximum of 2 cups a day as an excess induces vomiting.
- *Oil* (leaf) apply directly to scabies, (berries and leaves) for bruises and sprains. Added to bath water or used as a massage oil for tired limbs & to focus the mind, (berries) for dandruff, rheumatism, sprains and bruises.

CAUTIONS AND CONTRAINDICATIONS

Avoid during pregnancy (berries were used to promote abortion in the past). Do not use if you suffer from dermatitis.

Catmint (Nepeta cataria)

This herb has a stimulant effect on most cats, a property that led to its common name. It's not only cats, but also bees and butterflies that love it, perhaps strange considering vermin and many insects, including aphids, flea beetles and ants are repelled by it. A member of the mint family (as its name suggests), catmint is used as a flavouring in sauces and stews. The flowers are a great addition to salads, having a visual effect that will entice most children to daringly delve into the salad bowl.

MATERIA MEDICA

Anti-inflammatory, digestive, promotes perspiration, relaxant

GATHERING

Leaves and flowering tops can be collected and used fresh throughout the summer and into early autumn. To preserve for winter use, cut the stems when the flowers are in bud and hang in small bunches out of direct sunlight to dry.

PREPARATIONS

- *Crush* (leaves) rub on skin as a deterrent to mosquito or midge attack.
- *Infusion* to break a fever during colds and flu. As a relaxant to relieve excitability, palpitations, insomnia, bronchitis and nervous indigestion. To ease diarrhoea, stomach upsets, colic and flatulence. It also works as a mild antidepressant, lightening one's spirit. Its mild sedative action is an excellent remedy for infants and children who have trouble sleeping. Do not exceed 5 cups a day as high doses can induce vomiting. Externally it can be dabbed on bruises where the skin remains unbroken.
- *Poultice* to relieve swellings and give relief from rheumatism and arthritis.
- *Salve* for hemorrhoids, rheumatism and arthritis.

- *Syrup* for coughs.
- *Tincture* has the same action internally as an infusion.

HEALTHFUL COCKTAILS

Infuse with yarrow for the treatment of diarrhoea.

Infuse with lemonbalm for a relaxing and uplifting summer drink. Enjoy iced on a long summer's evening instead of a chilled chardonnay to bring a sense of calm after the day.

Infuse with elderflower and honey. Great for use with children to break a fever during a cold or the flu. It also eases gastric disturbances, helping children drift off to sleep.

CAUTIONS AND CONTRAINDICATIONS

Avoid during pregnancy or if suffering from pelvic inflammatory disease.

Chamomile (Chamaemelum nobile)

Found wild in the English countryside, it is closely related to German Chamomile (Matricaria recutita). They have similar properties and can be used interchangeably. It has long been used as a remedy for a multitude of ills and is safe to use on children. My friend weaned her son on a weak infusion of Chamomile: it worked a treat and he loved it. In the garden the pretty daisy-like flowers work as a deterrent to both aphids and flies.

MATERIA MEDICA

Antibacterial, antifungal, anti-inflammatory, pain relief , gentle de-stresser

GATHERING

Flowers can be collected and dried in the summer months, preferably 3-5 days after opening. They can only be stored and used for a year, after which time much of the potency is lost.

PREPARATIONS

- *Baths* for irritated, sore skin. It makes a relaxing soak after a stressful day. It can help ease children and infants to sleep, especially if they are hyperactive, over excited or teething.
- *Compress* (cool) for irritated and inflamed skin, burns and bites.
- *Eyebath* for red, irritated, dry eyes and stye relief. If you have manufactured teabags (Chamomile, of course) this would be a good time to use them. Wet them and leave them over closed eyes for a few moments.
- *Facial Steam* to be inhaled during colds, flu, sinusitis, throat infections, nasal catarrh and hay fever.
- *Infusion* to relieve stress, irritability, frustration, nervous tension, insomnia, and hyperactivity. It will also treat inflammations including sore throats, and those of the

uterus, anus and vagina. By calming inflammations of the gastrointestinal lining it will ease inflammatory bowel disease, ulcers and gastritis. In the digestive tract it will additionally ease heartburn and nausea, especially when caused by stress, colic, diverticulitis and morning sickness. It is also an option to ease painful menstruation, and when suffering a fever. Externally as a skin rinse it relieves sunburn or minor burns, calming inflammation, providing pain relief and preventing infection.

- *Mouthwash* for toothache.
- *Oil* applied externally to painful joints and swellings, also to inflammatory skin conditions including eczema and psoriasis.

HEALTHFUL COCKTAILS

Infuse with peppermint for tasty relief from minor stomach complaints.

CAUTIONS AND CONTRAINDICATIONS

Avoid during pregnancy, whilst breast feeding, with anti-coagulant medication, or hyper-sensitivity to compositae/ asteraceae family.

Chervil (Anthriscus cerefolium)

Loved by gardeners for its ability to repel slugs, ants and aphids. The leaves, flowers and roots are all edible and found mainly in French cuisine, especially soups, stews, potato, fish and egg dishes. Chervil is also often used in salads and as an edible garnish due to the attractive and dainty nature of its foliage. It has a high calcium content and is therefore even more worthy of a regular appearance on your kitchen table.

MATERIA MEDICA

Antidepressant, anti-inflammatory, blood purifier, digestive

GATHERING

Only the leaves are used in medical preparations. They can be collected throughout the growing season as needed, taking outside stems first and leaving the new centre leaves to grow. Stems cut before flowering contain stronger medicine. Chervil does not preserve well, but if you choose to do so, freezing finely chopped leaves in a little water in an ice cube tray works better than drying them. Chervil readily self-seeds so leave flowering heads to mature if you want the plant to spread, maintaining an abundant crop for future harvests.

PREPARATIONS

- *Eyebath* for conjunctivitis and inflamed eyelids.
- *Infusion* as a spring tonic to clean and detoxify the blood, liver and kidneys. It stimulates digestion, improves memory and eases depression. It also helps reduce high blood pressure and fluid retention and eases the symptoms of rheumatism, eczema and

jaundice. Additionally it acts as an expectorant helping to loosen phlegm in the respiratory tract.
- *Poultice* applied to bruises and swellings.

CAUTIONS AND CONTRAINDICATIONS

None known.

Coriander (Coriandrum sativum)

Fresh leaves finely chopped and sprinkled top many spicy dishes. It is especially common in Thai, Indian and Mexican cuisine. The seeds are used in curry powders, pickles and sauces. I frequently use the leaves as an essential ingredient in spicy salsas and salads. Grown in the garden it does tend to bolt for the sun so it's better kept in partially shady conditions. Coriander is a worthy garden companion as it repels aphids and carrot rust fly, whilst spraying infestations of spider mite with a strong infusion will serve to clear up the inflicted plant.

MATERIA MEDICA

Antibacterial, anti-inflammatory, digestive, expectorant, fungicidal

GATHERING

Collect flowers in late summer and dry upside down in a paper bag so seeds can ripen and be collected as they fall. Fresh leaves are collected throughout the growing season.

PREPARATIONS

- *Chew* (leaves) for nausea, (seeds) for mild digestive complaints.
- *Eyebath* to reduce swelling, pain and relieve conjunctivitis.
- *Infusion* (bruised seeds) for upset stomach, flatulence, stimulating appetite, as a mild sedative, reducing fever and as an expectorant to loosen phlegm. It also has diuretic properties which stimulate the kidneys and may lower cholesterol.
- *Juice* (leaves) apply directly to inflamed, sore skin and acne. Drink small amounts throughout the day to ease hay fever, allergies and skin rashes. Simply add a small handful of leaves to fruits or vegetables, juice and drink 3 times daily until symptoms have cleared.
- *Oil* (bruised seeds) used as a massage oil to ease muscular aches, poor circulation, neuralgic pain and in cases of nervous exhaustion.
- *Poultice* (bruised seeds) for painful joints and rheumatic pains.

CAUTIONS AND CONTRAINDICATIONS

None known.

Dill (Anethum graveolens)

High in calcium and rich in mineral salts (reducing the need to add extra salt), dill is a healthy and useful addition in the kitchen. Both the seeds and the feathery leaves are used in Scandinavian recipes and when cooking with fish. Like many of the culinary herbs, dill supports the digestive system. The flowers attract many beneficial insects to the garden, some of whom love to feast on aphids, so it can be a handy companion plant.

MATERIA MEDICA

Digestive, relaxant

GATHERING

Leaves can be collected as needed throughout growing season. If leaves are not regularly cut, dill will go to seed more quickly. Gather seeds when they ripen in autumn, then dry to preserve for later use.

PREPARATIONS

- *Chew* (seeds) after meals to freshen breath and aid digestion.
- *Infusion* (bruised seeds) before meals in small quantities for colicky infants or simply mash a few leaves in with food if on solids. Aids relaxation and acts as a gentle sedative assisting sleep. Eases intestinal spasms, menstrual cramps, nausea, indigestion, flatulence, hiatus hernia, stomach upsets, hiccups, colds and flu. Additional benefits are that it stimulates milk production in nursing mothers and promotes appetite. It is said that dipping fingernails in an infusion will help strengthen them due to the high calcium ontent, although you would get the benefit of the calcium throughout your system were you to drink the brew.

HEALTHFUL COCKTAILS

Infuse with ginger or peppermint for digestion.

Infuse with fennel to increase breast milk flow.

CAUTIONS AND CONTRAINDICATIONS

Not suitable if following a low sodium diet.

Fennel (Foeniculum vulgare)

The flowers of fennel attract beneficial insects to the garden. Perhaps the insects are attracted by its pungent aroma which is released even when you just brush the plant in passing. It's a plant that always draws me to pull off a section of the feathery foliage to rub between my fingers and inhale as I continue on my way.

The seeds are used in baking to flavour biscuits and bread, whilst the leaves and stems are eaten raw in salads. Florence fennel is a variety grown specifically for the large base of the stem, which can be prepared in many ways including steaming and roasting.

The Romans noted that snakes rub their eyes against fennel after shedding their skins and this was thought to get their sight back to normal and remove the milkyness that occurs during this process (Lipp, 1996). This point is interesting to note as it is used as a remedy for conjunctivitis and other sore and inflamed eye conditions.

MATERIA MEDICA

Antibacterial, anti-inflammatory, digestive, expectorant, increases milk flow, relaxant

GATHERING

The leaves are collected throughout the growing season and must be used fresh as they lose potency when dried. Roots are lifted in autumn and dried for decoctions. Unripe seeds can be used fresh. Ripe seeds are collected by hanging the whole seed head upside down to dry in a paper bag, which will then catch the seeds as they fall.

PREPARATIONS

- *Chew* (seeds) to allay hunger.
- *Crush* (leaves) rub onto the coat of dogs and cats or put leaves directly in their bedding to deter fleas. Although this is not directly a medicinal use it may save your sanity or at least energy when you discover that fleas have migrated from your animal onto the carpet during the hot summer months, and help you avoid using chemicals to do the job at that point.
- *Compress* for conjunctivitis.
- *Decoction* (root) for urinary disorders.
- *Eyebath* reduces inflammation in sore eyes and relieves symptoms of conjunctivitis.
- *Gargle* for sore throats.
- *Infusion* (bruised seeds) limit to one cup a day. Will increase milk flow in mothers and ease indigestion, wind, colic, intestinal cramps and menopausal symptoms. It's an expectorant and so will ease coughs and a liver tonic so will reduce body odour caused by congested intestines. It may compliment conventional prostate cancer treatments, although check with your health care professional before commencing fennel as a medicinal treatment.
- *Mouthwash* for gum disease.
- *Oil* (seeds) used to massage muscular and rheumatic pains.
- *Poultice* (crushed leaves and stems) for breasts sore and swollen due to breast feeding.

- *Syrup* (leaf juice) acts as an expectorant clearing mucous from lungs easing chronic coughs.

CAUTIONS AND CONTRAINDICATIONS

Avoid during pregnancy.

Ginger (Zingiber officinale)

This is the only plant I have chosen to include that is not fully hardy outside. In fact it won't even tolerate temperatures below 10°C, so if you do choose to grow it it must be inside for all but the hottest weeks of summer. Ginger is, however, available in most green grocers and supermarkets as a piece of fresh root. You can make all of the preparations I have included with such a piece. Alternatively you can plant the fresh root and let it grow. Either way I find ginger indispensable in my kitchen apothecary, which is why it has been included.

I love the strong spicy taste and add it raw into the blender with homemade winter soups. It really warms you up from the inside. Containing calcium, magnesium, phosphorus and potassium it is nutritious and beneficial to eat during convalescence. One of the additional benefits is that it is safe to use for children over the age of two in small amounts.

MATERIA MEDICA

Antibacterial, anti-inflammatory, antiseptic, eases nausea, expectorant, pain relief, promotes sweating, relaxes spasms, stimulates circulation

GATHERING

Unearth young sections of root as needed during the growing season until just after the leaves die back in autumn.

PREPARATIONS

- *Chew* for motion sickness, nausea (including that resulting from chemotherapy), morning sickness and to alleviate toothache.
- *Decoction/ Infusion* Infusions work but I find that if you simmer the chopped, mashed

piece of root for 10 minutes, more of the medicinal properties are released. It breaks fevers by promoting perspiration and so is useful in colds and flu. Ginger's expectorant action helps clear phlegm in coughs. It stimulates circulation, relieves all kinds of nausea, indigestion, flatulence, colic, improves liver function and is a natural blood thinner (which is why it helps circulation when it's cold and the blood naturally thickens). In fact the blood thinning action is potentially preventative against heart attack and stroke. In addition it lowers blood pressure and cholesterol. It's anti-inflammatory properties help in the treatment of arthritic conditions. It is a reproductive tonic for both men and women, improving poor circulation in the pelvis whilst easing the painful, cramping, muscle spasms that often accompany menstruation. It will help kill parasites in the digestive tract, whilst warming and stimulating the stomach, aiding weak digestion.

- *Footbath* for chilblains (Peterson, 1995).
- *Gargle* for sore throats.
- *Juice* has the same properties as making a decoction or infusion and in addition can be applied directly to minor burns for pain relief (after they have been held under cold running water for some time).
- *Oil* gently rubbed on swollen, painful and arthritic joints, sprains, rheumatism, lumbago and other localised pain such as menstrual cramps.
- *Poultice* (or warm compress) on painful and arthritic joints.
- *Syrup* for nausea, coughs, colds and sore throat.

HEALTHFUL COCKTAILS

Freshly juiced ginger can be added to all fruit or vegetable juices to give them a healthy kick, favourites being carrot and apple or beetroot and cucumber. Experiment to find one which suits your tastebuds.

Decoct with marshmallow to shift lingering chest infections.

Infuse with a squirt of fresh lemon and a spoonful of honey for a comforting and warming cold remedy.

CAUTIONS AND CONTRAINDICATIONS

Do not use if suffering from inflammatory skin conditions, digestive ulcers or a high fever. During pregnancy use with caution and do not extend use of medicinal doses beyond four consecutive days. As a natural blood thinner caution must be taken if concurrently on medication for this purpose.

Houseleek (Sempervivum tectorum)

A beautiful looking succulent that grows well in the UK, especially on gravelly patches, rockeries, and cracks in walls or paving. When mine flowered for the first time a couple of years ago I was so excited by its curious and alluring flower. It is the cooler climates' answer to Aloe vera, although not as strong in its properties and can be grown outside all year round without winter protection or watering in all but the driest spells.

MATERIA MEDICA

Anti-inflammatory, cooling, soothing

GATHERING

The fleshy leaves can be collected as required throughout the year.

PREPARATIONS

- *Chew* for toothache.
- *Crush* on temples for headache. Slice leaf through centre and apply inner pulp directly to warts, bites, stings, minor burns, sunburn and inflamed or itchy skin.
- Gargle for sore throats and mouth, but avoid swallowing too much as an excess will induce vomiting and diarrhoea.
- *Poultice* for corns, leave in place for a couple of hours, then soak foot in hot water and attempt to remove the corn.

CAUTIONS AND CONTRAINDICATIONS

None known.

Lemonbalm (Melissa officinalis)

A delicious, fragrant herb, you feel uplifted just running your hands through the foliage and taking a deep lungful. I personally love lemonbalm and its delicate feminine air. It makes you feel like you're being wrapped in mother's arms; protective, relaxing and safe to sleep. As such it is gentle and safe to use with children. It can be added raw to flavour salads and a sprig doesn't go amiss in a jug of Pimms, or an old fashioned summer lemonade.

MATERIA MEDICA

Antidepressant, antiviral, promotes sweating, relaxant

GATHERING

Collect fresh leaves throughout the growing season. Do not try to dry as it loses potency extremely quickly.

PREPARATIONS

- **Crush** on lips as soon as you feel the tingling onset of a coldsore. You can also apply to insect bites.
- **Infusion** can be consumed freely. Useful for tension headaches, nervous tension, insomnia, unsettling dreams, fatigue, nervous exhaustion, palpitations, upset stomach and morning sickness. It's a great general and nerve tonic, working wonders during periods of convalescence. Lifting one's spirits and improving one's sense of wellbeing, it is also great in times of depression and feeling stuck, smoothing the edges, restoring a sense of calm and clarity. It is useful for women during menopause, relieving hot flushes and helping to regulate menstruation at earlier times in womens' lives. Taken hot it can induce sweating and thereby break a fever, which when considered alongside its antiviral effect is great for colds and flu. In addition it can complement conventional treatment for an over active thyroid.
- **Solar** infusion for an uplifting yet relaxing evening drink and cooling on a summer's day.
- **Syrup** for feverish colds and flu, helps break a fever and alleviates bronchial catarrh.
- **Tincture** has the same action internally as an infusion and is a handy way to preserve the leaf for use during the winter when most people are more likely to need a bit of an uplifting elixir.

HEALTHFUL COCKTAILS

Infusion chilled and served with honey and a slice of lemon becomes a refreshing and cooling summer drink.

Infuse with rose for a really uplifting, heart opener.

Make a solar infusion and add a sprig or two of peppermint to the jug in the morning for a really refreshing and uplifting beverage.

Infuse with chamomile or lavender for a soothing bedtime tea.

CAUTIONS AND CONTRAINDICATIONS

Do not take concurrently with barbiturates for insomnia or anxiety.

Lovage
(Levisticum officinale)

Occasionally used in salads, it has an extremely strong flavour. I would recommend not using more than 2 leaves or that is all you will taste. I find the flavour overpowering and not to my taste so have certainly never tried grating the fresh root into a salad which is an alternative way to eat lovage. It makes a huge statement in the garden, growing up to almost two metres in height, so make sure you have room for this potential giant. Fortunately for our gardens, unlike me beneficial insects are attracted to lovage.

MATERIA MEDICA

Digestive, diuretic, expectorant, relaxant

GATHERING

Leaves are collected throughout the growing season. Roots can be lifted in the 3rd year and used fresh or dried for decoctions. Seeds are collected by chopping off the whole seed head when ripe and drying upside down in a paper bag to catch the seeds.

PREPARATIONS

- *Bath* for skin irritations.
- *Chew* (dried root) for increased level of alertness.
- *Decoction* (seeds)/*Infusion* (leaves) for indigestion, colic (safe to use for infants), flatulence, appetite stimulant, cystitis, kidney stones, urinary tract infections, regulation of menses and painful menstruation. In addition it acts as a mild sedative, is a blood cleanser, increases perspiration and is helpful for bad coughs as it both loosens phlegm and relaxes spasms.
- *Eyebath* (decoction) for sore eyes.
- *Gargle* (decoction) for throat and mouth infections.
- *Syrup* for chest complaints and coughs.

HEALTHFUL COCKTAILS

Can be combined in a syrup with thyme or marjoram for chesty coughs.

CAUTIONS AND CONTRAINDICATIONS

Avoid during, or if planning, pregnancy.

Marjoram
(Origanum vulgare)

Adored by bees, it's a great plant to grow in such troubling times for the bee kingdom. It imparts a strong but light flavour and is used widely in pasta dishes. I love to throw a few leaves and some of the flowers into my salad bowl. Surprisingly this popular culinary herb has a wide range of medicinal properties.

MATERIA MEDICA

Antifungal, anti-inflammatory, antioxidant, digestive, expectorant, relaxant

GATHERING

Leaves can be collected throughout the growing season and the tops just before flowering.

PREPARATIONS

- *Bath* as a relaxant for tense, sore muscles and joints, to ease anxiety and induce restful sleep.
- *Compress* for rheumatism, swellings, abdominal cramps and colic.
- *Crush* (leaves only) into temples for headache relief.
- *Facial steam* inhale for sore throats, laryngitis, and sinus congestion.
- *Gargle* for mouth ulcers.
- *Infusion* relieves hay fever, indigestion, colic, flatulence, stomach upsets, nervous headaches, insomnia, anxiety, irritability, menstrual pains and regulates menstruation. The antioxidant effects ease arthritis by clearing build ups of toxins in the joints. It's particularly useful when suffering from colds or flu as it helps break the fever, loosens phlegm, soothes coughs and clears congested sinuses.
- *Oil* gently massaged onto areas of muscular pain and stiff arthritic joints.
- *Poultice* (leaves only) mash the leaves with a hot infusion to make a paste, then apply to relieve arthritis, rheumatic aches and sprains.

CAUTIONS AND CONTRAINDICATIONS

Avoid during pregnancy.

Oregano (see marjoram)

Parsley (Petroselinum crispum)

The herb you are most likely to find on your plate as a sprig of green garnish, but whatever you do don't throw it aside. Tuck in and ask for more as it contains a large number of vitamins, minerals (A, B, C, E, iron, magnesium, calcium, sodium) and chlorophyll, hence it's highly nutritious. Flat leafed varieties do taste stronger, so if you don't like the taste go for small amounts of curly leafed ones. It is definitely worth growing if you have the space, but sow it where you intend to grow it as it really dislikes being transplanted. Not only is it fussy about being moved but it really needs coaxing to appear from its seeds at all in my experience. I have found the best method is to soak the seeds, preferably overnight, before sowing to give them the best chance of germination.

MATERIA MEDICA

Antioxidant, antiseptic, diuretic

GATHERING

Pick the leaves throughout the growing season leaving some stems to flower and develop seeds to self-broadcast your next crop. Roots can be collected in the autumn of the second year then dried. If you have a glut of leaves in summer and want to preserve them, either make a tincture or chop finely and freeze with a little water in the ice cube tray as the properties are soon lost through drying.

PREPARATIONS

- *Chew* (leaf) after meals (even garlic) to neutralize and freshen breath.
- *Crush* (leaf) and place on broken skin as a temporary wound dressing.
- *Decoction* (root) for water retention, urinary tract infections, cystitis, kidney stones, anemia, arthritis and rheumatism.
- *Infusion* (leaves) a mild digestive, relieving stomach cramps and gas. It alleviates water retention, encourages urination, is a kidney tonic and helps clear kidney stones. It also helps detoxify the body, improve circulation, ease lung congestion and relieve asthma. It also stimulates milk production and menstrual flow and lowers blood pressure.
- *Juice* this is the strongest preparation and the quickest way to get a good blast of any of the actions that you receive by drinking the infusion.
- *Tincture* probably worth making in the case of parsley as it is such a beneficial herb and will mean the health giving properties can then be accessed easily all year round.

HEALTHFUL COCKTAIL

A few sprigs of freshly juiced parsley mix well with an infusion of lemonbalm and, when taken 3 times daily, will help alleviate menstrual irregularities, pains and PMS.

CAUTIONS AND CONTRAINDICATIONS

Avoid during pregnancy or kidney infection/ disease.

Peppermint (Mentha spp.)

A garden favourite, but so vigorous it is best kept in a pot unless you don't mind it popping up all over the place. True peppermint has the strongest medicinal action of all the mints, although menthol, the main active ingredient, is present in all varieties. Its use as a flavouring is incredibly widespread so nearly everyone is familiar with it. The flavour infuses out of the leaf readily and so finds itself as a favoured candidate for solar infusions or floating as a flavoursome garnish in almost any jug of drink prepared in the summertime. Peppermint tea is widely enjoyed as an alternative to caffeinated teas and will still clear your head and perk you up. I drink it frequently. It is gentle enough for use with children too and high in vitamins A and E and iron, so it's a very tasty way to get the goodness in.

MATERIA MEDICA

Antiseptic, anaesthetic, decongestant, digestive , pain relief, relaxes spasms

GATHERING

Leaves are collected as and when needed throughout the growing season.

PREPARATIONS

- *Crush* against temples for headaches and directly onto insect stings.
- *Chew* after meals to freshen breath.
- *Compress* for rheumatic aches.
- *Facial steam* inhale for blocked nose, sinuses, catarrh and to cleanse skin pores.
- *Gargle* for sore throats.
- *Infusion* stimulates secretion of bile and digestive juices so eases indigestion, flatulence, gastric ulcer, gastroenteritis, IBS and colic. Relieves nausea due to motion sickness, morning sickness and migraine. Promotes sweating so is used for flu and colds. Iced, it makes a cooling and refreshing summer beverage.
- *Juice* directly applied to skin for acne, excema, scabies and dermatitis.
- *Solar infusion* will have the same action as a regular infusion.

HEALTHFUL COCKTAILS

Simmer elderberries as a decoction, then add peppermint leaves to infuse, a great way to promote sweating at the onset of cold or flu.

CAUTIONS AND CONTRAINDICATIONS

Do not use as a steam inhalant if suffering from asthma as it may irritate the chest. Do not give to children under the age of 5. Avoid during pregnancy.

Rosemary (Rosmarinus officinalis)

Rosemary's flowers can be sprinkled on salads or other food as an edible garnish. The leaves are used in cooking, especially with lamb, or with chunks of sea salt on roast potatoes. It contains useful levels of iron, calcium, magnesium, phosphorous, sodium and vitamin B6, but should be ingested in moderation because in excess it can irritate the stomach. Rosemary has cleansing properties. I have dried the leaves and burnt them as incense to clear the air. There is something very satisfying about using it in this way; I think the rosemary likes it.

MATERIA MEDICA

Antibacterial, antioxidant, antiseptic, diuretic, improves circulation

GATHERING

Collect leaves as needed throughout the year.

PREPARATIONS

- *Bath* for muscular aches, fatigue and to stimulate and tone skin.
- *Facial* steam to unclog skin pores, relieve fatigue, nervous exhaustion, headaches, de-stress and increase mental alertness.
- *Infusion* (maximum 3 times daily) eases indigestion due to tension and emotional upsets whilst stimulating a weak digestion. It eases mild depression and self-doubt, headaches and water retention. It's good to drink during colds and flu as it induces perspiration. Rosemary has long been known to improve memory, mental clarity and focus, probably due to the boost it gives the micro-circulation of the brain. As a liver stimulant it leads to faster processing of toxins, leaving you feeling energized. It improves circulation in the extremities, helping to keep fingers and toes warm in winter. In addition it offers protection against free radicals (implied in the development of heart disease, cancer and premature aging, amongst others).
- *Oil* for well perfumed but antiseptic body moisturiser. It feels like you are cleaning your skin as you moisturise. Can also be rubbed into muscular aches, arthritic and rheumatic pains and dry itchy scalp.

HEALTHFUL COCKTAILS

Infuse with sage and a tiny sprig of thyme and drink for the duration of a cold, or when glands are swollen.

Infuse with dandelion leaf after overindulging in a heavy meal to stimulate your digestion.

Infuse with lemonbalm to feel uplifted and relieve feelings of self-doubt.

Infuse with yarrow at the onset of flu.

Combine with thyme and make into a slave to rub on the chest when suffering a cold.

Combine with ginger and make a salve to rub onto rheumatic pains.

CAUTIONS AND CONTRAINDICATIONS

Avoid during pregnancy, breast feeding and if you suffer from high blood pressure or epilepsy.

Sage (Salvia officinalis)

The herb I probably use most frequently, especially if I have even the faintest sniff of a cold. It has a pleasant flavour, although if made too strongly it becomes a bit bitter. Favoured for use in stuffings, soups and stews it is a popular culinary herb. If planting in the earth make sure there is enough room around into which it can mature, otherwise it will crowd out and potentially kill off other plants that are too close. It's another favourite among the bees, keeping the garden buzzing with activity.

MATERIA MEDICA

Antibacterial, antidepressant, anti-inflammatory, antiseptic

GATHERING

The leaves can be collected throughout the year as needed.

PREPARATIONS

- *Bath* stimulates and cleanses skin and scalp, soothes tired muscles (Lipp, 1996).
- *Facial steam* inhale for head colds, soothing to mucous membranes and cleansing to skin pores.
- *Gargle* for sore throat.
- *Infusion* suppresses perspiration, salivation and lactation (useful when weaning). It improves liver and kidney function, digestion and memory. It eases colds, flu, flatulence, anxiety and depression. It contains plant oestrogens which help combat night sweats and other menopausal problems. Useful for throaty coughs by relaxing spasms and soothing mucous membranes. Drunk cold it is an effective remedy for menopausal hot flushes. It can be used as a skin wash for insect bites and skin infections.
- *Mouthwash* for mouth ulcers, inflamed gums, laryngitis and tonsillitis.
- *Rub* top side of leaf over teeth and gums for its antiseptic cleansing action.

CAUTIONS AND CONTRAINDICATIONS

Avoid during pregnancy or if you suffer from epilepsy. Toxic if taken in excess or over extended periods.

Thyme (Thymus vulgaris)

Loved by bees, thyme is a hardy plant and will grow in walls and cracks between paving slabs. It can even take a bit of trampling, which simply bruises the leaves and releases its fragrance. It is used in French cuisine, but sparingly due to its strong flavour. Wearing a sprig will enable you to see faeries (Cunningham, 1985). After a lot of practice I am fortunate enough to see them without adorning myself thus.

MATERIA MEDICA

Antibacterial, antibiotic, antifungal, antioxidant, antiseptic, digestive, expectorant, relaxes spasms

GATHERING

Can be collected throughout the growing season and dried for infusions over winter.

PREPARATIONS

- *Bath* to impart courage and inspiration for times of withdrawal and self-doubt. Eases coughs, including whooping cough.
- *Crush* wipe the oily residue between the toes to treat athlete's foot.
- *Facial steam* inhale for asthma, all types of cough, bronchial problems and congestion.
- *Gargle* for tonsillitis and oral thrush.
- *Infusion* (maximum of 2 cups per day) decreases thickness of bronchial secretions, helps loosen phlegm and relaxes spasms, all making it ideal for dry coughs, whooping cough, bronchitis, bronchial catarrh and chest infections. It eases headaches, asthma, laryngitis, indigestion, gastritis, and upset stomachs.
- *Mouthwash* for gum disease.
- *Poultice* for skin inflammations, rheumatism and arthritis.
- *Salve* for cuts, bruises, acne, rash.
- *Syrup* for coughs, colds and sore throats.
- *Tincture* for vaginal thrush. Dilute 40 drops in water and use as a douche 3 times daily.

HEALTHFUL COCKTAILS

Infuse with sage and gargle for sore throats.

CAUTIONS AND CONTRAINDICATIONS

Avoid during pregnancy.

Lawn

I recall throughout my childhood my fathers constant battle with his lawn. It was full of moss and daisies, with the odd dandelion. It always broke my heart when it was mowed as all the smiling daisy flowers were gone in the flicker of an eye. I think the moss was the main frustration for my dad who religiously applied herbicide every season, only for the moss to persevere and grow back, strong as ever.

Bill Mollison, co-founder of the permaculture movement, once famously coined the phrase of lawns being nothing but 'green deserts.' The well manicured lawns of suburbia can often be this way, unless the 'weeds' are as determined as they were in my parents' back garden. However, it just takes a minor change of attitude to see your lawn as a resource, no longer an enemy to battle with and trimmed mechanically to within an inch of its life. Allow it to grow just a little longer than normal and see what volunteers wind their way to you.

Personally I never realised how incredibly diverse and complex a piece of 'grass' could be until, as part of my degree dissertation, I found myself flinging $1m^2$ grids known as quadrats over grazed hillsides in the highlands of Scotland for a month. Each $1m^2$ was broken down into one hundred $10cm^2$ sections and, by identifying and counting the number of species within each, I finally got a total for the whole square metre. What amazed me was that to the untrained eye it just looked like grass, but in my most diverse quadrat I actually found 75 species and that was in just $1m^2$. Incredible! Never overlook 'grass' because, unless chemically manipulated to be a monoculture, a 'green desert' it may indeed be, but it can also be a treasure chest of medicines and nutritional treats.

Clover, Red (Trifolium pratense)

A popular lawn volunteer which has kept countless children and adults alike absorbed in the search for a 'four leafer,' a well known talisman bringing great fortune to the lucky finder! Flowers, leaves and sprouted seeds can all be added to salads. If you want sprouts it is recommended that you buy a pack of seeds from the health store, otherwise you would probably spend all summer trying to collect enough seed for one serving. Attractive to bees, they keep your garden aglow with a healthy buzz all summer long.

Clover is gentle enough to be used with children, and yet has the power to treat certain cancers. Red clover has a long corolla which means that only certain long tongued bees can pollinate it. Wild bumble bees are the most adept, but their presence is unreliable. Honey bees, despite having a shorter tongue, can also pollinate it, but tend to prefer other flowers that are easier for them. So as the bee numbers decline we may be in danger of losing red clover. It is important not just to us but to other plant life too as its roots are covered in nitrogen depositing nodules, giving vital nutrients back to the soil which are needed for the healthy growth of other plant life. Once you start to look at individual species and the important role they play it becomes even more of a tragedy that we are losing our bees. It makes you realise just quite how delicately balanced the whole web of life is, and our place within it.

MATERIA MEDICA

Blood cleanser, detoxifier, diuretic, expectorant, relaxant, relaxes spasms

GATHERING

Only the flowers are used in medicinal preparations and should be collected just as they open. This will be ongoing from May until September. Dry the flowers away from direct sunlight to preserve them for the winter season.

PREPARATIONS

- *Crush* on insect bites and stings.
- *Compress* for arthritic pain and gout.
- *Infusion* (fresh or dried) for relief of menopausal symptoms, especially hot flushes. It is useful as a spring tonic, cleansing the liver, blood and lymph, clearing out heavy metals and chemicals, especially useful after drug therapy, giving increased levels of vitality. It can be cleansing on emotional levels too, releasing old traumas, and acting as a relaxant, easing stress induced headaches, hyperactivity and muscle tension. Clover can also ease inflammatory skin conditions such as eczema, psoriasis and rashes. Also for chest infections, loosening phlegm, whooping cough and dry coughs. It provides support for degenerative diseases including some cancers. It is claimed that it can break down tumours and help prevent their spread. By preventing the loss of calcium it can help guard against osteoporosis. In addition it may help lower blood sugar, thin blood (thereby improving circulation), ease mastitis and gout. Externally the infusion can be used as a skin wash for eczema and psoriasis, although it is not to be used on open wounds.
- *Salve* for eczema and psoriasis (not on open wounds).
- *Syrup* for coughs to loosen phlegm and calm bronchial spasms.
- *Tincture* has same action internally as an infusion.

HEALTHFUL COCKTAILS

Infuse with elderflowers, leave to cool and drop in some ice for a cooling beverage on a hot summer's day.

Infuse with cleavers for a spring time lymphatic cleanse.

Infuse with nettle to clear minor skin outbreaks.

CAUTIONS AND CONTRAINDICATIONS

The action of clover may interfere with drug absorption in the liver, so check with your health care professional before using if you are currently on drug therapy. Avoid during pregnancy and breast feeding.

Daisy (Bellis perennis)

Not just for daisy chains, this robust little flower will return again and again to the lawn, seemingly untouched by slugs or other plant predators. It is said by some to bring love (Cunningham, 1985). Perhaps you can feel it as your heart gives a little jump when seeing a lawn adorned by the daisy's sunny flowers. The hairy leaves, although edible, are a little tough and sour and have a kind of lime tang. I add both the leaves and a few of the flower heads to my salads. The flowers always seem to cheer the presentation up.

MATERIA MEDICA

Anti-inflammatory, expectorant, relaxes spasms

GATHERING

Collect the leaves and flowers as needed throughout the summertime.

PREPARATIONS

- *Bath* for bruises, sore or aching muscles and rashes.
- *Eyebath* for sore eyes.
- *Infusion* for coughs, mucous, catarrh, bladder ailments, digestive problems and colic. It's a gentle laxative and paradoxically is also useful in mild diarrhoea. It is also good to drink as a tonic, cleansing the blood.
- *Salve* (leaves) for swellings, burns, minor skin wounds, varicose veins and bruises.

CAUTIONS AND CONTRAINDICATIONS

Avoid during pregnancy and breast feeding.

Dandelion (Taraxacum officinale)

It is said to contain the spirit of fairies (Kircher, 2001) which is hardly surprising when you have blown the beautiful seed heads and watched the seeds dissipate in the breeze like fairies. Popular with bees, the flowers are antioxidant and the petals can be pulled off and scattered on food as a colourful garnish. The flowers also contain leutin, a nutrient which is beneficial to eye health. I know that when my carefully nurtured rocket leaves are suddenly decimated by flea beetle I can rely on dandelion to add flavour to my salad bowl. The leaves are high in beta-carotene, potassium, iron, calcium and vitamins A & C and so are super nutritious, although best picked when small or in winter when they are less bitter. Leaves can also be added to a blender and made into a green smoothie using just a couple of leaves blended with other greens such as nettle along with water or fresh apple juice.

MATERIA MEDICA

Antibacterial, anti-inflammatory, antiviral, blood cleanser, digestive, powerful diuretic (I always remember being told that if you picked dandelions you would wet your bed!).

GATHERING

Harvest the leaves more or less throughout the year. Roots are best collected in the autumn and winter.

PREPARATIONS

- *Crush* (juice from stems) on warts and bee stings.
- *Decoction* (root) for menopausal women, as a liver cleanser, for gall stones and gall bladder inflammation, as an appetite stimulant and digestive aid.
- *Infusion* (leaves) for bruises, muscular rheumatism, stiff joints, gout, sleeplessness, anemia and upper respiratory tract infections. Increases the production of bile which supports the digestion easing heartburn, flatulence, dyspepsia and constipation. Helps clear skin conditions including eczema, psoriasis and acne, especially when resulting from a congested digestive system. It acts as a mild laxative also lowering blood pressure and cholesterol. A powerful diuretic easing premenstrual fluid retention and unlike with manufactured diuretics you will not lose minerals as by drinking dandelion you will be replacing them as you go.

HEALTHFUL COCKTAILS

Juice a couple of leaves with beetroot and carrot for a great liver and blood cleansing drink.

CAUTIONS AND CONTRAINDICATIONS

Avoid if planning or during pregnancy and whilst breast feeding. Do not use if your bile ducts are blocked (Vaughan, 2003).

Plantain (Plantago major)

Several years ago I went on a wild plant walk in an inner city area of Bristol. I was amazed that the information started in the car park. The guy leading the walk bent down and pulled up a plantain leaf pushing up through a crack in the concrete. He crushed it and rubbed it on his skin where we could see a light green juice. It was, he announced, the perfect antidote to a bite or sting.

There are two types of plantain you will commonly see dotted around lawns and wild areas; broad and narrow leaf (Plantago lanceolata). Their properties are quite similar and they can be used interchangeably in any of the preparations. The leaf is edible but best consumed young as they toughen and get more fibrous with age. Rich in silica, the leaves assist in tissue repair. Probably the most widespread medicinal use of plantain is from the psyllium variety where the seeds are used as a laxative and to soothe irritations in the gut lining. Unfortunately that variety is native to the Mediterranean and does not grow well in the UK.

MATERIA MEDICA

Antibacterial, antibiotic, anti-inflammatory, astringent, diuretic, expectorant

GATHERING

Leaves can be collected as needed throughout the growing season.

PREPARATIONS

- *Crush* and rub on a sting or bite.
- *Eyebath* for eye inflammations.
- *Infusion* for diarrhoea, gastritis, gastric ulcer, IBS, cystitis, bronchitis, dry cough, catarrh, sinusitis, asthma, hay fever and ear infections. It makes a great spring cleanse, clearing mucous, cleansing blood and stimulating the digestive tract. It can also reduce excessive menstrual flow. It is a restorative tonic and will help build up convalescents. It provides an earthy and grounding brew, helpful after an emotional shock or trauma. Used as a skin wash it's great for rashes, acne, wounds, insect bites, ulcers and bruises.
- *Juice* apply directly to relieve sun burn and nappy rash. For use in cases of IBS, juice 4-5 leaves every morning, mix with another juice to disguise the taste and drink before eating. It not only heals damaged tissue but also pulls out toxins. You will notice a great improvement in your condition within 2 weeks. You may need to continue this juice for 6 - 8 months if you have been suffering with longterm gastrointestinal problems.
- *Oil* for rashes, swellings and sprains.
- *Poultice* prepared on the spot by chewing leaf and applying directly to wounds to stop them bleeding and for its antibacterial properties.
- *Salve* for rashes (including nappy rash), cuts, swelling, sprains, burns and eczema.
- *Syrup* as a digestive and appetite stimulant. It also helps in cases of gastritis, diarrhoea, asthma, whooping cough, catarrh, bronchitis and throat inflammation.

HEALTHFUL COCKTAILS

Infuse with elderflower to strengthen and protect the mucous membranes, easing the symptoms of hay fever.

CAUTIONS AND CONTRAINDICATIONS

None known.

Selfheal (Prunella vulgaris)

It is quite easily overlooked amongst the green expanse of lawn, but once flowering you will notice the beautiful purple flower spikes punctuating the green. Young leaves are edible and a useful addition to a wild salad bowl or cooked in soups and stews. Bees will happily buzz around lawns collecting the pollen.

MATERIA MEDICA

Antibacterial, anti-inflammatory, antioxidant, astringent, diuretic, liver tonic, lowers fevers

GATHERING

The aerial parts (leaves, stems, flower heads) can be collected throughout the growing season. Flowers from mid to late summer.

PREPARATIONS

- *Crush* (leaf) on temples for headache.
- *Eyebath* for inflamed or sore eyes and sties.
- *Gargle* for sore throats and laryngitis.
- *Infusion* to reduce excessive menstruation and fever. It stimulates the liver and so is used as a spring tonic and is also useful for periods of convalescence. In addition it eases diarrhoea. Used as a skin wash it is good for sores, burns and bruises.
- *Mouthwash* for mouth inflammation and ulcers.
- *Poultice* for cuts, wounds and sprains.
- *Salve* for hemorrhoids and wounds.

CAUTIONS AND CONTRAINDICATIONS

None known.

Yarrow (Achillea millefolium)

Yarrow has long been associated with magic and ingesting it is said to improve your alertness and psychic abilities. The dried stalks are cast in traditional I Ching for divination, adding to its magical allure. It is edible but has a bitter taste, so is best cooked in a soup or stew. Loved by butterflies, hoverflies, ladybirds and parasitic wasps, all of whom help keep the garden free of pests, especially aphids, making it a great plant to have around.

The Medicine Garden

MATERIA MEDICA

Anti-inflammatory, antiseptic, antimicrobial, astringent, diuretic

GATHERING

Collect leaves throughout the growing season as needed. Leaves can be used fresh or dried.

PREPARATIONS

- *Bath* for inflamed skin.
- *Chew* (fresh leaf) and hold onto a bleeding wound; it not only stops the bleeding but, if held in place with a plaster or tape for a while, it heals the wound so quickly you will be left wondering what all the fuss was about. The chewed wad can also be inserted in a nostril to stop a nosebleed or kept in the mouth for a toothache.
- *Infusion* for diarrhoea, stomach ulcer, recurrent urinary tract infections, cystitis, provides relief from bladder irritations and promotes urination. It helps reduce the symptoms of PMS including irritability, cramps, regulates menstruation and reduces excessive bleeding during menstruation. It thins the blood and lowers blood pressure, so is a preventative measure against thrombosis after a stroke or heart attack (Brown, 1995). As an immune stimulant it's great to start drinking at the first sign of a cold or flu, or even when a colleague or family member gets it as you may then manage to totally avoid the cold yourself. During a cold or the flu it will stimulate perspiration and help lower fever. Drinking will tone the digestive tract, easing diarrhoea, reducing food sensitivities and helping to heal leaky gut syndrome. The infusion can be used as a skin wash on wounds, cleaning them and helping to prevent infection.
- *Liquid extract* juice the fresh leaves and make a 1:1 mixture with alcohol (40° vol. min.). This preserves the medicinal properties and makes them readily available, so that on a dark winter's evening when you begin to feel the first tingle of a virus you will not need to grab your coat and torch and scurry about the lawn looking for a few leaves, but can simply squirt a dropper full into warm water or another complimentary tea and drink it with the self-assured satisfaction that you are receiving the medicine you need.
- *Mouthwash* for toothache and gum inflammation.
- *Oil* for earache.
- *Poultice* for minor cuts and abrasions (see chew).
- *Salve* for skin wounds and hemorrhoids.

HEALTHFUL COCKTAILS

Infuse and add a spoonful of elderberry syrup at the onset of colds and flu.

Infuse with raspberry leaf and lady's mantle to lessen heavy menstrual bleeding.

CAUTIONS AND CONTRAINDICATIONS

Exercise caution if sensitive to asteraceae family. Not for internal use during the first 3 months of pregnancy or whilst breast feeding.

Flower Borders

The pride and joy of many a British household is the flower garden. We are world famous for our use of flowering plants to brighten up our outside living spaces. From cottage gardens to beds stuffed full of short lived annuals, this is where our individual style can be shown off to the world in all its glory. Not surprisingly I tend to err on the side of perennials; very low maintenance but with lots of medicinal and edible uses. I do love a good splash of brightly coloured flowers, though, and have been learning more and more that they too hold medicinal gifts for us.

Using hardy perennials, especially those as close to their wild form as possible, where they readily self-seed, will mean easy gardening for you. The less hybridized, the better, as they will be naturally strong, needing very little attention and no feed or herbicide, even organic ones, as they have naturally evolved to survive. Alongside a little selective weeding now and then, the most time consuming part may end up being pulling up the seedlings of those that have multiplied too enthusiastically. You can always pot these babies up and give them to friends and family throughout the summer. I always feel a bit subversive when asked to plant up and fill space in people's borders as I tend to choose plants that I love to use in my kitchen apothecary rather than the more fancy showy blooms that one would assume to be preferred. These time proven herbal remedies, of course, are also friends of the bees and butterflies, and as no flowering bed is complete without the healthy buzz and flutter of a whole host of winged friends on a long hot summer's day, I always manage to create the desired effect whilst sneaking a few medicinal favourites in for good measure. By doing the same yourself you will in no way reduce the visual impact of a stunning border, but you may just be preparing yourself with some valuable back up for an uncertain planetary future. Growing in this way provides living nutritional and medicinal resources to compliment those that currently come wrapped in plastic from overseas for our convenience. The original cottage gardens were indeed a multi-layered treasure trove of food and home remedies, not just a sensory delight. We have now just gone full circle.

Arnica (Arnica montana)

Arnica is known for its ability to provide pain relief and reduce swellings. I had the opportunity to put this sunny little flower to the test the day before my brother's wedding when I hit my eyebrow on a metal bar in a big industrial greenhouse, almost knocking myself out. Once I had recovered enough to stagger to a patch of flowering arnica I pulled off a few blooms, chewed them up a bit, then sat in the shade holding them to my eyebrow for the next 30 minutes as I recovered. Despite the fact it was a big old bump at the time, when the photos came back you could hardly notice it at all.

It has been imbibed in Germany for hundreds of years for heart conditions. It is, however, an irritant to mucous membranes, especially of the gastrointestinal tract, and is consequently restricted to external use in the UK. I was surprised to learn of that restriction, having been given homeopathic arnica pills on several occasions for internal bruising resulting from falls or particularly heavy going chiropractic, acupuncture or massage sessions. In fact it is available in its homeopathic form from health stores for internal shock, pain and bruising, having a negligible effect on mucous membranes in such tiny quantities.

To find arnica in the wild is rare . If you would like to make preparations with this wonderful sunny plant you would be well advised to grow it for yourself to preserve what's left in the wild. Being quite low growing at only 10-60cms, it would easily slip into the front of a border flush with blooms from the yellow part of the spectrum.

MATERIA MEDICA

Anti-inflammatory, pain relief

GATHERING

The flowers are picked when fully open, from early to late summer, and can be used fresh in preparations or dried before processing.

PREPARATIONS

- *Compress* for joint pains, muscle pains and even broken bones. Make either by diluting the tincture 1:4 with water, or using an infusion made with either fresh or dried flowers.
- *Gargle* for sore throats and laryngitis.
- *Oil* to massage athletic members of the family after big exertions such as competitive events. It's anti-inflammatory and gives relief from the pain of bruising, sprains and dislocations. It can also be massaged onto arthritic joints, rheumatic pains and muscle soreness.
- *Poultice* for bruises and painful swellings.
- *Salve* for varicose veins and chilblains. For immediate relief from a bump with swelling and to speed up the healing of bruises. Use regularly on painful arthritic joints.
- *Tincture* for external use only on chilblains, bruises, sprains but only use if the skin remains unbroken. To reduce severe swellings repeat application at 20 minute intervals until you get the required results.

CAUTIONS AND CONTRAINDICATIONS

Do a skin test first with any preparation as it may cause a skin rash or irritation. Do not use on broken skin. Do not use internally.

Balloon Flower (Platycodon grandiflorus)

This plant has rather cute flowers, especially before the blooms open. I guess they look a bit like hot air balloons and certainly look inflated. Being only small at a maximum height of 90cm (often much lower depending on variety), they look good at the front of borders. Their preferred and more natural position would be in a rock garden or rocky border. Balloon flowers were introduced from China where they have been used medicinally since antiquity. Not confined solely to eastern medicine, platycodon is also a flavouring for Japan's most famous drink, sake.

MATERIA MEDICA

Anti-inflammatory, expectorant, pain relief

GATHERING

Roots are lifted from plants 3-4 years old, and peeled. They can then be used fresh or dried.

PREPARATIONS

- *Gargle* for sore throats, laryngitis and tonsillitis. Use honey to improve the taste as it is rather bitter and a little unpleasant.
- *Syrup* the roots cause the bronchial tubes to dilate, making it an ideal remedy for coughs with lots of sticky phlegm, bronchitis, pleurisy, colds and throat infections.

CAUTIONS AND CONTRAINDICATIONS

Do not take for extended periods (longer than 3 weeks). Do not use if you have a long term cough, are vomiting blood, suffering from liver disease or are pregnant.

Bergamot (Monarda didyma)

Hmm......the unmistakable aroma of a fresh pot of Earl grey tea is the perfume belonging to bergamot. The flowers, like pompoms, remind me of fireworks bursting forth, especially the double blooms, one flower exploding in colour directly above the next. They are highly attractive to butterflies and are also known as beebalm, so obviously they are rather attractive to our buzzing friends as well. They are a colourful addition to any garden, reaching 1.2m and can be used as an architectural plant for height and colour at the back of a border.

The leaves can be eaten raw in salads or chopped finely and used as a floating garnish in summer drinks and cocktails where their cooling action will be more than welcome on a long hot summer's afternoon. Flowers can also be eaten raw, bringing a splash of colour to your plate. They belong to the mint family and are rich in the volatile oil thymol, the active ingredient in thyme, which has antiseptic and expectorant qualities.

MATERIA MEDICA

Antiseptic, antiemetic, digestive, expectorant, lowers fever, sedative

GATHERING

Collect the blooms when flowering (from early summer until mid-autumn depending on the plants' position in the garden) and the leaves prior to the opening of the blooms. They can be used either fresh or dried for infusions.

PREPARATIONS

- *Bath* is revitalising, and will help clear the mind, bringing clarity to a situation.
- *Crush* directly on pimples.
- *Infusion* for minor digestive complaints, nausea, to stop vomiting and flatulence. It relieves insomnia, promoting restful sleep, relaxing nerves and reducing tension. It induces perspiration, lowering fevers and easing colds, bronchial complaints and sore throats. It reduces pain and is helpful for painful periods and rheumatic aches.
- *Tincture* has the same effect as an infusion, but is stronger in its action.

CAUTIONS AND CONTRAINDICATIONS

Avoid during pregnancy.

Carnation /Pinks (Dianthus chinensis)

Most often with a silvery grey foliage, the flowers having a fringed edge in colours ranging from deep red to white and every shade of pink in between. They make a great cut flower, but I can never bring myself to remove them from their happy home, waving around with all the insects and other flowers in the garden. The fresh petals can be eaten but be sure to remove the bitter petal base or it won't taste so good. They are surprisingly easy to grow and make a great low growing and colourful edge to any planted area.

MATERIA MEDICA

Antibacterial, anti-inflammatory, diuretic, nerve tonic, reduces fever

GATHERING

The whole of the aerial part of the plant is used and collected when flowering throughout the summer. The blooms can subsequently be dried for later use.

PREPARATIONS

- *Bath* adding a few fresh or dried blooms will help to boost energy.
- *Infusion* as a nerve tonic and to reduce blood pressure. It stimulates the urinary system and is useful for urinary tract infections, urinary stones and cystitis. It helps control bacterial infections and reduce fever. Stimulating to the digestive system and bowels, it helps relieve constipation. In addition it helps encourage delayed menstruation. The infusion can be used externally as a skin wash for skin inflammations, swellings and eczema.

CAUTIONS AND CONTRAINDICATIONS

Avoid during pregnancy.

Columbine (Aquilegia vulgaris)

This grows like a weed in my garden, self-seeding like crazy all over the place. It is just as well I love it so much. The flower has a delicate flavour. I love to nibble on them while spending time in the garden, although they work great on a plate too. The beautiful otherworldly flowers, also known as Granny's bonnet, are in bloom throughout May and June. Due to mild levels of toxicity in all parts but the flower, aquilegia is rarely used internally except under expert supervision.

MATERIA MEDICA

Head lice control

GATHERING

The seeds are collected as they ripen in mid-summer. Once the flower has died off a green seed head remains. If the seeds inside are black it means they are ripe. You can wait for the seed heads to go brown but by then many will already have fallen from the pod, meaning you will have to harvest more heads to get the number of seeds you need.

PREPARATIONS

- **Crush** onto skin to get rid of lice. You can also crush the seeds with a pestle and mortar. Add a tiny amount of water to create a paste, this can be rubbed into hair and scalp to eradicate head lice. Knowing the desperation parents go through trying to rid their children of lice I thought this was worthy of a mention despite being a bit messy, even if it's only used when all else has failed.

CAUTIONS AND CONTRAINDICATIONS

Do not use internally.

Crocus (Crocus sativus)

One of the first flowers of spring, they can even poke up through a light snow, reminding us of the world of colour that's soon to come. The medicinal parts of a crocus are the stigmas. You can see the stigmas when you look into the flower; they are the bright orange threads. Once gathered, the stigmas are collectively known as saffron which has been used for over 4000 years. Each flower has so few strands it is soon easy to understand why saffron is so expensive. Most people have a few clumps of crocus peppering their early spring garden.

You will never manage to collect kilos from such a small amount, but depending on how many you have you may get a precious handful or two.

It is highly valued in Asia and the Middle East for its reported aphrodisiac properties and is used extensively in food during Indian weddings and other celebrations as a show of wealth. You are most likely to have come across saffron in a culinary context as it is often used as a colouring and flavouring in rice dishes such as paella, risotto and biryani. It is occasionally used in cakes and biscuits too.

MATERIA MEDICA

Antibacterial, antiseptic, antiviral, digestive, diuretic, improves circulation, increases perspiration, relaxes muscle spasms

GATHERING

Saffron can only be collected when the crocus is in flower, for obvious reasons. Dry for storage and use within the year as the properties will not last for longer than this. It is best to store them whole as powdering will create more surface area to oxidize and the medicinal properties will be lost as it does so.

PREPARATIONS

- *Infusion* only use a tiny pinch, never more than 10 strands. Dissolve in a glass of warm water or milk, sweeten with honey and drink daily over several weeks to reap the benefits. It's used to stimulate circulation, reduce blood pressure, reduce cholesterol and reduce atherosclerosis, guarding against heart attack. Also for asthma, coughs, colds and to clear the lungs. It will help relieve tension, depression and insomnia. It's a stimulant to the digestive system, calming indigestion, improving appetite and relieving stomach cramps. It also stimulates the uterus, helping to induce menstruation and relieve cramping period pains.
- *Tincture* making a tincture straight after gathering the saffron will help preserve the medicinal properties in a more stable way. A dropper full can be used once a day over several weeks as a tonic for the system and for the same complaints as the infusion.

CAUTIONS AND CONTRAINDICATIONS

Excessive intake can be harmful. Avoid during pregnancy.

Echinacea (Echinacea purpurea)

A vibrant, bold flower brightening up gardens from mid-summer until early autumn. I recommend a close look at the centre of the flower head. It's actually quite stiff and bristly, so don't lean down too close and get it in your eye or you will surely know about it!

Echinacea angustifolia, I have been assured by a master herbalist in the States, is the superior herb to use, however it appears that purpurea is the more easy to grow in our climate and is the one used in most of the preparations that you can purchase. Echinacea did originate in North America so I would trust the original knowledge offered by my friend that angustifolia is the more potent. I have seen purpurea, angustifolia and pallida plants and seed for sale, so when stocking your borders the choice will of course be yours. The three species have similar actions and can be used interchangeably.

Many people over use this wonder plant believing that constant use will keep their immune systems pumped up and protect them from any infection or virus doing the rounds. To do this would be ill-informed and might in fact produce side effects imitating the symptoms this behaviour was undertaken to avoid. For example, echinacea provides a boost to the system and is a tonic when suffering from exhaustion, but if taken for longer than two weeks it will inadvertently cause exhaustion. The good news is that when taken respectfully and for short periods it is exceptionally powerful and yet still safe to use with children. In fact it is so highly regarded that it is often considered the most effective detoxicant for the circulatory, lymphatic and respiratory systems that is readily available to us.

MATERIA MEDICA

Antibacterial, antifungal, anti-inflammatory, antiviral, immuno-stimulant

GATHERING

The roots of mature plants (4 years or older) are collected in autumn. They can be preserved by drying, freezing or processing into a tincture or infused oil. The aerial parts can be used in the first couple of years whilst waiting for the root to mature and can be made into a liquid extraction used as you would the tincture, although the effect will not be as strong.

PREPARATIONS

- *Decoction* (root) make using a fresh or dried piece of root. If you have frozen the root, simply grate a teaspoon full into hot water and leave to steep for 10 minutes before drinking. Use for the same conditions as the tincture.
- *Gargle* (diluted tincture, liquid extraction or decoction) for sore throats, tonsillitis, laryngitis.
- *Liquid Extraction* (aerial parts) use as you would the tincture, although expect less dramatic results.
- *Mouthwash* (diluted tincture, liquid extraction or decoction) for inflamed gums.
- *Salve* (root) for minor cuts, infected wounds, acne, herpes and psoriasis. For stronger action make a double or triple infused oil to use as the base.
- *Tincture* (root) the indication of a good tincture is a tingling on the tongue. This will provide a powerful impact on the nervous system. It acts most strongly within the blood and lymph, removing toxins and stimulating the immune system and is a great remedy when there is a low fever, swollen glands and skin eruptions associated with toxicity such as pimples, boils and abscesses. It contains flavenoids which strengthen blood vessels and destroy free radicals, protecting against premature aging and some cancers. It is most commonly used at the first sign of a cold or viral infection. At this

point it's recommended to take 15-30 drops every 3 hours for up to 24 hours. Also used for coughs, catarrh in the nose, sinus and lungs, laryngitis and tonsillitis. To clear up chronic or minor infections, septicemia, septic fevers, slow healing wounds, venereal diseases and fungal infections. Brings relief from exhaustion and chronic fatigue syndrome. Applied topically it can clear fungal infections such as athlete's foot, and relieve bites and stings.

HEALTHFUL COCKTAILS

Infuse grated root with yarrow for a powerful impact on the immune system at the first sign of a cold or viral infection.

CAUTIONS AND CONTRAINDICATIONS

Use with caution if sensitive to asteraceae family. Excess causes throat irritation. It may interfere with drugs taken for hiv and tb and is not necessarily helpful for auto-immune diseases, so, as always, check with a healthcare professional first if you are already undergoing drug therapy or are suffering a chronic illness. Do not take continuously for longer than an absolute maximum of 8 weeks at a time.

Elecampane (Inula helenium)

It's quite tall, growing up to 2 metres and is a handy plant for the back of a border, its generous leaves cutting light to anything below, shading out weeds in those hard to get to areas. The bright yellow blooms seem somehow out of proportion with the leaf size despite reaching up to 10cm in diameter. I, however, like Inula for the light green leaf itself, being deeply patterned by veins and for their incredible size, reminding me a little of elephants' ears, although I doubt any self-respecting mahout would agree. A very useful plant medicinally and safe to use for children. One of its more alternative uses is the sharpening of psychic powers which is achieved by allowing the leaves to smoulder like incense on a charcoal disc (Cunningham, 1985).

MATERIA MEDICA

Antibacterial, antifungal, anti-inflammatory, antiparasitic, antiseptic, diuretic, expectorant, induces perspiration, immuno-stimulant, pain relief

GATHERING

Dig up the roots in the autumn of plants 2-3 years old. After this age the roots become rather woody. The root is best frozen fresh as this will preserve the volatile oils and is the most reliable method of preserving the medicinal qualities without further processing. The flowers are collected whilst open, from June until August, and dried or used fresh.

PREPARATIONS

- *Decoction* (root) the taste is rather unpleasant so be prepared and perhaps mix in a spoonful of honey, or mix with other plants that have similar uses and strong flavours that will disguise the bitterness a little. Being antibacterial and expectorant it is a popular remedy for the chest and respiratory tract, helping to soothe inflamed airways and reduce coughing whilst loosening and helping to expel phlegm. It brings great relief from chest infections, bronchial diseases, pleurisy, whooping cough, emphysema, asthma and allergies that are affecting breathing such as hay fever. It can be used as a lung tonic, cleansing and toning the mucous membranes. It will also stimulate the uterus, promoting menstruation, help treat anemia and increase the flow of bile. Apply externally as a skin wash to scabies, itching skin and eczema.
- *Infusion* (flowers) for nausea, diarrhoea and stomach complaints.
- *Syrup* (root) begin use at the first sign of a respiratory infection and take up to 4 tablespoons daily.
- *Tincture* (root) add to warm water and use as you would the decoction.

HEALTHFUL COCKTAILS

Decoct with echinacea or add a little yarrow to the hot decoction and allow to infuse at the onset of a cough, cold or viral infection.

Stir a spoonful of the syrup in with a ginger decoction to loosen phlegm.

Combine in a syrup with thyme to soothe and fight chest infections, or with fennel to clear mucous and ease chronic coughs.

CAUTIONS AND CONTRAINDICATIONS

Use with caution if sensitive to asteracacae family. Avoid during pregnancy.

Evening Primrose (Oenothera biennis)

Another tall plant reaching 1.2 metres in height, although if not propped up by surrounding plants or a thin stake it has a tendency to lean over. Although only biennial, evening primrose will successfully self-sow if it's left to go to seed. It is loved by moths who do their pollinating during the evening and at night, which may be a clue as to how it received its common name.

It has achieved an increasing amount of interest in recent years due to its high gammalinolenic acid (GLA) content. This essential fatty acid is contained in the seeds, which are pressed for their oil. The oil helps regulate hormonal systems and is especially used by menopausal women and those who suffer pre-menstrual syndrome (PMS). It's also widely used in inflammatory conditions such as eczema and rheumatoid arthritis. Unfortunately the seeds are relatively tiny and so collecting and pressing them at home to extract usable quantities of this oil would be an almost impossible task. Luckily you can eat the young seed pods and by doing this you will absorb some of the benefits of the extracted oil. The seed pods are best eaten when still a little immature as the older they get, the tougher they get. Try chewing on a fresh one or eat them steamed. The leaves, flowers and roots are also edible and young leaves can be added to salads or cooked as a green leaf ingredient in many dishes. The flowers are a bright addition to any salad or as an edible garnish. The roots have a parsnip like flavour and can be lifted in the second year for use in soups and stews.

MATERIA MEDICA

Astringent, expectorant, pain relief, sedative

GATHERING

Collect all the aerial parts (leaves, stems and flowers) in the second year as the flowering spike makes its appearance. The root is collected in the autumn of the second year.

PREPARATIONS

- *Decoction* (root) as an expectorant to loosen and expel phlegm in stubborn coughs and bronchitis. To bring pain relief for arthritic and rheumatic conditions.
- *Infusion* (leaf & stem) for asthma and whooping cough. It will help balance out menstrual problems, easing the symptoms of PMS. It acts on the gastrointestinal tract, soothing and aiding problems associated with digestion. It can be used externally as a skin wash on dry, itchy, irritated skin, notably rashes and eczema. Use the flower to bring pain relief for headaches.
- *Poultice* (leaf) on boils, abscesses and rheumatic pains.
- *Tincture* (flower) to relieve anxiety and insomnia.

CAUTIONS AND CONTRAINDICATIONS

Virtually non toxic, although it may be worth avoiding during pregnancy.

Feverfew (Tanacetum parthenium)

The flowers are daisy-like in appearance and self-seed readily, so you may want to keep on top of any new seedlings. If it starts to take over you could always pot these up and give them away to friends. It is a strong little plant, a survivor, and will still happily flourish despite ongoing neglect and poor soil, an easy triumph for the lazy gardener. A very useful plant to have around, especially if you are a migraine or arthritis sufferer.

MATERIA MEDICA

Antibiotic, anti-inflammatory, digestive, helps kill and expel worms, lowers fever, pain relief, relieves spasms

GATHERING

Pick the leaves as needed throughout the spring and summer. Save some for infusions during the winter months when the foliage has died back, although they do not dry well, losing their potency rather quickly, so it is best to freeze them. Collect the flowers when in full bloom and process into a tincture immediately to avoid losing any medicinal potency.

PREPARATIONS

- *Eat* (leaf) to prevent migraine and alleviate rheumatism and arthritis. Just take a couple of decent sized leaves and eat them on a daily basis. You can put them in a sandwich or chop them into a salad if you want to disguise the bitter flavour. This will act as an effective preventative for migraine, but if you do feel one coming on, eating a couple of extra leaves will also ease any nausea or vomiting that may accompany the attack.
- *Infusion* (leaf) can help ease depression and soothe you into a restful sleep. It will promote good digestion, alleviating indigestion, flatulence, colic, bloating and stomach cramps. It helps rid the digestive system of worms and acts as a mild laxative. It is used for both asthma and bronchitis and, by dilating the blood vessels, helps to improve circulation and lower a fever. It stimulates the uterus, helping induce delayed menstruation and is even used to aid in the expulsion of the placenta after child birth.
- *Washed* over the skin it will act as an insect repellent.
- *Oil* (leaves) rub into the skin as an insect repellent.
- *Tincture* (flowers) apply directly to insect bites for instant relief. Dilute a teaspoon of the tincture in a tea cup of water, then rub over the skin as an insect repellent. If this is not effective use less water to dilute the mixture before applying to your skin.

CAUTIONS AND CONTRAINDICATIONS

Use with caution if sensitive to asteracacae family, or on medication for blood thinning. Do not take continuously for periods exceeding 4 months. If you start to develop mouth ulcers discontinue use. Avoid if pregnant, breast feeding or under 2 years of age.

Gentian, Yellow (Gentiana lutea)

Several species grow wild in the British Isles, the most prolific being pneumonanthe. However, if you are choosing one to grow in your garden rather than collect from the wild then you are only limited by the seeds or ready grown plants that are available, the individual climatic conditions of your back garden and your skill as a gardener. They are renowned as being tricky to grow. Lutea is native to the mountainous regions of France and Spain, but it grows well here and is better known for its medicinal value than our own native varieties.

Gentian has been used since ancient times, especially to benefit the digestive system. It contains the glycoside amarogentin, one of most bitter substances known. Angostura bitters, a cocktail ingredient, is more or less a gentian tincture and was traditionally added to drinks to aid digestion prior to a particularly rich or heavy meal.

MATERIA MEDICA

Anti-inflammatory, antimicrobial, antiparasitic, antiseptic, lowers fever, relieves pain, sedative

GATHERING

The roots are lifted in autumn and dried for use in decoctions, or processed into tinctures. To dry the root thoroughly it must first be sliced and then dried slowly, out of direct sunlight.

PREPARATIONS

- *Chew* to reduce tobacco cravings.
- *Decoction* make with only ½ teaspoon. The taste is extremely bitter so you may have to start with a weaker decoction and slowly build up to this strength. Drink 30 minutes before eating if using for its beneficial effects on the digestive system. It will stimulate gastric secretions, improving a sluggish digestion, flatulence, heartburn and dyspepsia. It will treat gastritis, diarrhoea and nausea, can help stimulate appetite in the sick, elderly and recovering anorexics, helps to prevent and clear intestinal infection whilst maintaining a healthy balance of intestinal flora, essential for optimum body function. It can also be used to kill and expel worms resident in the gastrointestinal tract. The increase in gastric secretions that is stimulated by drinking gentian will help the body absorb nutrients from food, this can help anaemics as the iron absorption rate improves, but also vegans and others whose diets are naturally low in vitamin B12 as this will also be more efficiently absorbed from any ingested source. As gentian tonifies the entire gastrointestinal tract, it also stimulates peristalsis (wave like muscular contractions), helping to evacuate the bowel. It stimulates nerves and muscles throughout the body, having a tonic effect, and so is useful in the treatment of exhaustion. It improves the function of the gall bladder and liver, increasing the secretion of bile (essential for the digestion of fats). It increases pancreatic activity, improves blood circulation and stimulates menstruation, basically making the whole body more alive and work more efficiently. It has even been used for the successful treatment of malaria, although one must seek immediate medical attention if malaria is even suspected as it can be and often is fatal.
- *Poultice* for abscesses and boils.
- *Tincture* it is recommended to take ½ a teaspoon 3 times daily, one hour before meals as a digestive tonic. In 'A Modern Herbal' Mrs. M. Grieve recommends making the tincture with an aromatic to disguise the terribly bitter flavour. Her recipe uses 60g of root, 30g of orange peel and 15g of bruised cardamon seeds in brandy. Continue as you would any tincture by leaving to infuse for 3 weeks and shaking daily before squeezing through muslin as you bottle it up.

HEALTHFUL COCKTAILS

Decoct with ginger to allay nausea.

CAUTIONS AND CONTRAINDICATIONS

Avoid if pregnant, suffering nervous conditions, high blood pressure or gastric or duodenal ulcers.

Geranium (Geranium maculatum)

There are many varieties of geranium well known for their scented leaves. It is very easy to take cuttings from geraniums. I remember my very first experiments with plants at infant school; one was taking a cutting from a geranium. It was a success and my mother still has the plant alive and well. The other was growing a broad bean between a sheet of blotting paper and the clear glass walls of a jam jar so that you could see the moment by moment changes as it germinated, but that is another story...

Also known as cranesbills, they are not to be confused with the highly scented pelargoniums which have adopted geranium as their common name. They have a whole set of different actions on the body. Herb Robert, a freely self-sowing, pink flowered member of the geranium family can be used more or less interchangeably with maculatum for physical afflictions. I use herb Robert all the time in my practice. It has a special significance within the Plant Spirit Medicine world (see resources) and as such I personally hold the little biennial in particularly high regard. Geraniums are highly astringent and consequently are most often used to stem bleeding, dry up discharges and promote healing.

MATERIA MEDICA

Antiseptic, astringent

GATHERING

The whole plant, including the roots, can be used and is collected in early summer as flowering begins. It can be used fresh or dried for storage.

PREPARATIONS

- *Douche* for thrush and vaginal discharge.
- *Gargle* for sore, inflamed throats.
- *Infusion* gentle enough to use for diarrhoea in children and the elderly, but strong enough to treat dysentery, gastroenteritis, colitis, peptic ulcers and cholera. Also used to stem bleeding in the case of haemorrhage and excessive menstruation.
- *Mouthwash* for inflamed mouth, gums and ulcers.
- *Salve* for cuts, bruises, scrapes, eczema, hemorrhoids and varicose veins.

CAUTIONS AND CONTRAINDICATIONS

Avoid if pregnant or have an auto-immune disease.

Giant Hyssop (Agastache foeniculum)

Extremely aromatic, attractive to bees and butterflies and, as the name suggests, it stands quite tall (up to about 1m). I love the fluffy looking flower spikes, which remind me of the kind of brush that cleans the inside of a clarinet or other similar wind instrument. The almost lilac flowers are a must for every self-respecting faerie lover's garden. Also known as anise hyssop, the long lasting flower spikes are edible and provide a lightly aniseed flavoured addition to a fruit salad with plenty of visual impact. The leaves share the sweet aniseed flavour and are also edible, although older leaves become tougher and less palatable. It has been used medicinally for many hundreds of years, from the native tribes of North America where it originated, all the way to China.

MATERIA MEDICA

Antifungal, anti-inflammatory, antiviral

GATHERING

The leaves are collected in spring and summer and the flowers in summer (from June until September). They are used fresh or dried for teas.

PREPARATIONS

- *Infusion* to relieve respiratory congestion, for coughs and colds. It increases perspiration, helping to break a fever. Improves digestion by increasing gastric secretions.
- *Poultice* for minor burns.

CAUTIONS AND CONTRAINDICATIONS

None known.

Golden Rod (Solidago virgaurea)

Having a swathe of golden rod in the garden is a bit like having your own mini nature reserve. In the summer months its flowering heads are smothered in tiny yellow blooms waving like yellow flames from across the garden. It attracts a whole host of beneficial insects which will feast on garden pests such as aphids. Once late autumn and winter arrives and most of the summer foliage has died back, the golden rods remain. Although no longer flowering their height, when left in situ, will give movement in the largely dormant garden whilst providing a playground for the birds that remain. The birds are most probably attracted by the fine seeds which provide food, but also maybe for the protection its feathery height gives, but who knows; maybe they just like it.

MATERIA MEDICA

Anti-inflammatory, antifungal, antiseptic, astringent, diuretic, induces sweating

GATHERING

Collect the leaves, stalks and flowering heads just before the flowers open between mid-summer and mid-autumn. They can be used fresh or dried.

PREPARATIONS

- *Douche* for vaginal thrush.
- *Gargle* for sore throat, laryngitis and pharyngitis.
- *Infusion* it's a kidney tonic, helping expel kidney stones and clear up kidney infections. Also a urinary antiseptic clearing urinary stones, infections and cystitis. Due to the cleansing and eliminative properties it is also effective against arthritis, rheumatism and skin diseases. Its expectorant qualities help treat chronic catarrh, long term sinus and nasal congestion (not related to an infection), and whooping cough. It promotes sweating, making it worth using during a bout of flu to break the fever. As an anti-fungal it helps kill off a Candida albicans overgrowth. It will also help stimulate menstruation where it is delayed or absent. Drunk cold as a digestive tonic it will ease flatulence, dyspepsia, relieve diarrhoea and improve digestion. It can also be used externally as a face wash to remove excess oils and treat pimples.
- *Mouthwash* for oral thrush and mouth ulcers.
- *Salve* the astringent action helps draw together the skin of open wounds, promoting the healing of wounds, eczema and skin ulcers. It can also be applied to insect bites and stings.

CAUTIONS AND CONTRAINDICATIONS

Avoid using during pregnancy, breast feeding or if suffering serious heart or kidney problems.

Hollyhock (Alcea rosea)

Depending on the cultivar, hollyhock can grow up to a stunning 2.5m tall and is a must in every cottage garden. Unfortunately it is very attractive to slugs, making positioning and vigilance key to its survival. It's only a biennial or short lived perennial, but is worth having for the impact it has when flowering. The young leaves, petals and flower heads are all edible, although the leaves especially are a bit rough textured and don't taste great.

MATERIA MEDICA

Anti-inflammatory, astringent, diuretic, pain relief, soothing

GATHERING

Flowers are gathered in July and early August, when it's in full bloom. Dry carefully in the shade.

PREPARATIONS

- *Gargle* for sore, inflamed throat.
- *Infusion* its soothing action brings relief from peptic ulcers, gastritis, IBS, colic, diarrhoea, diverticulitis and reduces excess stomach acid. It will stimulate the immune system, is helpful during colds and soothes sore throats. The soothing action will bring great relief from chest infections whilst helping expel catarrh, easing coughs and bronchitis.
- *Mouthwash* for sore, inflamed mouth and gums.
- *Poultice* to draw the poison from boils, abscesses, insect bites, infected wounds and even splinters.
- *Salve* to soothe and heal skin inflammation and rashes.
- *Syrup* will moisten and cool the lungs, bringing relief from chest infections, dry coughs, chronic catarrh and sore throats resulting from excessive coughing.

HEALTHFUL COCKTAILS

Combine in a syrup with mullein and/or thyme for coughs and chest complaints.

Infuse into an elecampane decoction for irritating coughs.

CAUTIONS AND CONTRAINDICATIONS

None known.

Hyssop (Hyssopus officinalis)

Being an evergreen it helps out during the leaf free months, keeping a little green in the taupe and brown of the late winter season. After a few years it becomes quite woody at the base which can be a bit ungainly if neglected, making it worthy of a harsh cut back at the end of every summer or in spring, so that it keeps a good shape. Both leaf and flower are edible and can be added to salads, soups and stews. They do, however, have a very strong flavour so taste a pinch first to see if you can handle it and even then only use sparingly. The highly aromatic qualities are what comes through when tasting hyssop, but are also what gives it its insect repelling properties. In fact it is so effective at this that is was used as a strewing herb in times past to deter insects from peoples homes. Unfortunately it does attract cabbage white butterflies (Fern, 1997), but this is OK if it's well spaced from any cabbages you may be growing, although if close they may divert them from your cabbages, preserving them from damage, who's really to say? Fortunately hyssop also attracts bees and other butterflies, making up for the cabbage whites.

MATERIA MEDICA

Anti-inflammatory, antiseptic, antiviral, expectorant, relaxes muscle spasms, sedative, soothing

GATHERING

Collect leaves and flowering tops when the flowers are at their fullest, from June until October.

PREPARATIONS

- *Bath* is purifying and cleansing, it will help lighten a negative mental state, ease anxiety and rheumatic aches.
- *Crush* directly onto cuts to speed healing.
- *Gargle* for sore throats.
- *Infusion* can assist a weak stomach, improving digestion, relieving gas, colic and to soothe the digestive tract. Drunk at the onset of flu or a head cold it will induce perspiration, breaking the fever, relieve a stuffy nose and ease congestion in the head and chest. It will help loosen and expel catarrh, soothe the lungs and chest, relieve asthma, bronchitis and coughs. As a diuretic it helps to flush the system, relieving the pains of rheumatism. It can also be drunk as a tonic for the nervous system due to its sedative effect.
- *Oil* to rub over areas of rheumatic pain.
- *Poultice* on minor wounds, cuts and bruising.
- *Salve* for rheumatic aches.
- *Tincture* for respiratory conditions, it will soothe chest problems and help expel catarrh.

CAUTIONS AND CONTRAINDICATIONS

Do not take for more than 2 weeks consecutively. The iodine content is rather high, so avoid if suffering thyroid conditions where iodine cannot be effectively processed. Do not use if suffering heart problems, during pregnancy or breast feeding.

Iris (Iris versicolor)

Yellow flag (Iris pseudacorus) is the native and abundant wild iris growing in damp places across Britain. Blue flag (Iris versicolor) is its American cousin, which can be grown in the UK too. It has a full history as a well loved and well used medicinal plant amongst native Americans, and has found its way into homeopathy as a migraine remedy.

Found mostly in wetlands, it actually helps to clean water. I have planted both yellow and blue iris as functional plants in a lower pond, part of a reed bed system. They were planted in this instance to clean toxins and pathogens from the waste water at a country house, making it clean and usable again, but avoiding the need for a sewerage connection or a septic tank.

The flower is the origin of the fleur de lys, the three inner petals representing faith, wisdom and valor, a symbol that has been used for many hundreds of years to represent different family lines (including the French Royalty) and secret societies. It even appears on the Prince of Wales' official badge.

MATERIA MEDICA

Anti-inflammatory, blood cleanser, diuretic, increases perspiration, laxative

GATHERING

Collect only rhizomes that are firm to the touch, not the ones that have dried up on the outside or the ones which, when you touch them, have a mush inside. Lift them in late summer or early autumn and dry out of direct sunlight.

PREPARATIONS

- *Decoction* it's stimulating to the liver, gall bladder, pancreas and gastrointestinal tract and also acts as a a powerful blood cleanser. It increases flow of bile and will help clear skin conditions that are resulting from a stagnant liver and internal toxicity including psoriasis, acne and septicemia. It will relieve migraines caused by a congested and sluggish liver. By stimulating the digestive tract it helps relieve nausea, heartburn, wind and constipation. The diuretic and anti-inflammatory action eases arthritis. In addition it will ease and reduce swollen glands, relieve fibroids and pelvic inflammatory disease.
- *Oil* rub onto rheumatic aches and inflamed joints.
- *Poultice* for inflamed skin conditions, psoriasis, herpes and infected wounds.

CAUTIONS AND CONTRAINDICATIONS

Toxic if eaten so use extreme caution and label clearly any you are storing or drying whilst keeping it out of the way of children's inquisitive little fingers! It can irritate the skin or be an allergen, so always test with a small piece, then leave for 24 hours before proceeding. Do not exceed recommended doses. Avoid during pregnancy.

Jacob's Ladder (Polemonium Caeruleum)

A member of the Phlox family, recognisable by its dainty blue flowers which bloom from early until mid-summer. If it is happy in its spot it will self-seed profusely. Loved by cats who, in their ecstasy may roll on it, thereby damaging it. Jacob's ladder is not widely used in medicine today, but nonetheless remains a valuable nerve tonic and makes a pleasant, relaxing infusion.

MATERIA MEDICA

Astringent, induces perspiration

GATHERING

Cut and dry the aerial part of the plant in summer and use fresh or dry.

PREPARATIONS

- *Infusion* will cause excessive perspiration, so is used to help break a fever. Drinking the infusion will treat dysentery. As a nerve tonic it will soothe nervous headaches and other nervous conditions, bringing a sense of calm. It can also be used externally as a skin wash for weeping skin conditions.

CAUTIONS AND CONTRAINDICATIONS

None known.

Lady's Mantle (Alchemilla vulgaris)

If you have ever seen the concertina leaves of this low growing, green little plant first thing in the morning, with a tear drop of early morning dew, you will never forget how fresh and beautiful it looks. The drop remains whole as it moves on the leaf like a droplet of mercury escaping from a thermometer. Drinking these drops carefully harvested in the early morning will give you a vibrant buzz of being truly alive, so get on your knees and give it a go! Alchemilla means 'little magical one.' I'm sure that meaning must have something to do with the droplets of dew. Perhaps drinking them is the secret to eternal youth, but you wont know unless you try! It blooms from June to August, is very small and yellowish green, appears like a haze and, although not showy, you wont miss them. It spreads quite well, working as a ground cover and grown more for its foliage and the magical droplets than the flower. The scientific reason for the droplets is that the leaves are in fact water repellent, their internal effect being to dry up and expel water from the tissues. The young leaves are edible (Fern, 1997) and can be chopped finely into salads or added as a green leafy vegetable to cooked dishes. Lady's mantle is most well known as a woman's herb.

MATERIA MEDICA

Anti-inflammatory, astringent, pain relief

GATHERING

Harvest the aerial part of plant as the flowers start to open from around late May. It can be used fresh or dried. Collect the roots in the autumn and dry away from sunlight.

PREPARATIONS

- **Decoction** (root) to stop excessive bleeding in menstruation, hemorrhage and to stop diarrhea.
- **Douche** (leaf) use a double strength infusion to treat vaginal thrush, dry up excessive discharge and relieve vaginal itching.
- **Gargle** (leaf) for laryngitis (Hoffman, 1996).
- **Infusion** (leaf) a mild but effective remedy that can be drunk up to 5 times a day. It's a tonic for the woman's reproductive system, will help to promote conception, regulate menses, reduce excessive bleeding during menstruation, reduce gynecological inflammations and treat fibroids. It increases the production of progesterone which helps to ease hot flushes and other uncomfortable changes associated with the menopause. It contains salicylic acid which provides pain relief and alleviates cramps, easing the symptoms of PMS. It can help treat a prolapsed uterus by strengthening and toning the tissues, for which it is also used after delivery, miscarriage, abortion and during the last few months of pregnancy. Externally it can be used as a wash for the skin treating acne, oozing wounds, cuts, scrapes, minor burns and eczema.
- **Mouthwash** (leaf) for sores, ulcers and bleeding gums.
- **Oil** (leaf) rub on painful joints affected by gout and arthritis.
- **Powder** (root) to stem bleeding cuts, scrapes and wounds.

CAUTIONS AND CONTRAINDICATIONS

Avoid during the first few months of pregnancy.

Lavender (Lavendula angustifolia)

There is a huge range of lavenders, each varying in shape, size and colour of flower and foliage. Despite their individual variations they are all quite bushy and incredibly aromatic. It is a wonderful sight to see a lavender farm where huge swathes of purple colour the landscape.

The flowers are edible and are creeping into some of the more upmarket cookies, marmalades and even ice creams. It is, however, better known for its essential oil than its culinary uses. The oft used oil is obtained through steam distillation and is therefore unobtainable in the kitchen pharmacy without a lot of extra knowledge and equipment. It is worth getting hold of a bottle, though, as it is the first thing I reach for when a minor burn or sunburn has occurred, being very effective in these circumstances.

Highly attractive to bees, I find it almost impossible to remove a single flower stem until the very last bee no longer seems interested. It is recommended to harvest the flowers before they have all opened, but to remove the late summer pleasures from a bee just seems too cruel to me, so I collect my flowers and cut back for winter when the last bee has gone. I still get the benefit of the medicinal and aromatic properties from the dried flowers despite the lower oil content later in the summer, so I am loathe to collect any sooner.

Making little bags for the dried lavender and placing them amongst your clothes will help repel moths and will of course impart their lovely fragrance to your clothing. The smell is so pleasing that I would recommend using lavender if you ever find yourself creating a sensory garden for someone who is visually impaired.

MATERIA MEDICA

Antibacterial, antifungal, antimicrobial, antiseptic, circulatory stimulant, pain relief, sedative

GATHERING

The flowers contain the oils that provide the medicine. The oil content is highest before the last flowers on each stalk are fully open. Flowering is ongoing from June until September, so you will need to remain vigilant to catch the optimum time to harvest. Hang to dry in a shady, well ventilated space. Once dried you can run your fingers down the stem and the flowers will come off easily. Store in an airtight container.

PREPARATIONS

- *Footbath* for relaxation and to relieve anxiety. Use cooled to relieve swollen feet and ankles.
- *Infusion* the flavour is quite strong so it's good to mix with other milder flavoured herbs (see healthful cocktails below). Drink to reduce anxiety, promote restful sleep, relax muscular tension, ease irritability, nervous headache and depression. It is strengthening to the nerves, having a restorative and balancing action on frayed nerves. It improves digestion, easing flatulence and colic.
- *Oil* for massaging tired, tense muscles, aches, sprains, rheumatism and lumbago.
- *Salve* rub on the temples for headaches and as a gentle assist to falling asleep. Will help kill off the fungus causing athlete's foot, bringing great relief. Will promote healing when applied to cuts, scrapes, rashes, blisters, and bruises.
- *Tincture* use directly on cold sores (Peterson, 1995).

HEALTHFUL COCKTAILS

Use in a bath with lemonbalm to calm anxiety, lighten depression, relax tension and induce a deep sleep.

Infuse with skullcap and limeflower for a sleep inducing tea.

Infuse with chamomile for relaxation, to relieve tension and to gently slip off to sleep.

Infuse with rosemary and skullcap to lift depression.

Infuse with wood betony to relieve stress and soothe headaches.

Infuse with passionflower for nervous tension and anxiety.

Mix with hops and make a sleep pillow for a sound night's sleep.

CAUTIONS AND CONTRAINDICATIONS

None known.

Marigold, French (Tagetes patula)

Not to be confused with Calendula which, although also known as marigold, has different properties. Native to Mexico, it's a wonder where the common name came from. I once planted some French marigolds erroneously thinking that they were a deterrent to slugs. I awoke the following morning to witness the only remaining part of my marigold was the stem and there was a slug precariously balanced on the top, I promise that I am not exaggerating. It is used to deter some garden pests with more success, such as white fly. In fact it is often planted with tomato for the specific function of repelling whitefly.

The flowers can be used in cooking for their flavour and colour and you can use them fresh or dried. Dead heading will prolong their flowering life so by collecting the flowers, whether for food or medicine, you will end up with a colourful display for longer. Unfortunately, they are only half hardy so you will have to grow from seed (or buy seedlings) every year, if you choose to grow them.

MATERIA MEDICA

Digestive, diuretic, sedative

GATHERING

Both leaf and flower are used, so you can take the whole aerial part of the plant when it's flowering or collect individual flowers as they come out, only taking the leaves at the end of the season. This way you will get a lot more mileage from each plant. The leaves and flowers can both be used either fresh or dried.

PREPARATIONS

- *Infusion* improves digestion, treating indigestion, colic, constipation and dysentery. It can also help calm anxiety and nervousness.

CAUTIONS AND CONTRAINDICATIONS

None known.

Pansy/Heartsease (Viola tricolor)

The flowers were once considered beneficial for diseases of the heart and for mending broken hearts, which is where the name came from. Now it is better and more accurately known as a cleansing herb. Pansy is the name often used for the larger bloomed, more showy varieties, whereas heartsease is the smaller wild pansy, still just as fun to look at, only more delicate. I love to top my summer salads with the edible flowers, especially when I have guests because they are always amazed that these flowers can be eaten. If you really want to show off, add them to summer drinks as a floating, edible garnish. Dead head frequently to extend the flowering season which begins early, alongside spring bulbs. Leave some to go to seed as they will self-seed, hopefully allowing a new crop to emerge the following year. By rights they are only annuals, although some of the more showy pansies have been engineered to be perennials.

MATERIA MEDICA

Anti-inflammatory, diuretic, expectorant, pain relief

GATHERING

Leaves and flowers are collected throughout spring and summer, whilst flowering. They lose potency quickly when dried, so either use them fresh, or swiftly process them into salves, syrups and tinctures to use during the winter months.

PREPARATIONS

- *Infusion* will help cleanse toxins from the system, making it useful for skin complaints such as acne, psoriasis and weeping eczema, whilst providing relief from gout, rheumatism and arthritis. It lowers fever, helps reduce blood pressure and atherosclerosis. It can be used for urinary complaints, specifically cystitis. It has a mild sedative effect, calming nervous complaints. It will soothe and ease coughs and sore, inflamed respiratory tracts. It is also mildly laxative.
- *Salve* for inflammatory skin conditions, itching skin, varicose veins, nappy rash and cradle cap.
- *Syrup* helps loosen and expel phlegm, easing painful coughs, whooping cough, and bronchitis. It will also soothe mucous membranes and the respiratory tract.
- *Tincture* has the same action as an infusion, but as you cannot effectively dry heartsease this is the preferred preparation when it is out of season.

CAUTIONS AND CONTRAINDICATIONS

High doses cause nausea and vomiting. Do not use in conjunction with prescription diuretics or asthma medication.

Periwinkle, Greater (Vinca major)

I love the eye catching violet blue, star shaped flowers that jump out of a scramble of green foliage and wink at you. The flower has a pentagon at the base of the five petals which surround the yellow reproductive parts. Periwinkle is a creeper and good ground cover in dark and shady parts of the garden that are notoriously hard to tame. It is invasive, spreading from the roots, so cut it back in the autumn if it has begun to encroach too much.

MATERIA MEDICA

Anti-inflammatory, astringent, sedative

GATHERING

Collect the aerial parts whilst flowering from March until early June. Dry before using as the fresh flowers are toxic and may cause diarrhoea. As they dry, the toxicity is reduced.

PREPARATIONS

- *Chew* (leaf only) to reduce anxiety and bring restful sleep.
- *Crush* and insert into nostril during a nosebleed to stem the blood flow.
- *Douche* to reduce excessive vaginal discharge.
- *Gargle* for sore throats and tonsillitis.
- *Infusion* will tone the digestive tract and help treat colitis. It will relax and thereby widen the blood vessels, helping to reduce high blood pressure. It will calm and soothe nervous disorders. It helps reduce excessive blood flow during menstruation and spotting between periods.
- *Mouthwash* for ulcers and bleeding gums.
- *Salve* for bleeding hemorrhoids, cuts, scrapes, sores and inflamed skin.
- *Syrup* works as a laxative for severe constipation.

CAUTIONS AND CONTRAINDICATIONS

Toxic if eaten fresh. Stick to recommended dose.

Rock Rose (Helianthemum nummularium)

An excellent plant to soften the edges of a gravel patch or rock garden. Flowering from early summer it forms a low mat of colourful blooms which intriguingly all close up at night. It seems to need very little attention to thrive and won't spread too far and wide, becoming a nuisance. Such a happy little plant, it's no surprise that it is used as a Bach Flower Remedy to treat terror, panic and extreme fright. In fact it is one of the ingredients in Bach's famous Rescue Remedy.

MATERIA MEDICA

Antibiotic, astringent, expectorant

GATHERING

Collect leaves and twigs from late spring until early summer. They can be used fresh or dried.

PREPARATIONS

- *Gargle* for sore throats.
- *Infusion* will reduce excessive menstrual bleeding and diarrhoea. Will help bring up catarrh.
- *Syrup* to allay diarrhoea. Will also help loosen and expel phlegm.

CAUTIONS AND CONTRAINDICATIONS

Excess causes vomiting and nausea.

Rose (Rosa spp.)

Ahh, the quintessential English country cottage! I can see it now; beautiful, big bloomed roses climbing around the door. Long associated with love, not only used in love potions and remedies for nurturing and opening a damaged heart (in the emotional sense), but also given as a romantic gesture on Valentine's Day. The red rose is traditionally the symbol of the love shared by a couple. The older pink and red varieties, still highly fragrant, hold the most medicine. Most of the highly hybridised varieties will have lost their heart lifting perfume and suffered a reduction in their medicinal attributes in the process. The first potion I ever made was probably my childhood version of rosewater, which consisted of a handful of rose petals crushed up in a jam jar with some water poured over them, I probably called it perfume, or more realistically magic perfume, and it probably was. The petals can be eaten raw in salads. I also use them whenever I do a facial steam, not only for their therapeutic effects and astringent action, but also for their light, delicate fragrance.

Hips from wild/dog rose (Rosa canina) have a significantly higher vitamin C content weight per weight than oranges, making them very valuable when suffering an infection or when feeling under par. They also have quite a high pectin content which means they potentially make a good jelly. I might try combining them with elderberries and blackberries to make a hedgerow jelly for a super charged antibacterial treat. Both hips and petals are safe to use on children.

MATERIA MEDICA

Antibacterial, antiviral

The Medicine Garden

GATHERING

Most roses flower between June and October. Collect individual petals after flowering when they have lost moisture, or the whole bud before it opens. If collecting whole buds be sure they are thoroughly dry before storing. They can of course also be used fresh. Collect hips after the first hard frost, preferably from wild/dog roses (Rosa canina) where the hip will have stronger medicinal qualities. It is important to remove the fine hairs and seeds before drying as they are an irritant.

PREPARATIONS

- *Compress* (buds/petals) across the temples and forehead will relieve a headache. Used cool over closed eyes it will have a soothing action and ease irritation, soreness and itchiness.
- *Decoction* (hips) the high vitamin C content will help boost the working of allergic responses, the production of adrenal hormones and help the body fight infections and colds. Drink as a spring tonic and to build up during convalescence and exhaustion. It will also remedy mild gall bladder problems, constipation and ease arthritis.
- *Gargle* (buds/petals) for sore throats.
- *Infusion* (buds/petals) has a mild taste and delicate fragrance. Drunk before bed it will help induce prophetic dreams (Cunningham, 1985). It benefits reproductive health in both males and females, treating infertility, impotence and low sperm count whilst balancing the hormones, regulating the menstrual cycle, easing painful menstruation and soothing the rough edges that come with menopausal changes. It has a restorative and uplifting effect on the nerves, calming and nurturing, soothing anger and irritability, whilst comforting and healing the heart on an emotional level, easing depression and grief. It also stimulates the liver, increasing the flow of bile, easing headache and migraine where congested liver is a causative factor. Drunk after eating it will aid digestion, having a mild laxative action and will help to maintain a healthy balance of bacteria within the gastrointestinal tract.
- *Salve* (buds/petals) for sore or dry skin. Chemically this will not be as strong as a manufactured product, where they have the equipment to extract the active ingredients more efficiently. However, it's always great to use something you have made, especially if you potentize it by asking the plant at each stage of the process for which purpose you wish to use it.
- *Syrup* (hips) remove seeds and hairs from hips before processing into syrup and use relatively freely as a high vitamin C content winter tonic, especially when a cold is threatening or lingering, or you are just feeling physically low. Also soothing for a sore throat. Vitamin C helps form connective tissue such as collagen which is vital for the healing of wounds, so use the syrup whenever you have a badly healing wound.

CAUTIONS AND CONTRAINDICATIONS

Avoid during pregnancy.

Skullcap (Scutellaria lateriflora)

The big blue spikes of flowers look lovely in a well stocked border and will increase in bushiness if cut back in spring. The name tends to put people off, but only until they see it. The name relates to the shape of the calyx at the base of the flowers and nothing more sinister, I promise you!

Although Scutellaria galericulata is in fact the native Skullcap for the UK and is widespread, it is the American cousin lateriflora that appears to have the most medicinal attributes. This may just be due to the skew of any research that has been undertaken. It is, however, possible to buy seeds and grow lateriflora in our climate, so that is what I would recommend if you would like to experience the deeply relaxing medicine of this blue flowered friend. Lateriflora has less showy flower spikes than some, but this is the sacrifice you will have to choose whether or not to make if you want the plant with the highest medicinal potency.

MATERIA MEDICA

Calms muscle spasms and convulsions, digestive, nervous system tonic, sedative

GATHERING

The aerial parts (leaves, flowers and stems) of this herb are collected when flowering (June until September) and can be used fresh or dried. When dried it retains a delightful bright green colour and looks entirely vibrant, unlike most plants that tend to look a little dull when dried.

PREPARATIONS

- *Infusion* it's main action is on the central nervous system which it renews and fortifies, calming nervous complaints, stress, anxiety, tension, hysteria, lifting depression and easing insomnia, neuralgia and sciatica. It promotes feelings of peace and relaxation, soothing tension headaches and rejuvenating after a breakdown, especially if caused by nervous exhaustion. It's often used as part of a treatment for withdrawing from drug addiction including tranquilizers and antidepressants. I would recommend asking a qualified herbalist for advice and support if you find yourself in this situation. It has been successfully used in the treatment of attention deficit disorder (ADD). Skullcap has a calming effect on the body, relieving tense muscles, menstrual cramps and involuntary twitches, giving it the potential for treating mild cases of Tourette's syndrome, and as a preventative in epilepsy. It eases premenstrual tension (PMT) whilst inducing menstruation and balancing menstrual problems. It strengthens and stimulates digestion and kidneys. It helps clear shingles and herpes. It can be added to other herbs in sleep mixes.
- *Tincture* for the same complaints as the infusion.

HEALTHFUL COCKTAILS

Infuse with passionflower for deep relaxation and restful sleep.

CAUTIONS AND CONTRAINDICATIONS

Avoid during pregnancy and breast feeding. Do not take alongside other tranquilizers or sedatives.

Speedwell (Veronica officinalis)

One of the common names is gypsy weed, which is quite lovely. It's all too easy to pull up in a weeding frenzy as it is a prolific self-seeder, but it fills in the gaps with its tiny blue flowers and seeing it make me feel quite merry: a happy little plant.

MATERIA MEDICA

Anti-inflammatory, astringent, diuretic, expectorant, induces perspiration

GATHERING

Aerial parts of the plants are cut when flowering and used fresh or dried for later use.

PREPARATIONS

- *Infusion* it has a bitter flavour so you may want to add a spoonful of honey to make it more palatable. It is blood cleansing and a diuretic, removing toxins from your system, improving skin conditions and easing arthritis and rheumatism. It helps loosen and expel catarrh, easing coughs and bronchial complaints. It will calm stomach upsets and help improve digestion. By encouraging sweating it will help reduce a fever. It is a nurturing brew for times of nervous exhaustion. It can be applied directly to the skin as a wash for itching skin and wounds.
- *Salve* for eczema and to speed the healing of wounds, cuts, scrapes and abrasions.

CAUTIONS AND CONTRAINDICATIONS

None known.

Sunflower (Helianthus annuus)

This must be the favourite of any child who has ever grown a seed, just due to the rapid rate of growth with the spectacular big yellow flower waving high above their heads. Some varieties can grow up to 5m tall, but if you want to achieve this you must be somewhat military in your protection of the freshly sprouted seedlings from slug and snail attacks! It doesn't take an expert to know that a sunflower is full of powerful sun energy; the flowers even follow the sun as it traces its daily arc across the sky. The flowers attract beneficial insects which in turn prey on garden pests, although unfortunately this does not extend to their nemesis, the slimy world of the slug and snail.

Seeds can number up to 1000 per flower head depending on the variety. I personally love looking at the spiraling arrangement of the seeds, an expression of the principles of sacred geometry that underly the architecture of all life, drawing one into the consciousness of universal interconnectedness. The seeds are high in iron, calcium, fibre and B and E vitamins. E vitamins are crucial to circulatory health, help protect against free radicals and give the skin a healthy glow. Dehulled seeds can be eaten raw, sprouted and added to salads, blended into healthy raw pates, or even fermented into seed yoghurts and cheeses. Alternatively you could grow trays of sunflowers until they become greens at about 3 inches tall. They can be cut at this point and used as a highly nutritious addition to salads, even in winter.

Oil extracted from the seeds is widely used, not only in cooking but also as a fine base for solar infused oils that are to be used for massaging. Unfortunately it is not practically feasible to grow the quantity required or to efficiently extract the oil oneself.

MATERIA MEDICA

Diuretic, expectorant.

GATHERING

Leaves are collected throughout the growing season and can be used fresh or dried. The seeds are collected after the flowering has finished. Cut off the seed heads and hang them upside down to dry with a newspaper beneath to catch the falling seeds. Whilst drying keep in a place that will be secure from birds and mice.

PREPARATIONS

- *Infusion* (seeds) soothing to the mucous membranes and expectorant, making a soothing treatment for coughs, whooping cough, bronchitis and bronchial infections. The vitamin E they contain has an anti-inflammatory action useful for the treatment of arthritis, rheumatism and asthma. It lowers cholesterol and is also a cold remedy. The leaves are a powerful remedy, so only take a tablespoonful at a time to treat diarrhoea, lung ailments and fevers.

CAUTIONS AND CONTRAINDICATIONS

None known.

Valerian (Valeriana officinalis)

Not to be confused with Red Valerian (Centranthus ruber) which unfortunately does not share the same medicinal qualities despite being extremely abundant, certainly in my locale. It has an unpleasant and somewhat nauseous odor, however, the relaxing medicine valerian imparts is well worth the odd malodorous whiff. It is a good idea to compost the steeped root straight away, otherwise it may stink out your kitchen. It is very difficult to grow from seed, but you can propagate by dividing the root. This will most often produce a new plant. Removing the flowering stems as soon as they appear will send the energy down into the root, giving you nice fat roots to harvest. Leaving them to flower is not a problem though and you will still get plenty of root, and by enjoying the flower too you will get the best of both worlds.

MATERIA MEDICA

Calms muscle spasms, pain relief, sedative

GATHERING

Lift roots in the late autumn of the second year after the leaves have died off. Use fresh or dried, although the root tastes better fresh. Do not store for more than one year as the medicinal properties will be lost.

PREPARATIONS

- *Decoction* cover whilst simmering as it is high in volatile oils which will otherwise be lost. It has a calming effect on the nervous system, reducing symptoms of stress, tension and anxiety. Helps bring calm after experiencing a shock, trauma or panic attack. It lowers blood pressure so is useful if suffering hypertension and calms palpitations triggered by anxiety. It relieves the pain of tension headaches, migraine, neuralgia and period pains. It relieves cramping, easing stomach aches, menstrual cramps and coughing fits. It relaxes muscular tension and will ease nervous dyspepsia. It is most widely used as a sedative to aid with insomnia, reputedly with no hangover, although I find the effects take an hour or two to shake off after first rising. Paradoxically it is actually stimulating if you are suffering from fatigue.
- *Salve* for eczema, sores and pimples.
- *Tincture* use for the same complaints as the decoction. Tincturing is a good way of preserving the root without losing the potency. It will last longer than the dried root alone. For serious cases of anxiety take a teaspoon of the tincture 3 times daily, but if using for sleeplessness take just one teaspoon an hour before bed.

HEALTHFUL COCKTAILS

Decoct and add passionflower for a deep sleep.

Infuse skullcap or hops into the decoction to relieve tension.

CAUTIONS AND CONTRAINDICATIONS

It is best to use in the evening or when at home as it may cause drowsiness. Do not use with other sedatives, antidepressants, or exceed the recommended dose. Do not drive after taking internally. Avoid during pregnancy.

Violet, Sweet (Viola odorata)

A cleansing herb, helping to flush toxins from the system, making way for improved health. It's fragrance was once prized amongst perfumiers and it was commercially cultivated on a relatively large scale for this purpose. The aromatic element can now be synthesized and, as a consequence, its demand has dropped heavily and it's currently grown on a much smaller scale.

Collect the heads as they flower. This will extend the flowering season, giving you more blooms to use or store. They spread by runners so removing the flowers will not mean they are unable to reproduce. The young heart shaped leaves and slightly spicy flowers are edible and, being high in vitamin C, are a healthy addition to salads.

MATERIA MEDICA

Antioxidant, antiseptic, astringent, expectorant, sedative

GATHERING

Collect the aerial parts when flowering, from March until May. The leaves can be collected throughout the entire growing season to be used fresh.

PREPARATIONS

All preparations can be made with a combination of the flowers and leaves unless otherwise specified.

- *Compress* to relieve headache.
- *Eat* (flowers) as a quick fix breath freshener.
- *Gargle* for sore, inflamed throats.
- *Infusion* it helps rid the respiratory tract of catarrh and has a soothing effect on coughs, bronchitis and asthma. It will ease headache, hangover, flu, urinary infections, eczema and insomnia. It has anti-cancer properties and is potentially useful in treating certain specific cancers such as those found in the digestive tract, stomach, lung and breast.
- *Mouthwash* for sore and bleeding gums.
- *Poultice* (leaves) for leg ulcers and eczema.
- *Salve* for eczema, rashes and sore, inflamed skin.
- *Syrup* (flowers) for coughs, mild constipation and insomnia.

CAUTIONS AND CONTRAINDICATIONS

None known.

Evening Primrose - Above Left

Holly Hock - Above Right

Hardy Geranium - Left

Columbine - Below Left

Fever Few - Below Right

Iris - Top Left

Lavander - Above Right

Echinacea - Left

Rock Rose - Below Left

Marigold Calendula - Below Right

Golden Rod - Above

Carnations/Pink - Above

Hyssop - Above

Heartease - Below

Rose - Below

Sunflower - Above

French Marigold - Below

Asparagus - Above

Elecampane - Below

Primrose
- Above Left

Borage
- Above Right

Comfrey
- Left

Nasturtium
- Right

Pumpkin Flower
- Below Left

Daisy
- Below Right

Honeysuckle - Above

Radish - Above

Elderflower - Above

Dandelion - Above

Lungwort
- Right

Chamomile - Below

Quince - Above Left

Bluebell Fields - Above Right

Red Clover - Left

Raspberry - Right

Rowan - Below Left

Blackberry - Below Right

Selfheal - Above Left

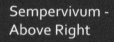

Sempervivum - Above Right

Watermint - Left

St Johns Wort - Right

Cowslip - Below Right

Wild Garlic - Below Left

COMMON "WEEDS" IN YOUR BORDERS

Chickweed (Stellaria media)

A great favourite of free food enthusiasts as it will grow just about anywhere and is not just edible, but also nutritious with a mild flavour. The leaves are neither tough nor hairy but are, in fact, rather tender; a pleasant surprise for a forager, I can assure you! It is an excellent source of vitamin C and will fill any recently weeded patch of bare ground with a light and easily removed covering of leaves peppered with tiny, white, star shaped flowers. Once you start using it you will be pleased to see it crop up between flowers or vegetables as it spreads quite widely providing a kind of living mulch which makes it harder for other weeds to get established. Both a salad crop and a medicine in its own right!

MATERIA MEDICA

Anti-inflammatory, antipruritic (reduces itching), diuretic, expectorant

GATHERING

The aerial parts can be collected all year round, but it grows much less abundantly in winter. It is in fact only an annual, but if the weather is mild it will overwinter.

PREPARATIONS

- *Bath* for itching skin, bringing soothing relief for children with chicken pox, whilst promoting the healing of areas they have scratched.
- *Infusion* works on the gastrointestinal tract easing acid indigestion, colitis and IBS (Kircher, 2001). It helps increase the excretion rate of waste products and toxins which will improve the appearance of skin eruptions, ease arthritis, rheumatism and water retention. Ridding the system of these waste products will bring an increased sense of vitality, improving energy levels. It will help soothe bronchitis and chest infections. As a skin wash it will provide cooling, soothing relief from severe itching and skin inflammations whilst promoting healing of any skin wounds or abrasions.
- *Juice* a small sprig in the juicer will help ease indigestion, arthritis, rheumatism, coughs and bronchitis.
- *Oil* for dry, itchy skin and eczema.
- *Poultice* for ulcers, boils,and abscesses. Make a hot poultice to relieve heat rash.
- *Salve* for cuts, wounds, hemorrhoids, psoriasis and nappy rash.

HEALTHFUL COCKTAILS

Juice with a sprig of nettle and cleavers as a spring tonic to boost your body's function and help expel toxins after the dark months of winter. To sweeten add either carrot, apple, beetroot or any combination. All of these have a detoxifying and rejuvenating effect and will absolutely complement the herbs in your spring tonic.

CAUTIONS AND CONTRAINDICATIONS

Avoid during pregnancy. Excess causes diarrhea and vomiting.

Ground Elder (Aegopodium podagraria)

If you find this sneakily creeping into your borders you will have a real challenge to rid them of it, especially if you are opting for a chemical free approach. It is heavily invasive and it can spread through even the tiniest bit of root left in the ground. So perhaps the most satisfying way forward would be to make friends with this prolific plant, or at least peace, and discover that it has uses beyond just exasperating the keen gardener. Also known as gout weed, this common name gives a clue to its medicinal use. Indeed it was apparently a once cultivated and highly valued plant, introduced by the Romans and subsequently grown as a garden vegetable, leading to it currently being so widespread in gardens and around the edges of settlements across the land .

The leaves have a distinctive flavour and can be used raw and fresh in salads when young, or cooked as a spinach like green vegetable. I have even seen a recipe for ground elder and vanilla muffins on the internet, so don't be shy of how they can be used as a free food in the kitchen; only the limits of your culinary creativity will restrain you!

I like the white lacy umbels of flowers and find them quite delicate and a pleasant surprise and contrast to the more stocky foliage, as long as they're not in my backyard, that is!

MATERIA MEDICA

Anti-inflammatory, diuretic, mild sedative.

GATHERING

The whole plant (including roots) is harvested when in flower from June until August. It can be used fresh or dried for later use. Store the roots in large pieces, but chop them finely before use, so that the medicinal properties can infuse easily into the preparations.

PREPARATIONS

- *Compress* for swellings.
- *Infusion* for sciatic pains, gout and otherwise achy, swollen joints.
- *Poultice* for gouty, painful, swollen joints.
- *Salve* for bites, stings, hemorrhoids and gout.

CAUTIONS AND CONTRAINDICATIONS

None known.

The Veggie Garden

I am a total believer in no dig gardening, not just because I want to put in minimum effort, but to preserve the integrity of my soil. In just one teaspoon of healthy soil there are over a million (some sources say closer to a billion!) bacteria, all living beings. Now that's incredible! By digging and turning the soil one ends up destroying the soil's very structure and all the ventilation that ants and worms have worked so hard to provide is damaged. When these previously covered sections are exposed to the air, some of the microbes are also killed.

Over winter you will find my designated beds under a thick blanket of mulch, and when it comes to planting in spring, not only are these areas weed free but they have an incredibly rich, friable soil ready for planting. Gardening with permaculture principles (see resources) in mind, I aim for as many perennial species as possible, creating a diverse patchwork of plants, each giving their unique gifts to the immediate environment, be it attracting bees or deterring black fly. I choose each plant for its function and by avoiding huge swathes of the same species, avoid the need for any kind of pesticide, allowing nature do the work for me.

The payback is, of course, eating a meal on a summer's evening and knowing that you personally have grown everything on your plate. Even if it wasn't miles (quite literally) fresher and tastier, the buzz I get from it would still be quite tangible. The health value of eating such lovingly nurtured, organic, local produce is apparent, not just on a personal level, but also its implications for our wider environment.

It is so easy to grow fruit and vegetables, even if you have no outside space of your own. There are local allotments, or if that is too daunting there is always your windowsill. If you are looking for just one or two easy things to grow in a small space I would recommend soft fruit (black currants, raspberries and/or strawberries). For a very minimum of effort, a little weeding and annual pruning, you will get incredible quantities of delicious fruit throughout the summer. My top tip is to have a wood fire at some point in the late winter, save the ash, sprinkle it around the base of your fruits in early spring and just watch as a bumper crop develops.

I started growing my own veg whilst living in a flat in East London with just a few pots on my postage stamp sized balcony. I implore you to try if you haven't already done so, you will soon be hooked! An additional benefit to growing your own is that many of the fruits and vegetables commonly grown at home also have a medicinal value that is often over looked, once again returning to the concept of one's food being one's medicine.

Amaranth (Amaranthus caudatus)

A stunning ornamental also known as 'Love lies bleeding' which has great nutritional properties. As an architectural plant it can be grown for its height and deep red dripping heads of colour in the flower beds or amongst the vegetables.

The flowering heads contain vast quantities of seed, up to 100,000 per plant (Fern, 1997). This seed can be cooked and treated as a grain. It has long been grown as part of the staple diet in Mexico, nourishing generations of Aztec and Mayan peoples long before the modern age. Perhaps surprisingly I saw it being grown as the main staple in mountainous parts of Kenya, with up to 2.5kg of viable grain produced from just the one plant. It is not native there, but when a plant produces such a large quantity of seed who can argue? The optimum time to harvest, if you are collecting for food, is when you see the seed starting to drop. Take a sieve and a bowl into which you cut the heads, or you will lose much of the seed on the ground. It is a great plant to grow if you would like to produce some of your own grains but don't have the space or conditions for wheat, barley, rice etc. The seeds on their own are a bit bland, so treat them as you would millet or quinoa, adding plenty of flavour before serving. Alternatively, add to soups and stews where its lack of flavour won't be a problem and it will act as a thickening agent. You can even put the seed through a coffee grinder to make flour, creating a valuable gluten free alternative to wheat flour, giving coeliacs and other gluten sensitive people a wider range of alternatives with which to bake breads, cakes and cookies. If you prefer to eat live, raw food, amaranth can be sprouted. It produces tiny sprouts similar to those you get from quinoa. There is no need to soak them, just rinse regularly (every 8-12 hours) and after a couple of days you will see tiny white hair-like sprouts emerging. Don't let them grow longer than the length of the seed. They will remain somewhat crunchy and can be mixed with olives, sun dried tomatoes, herbs and other yummy, highly flavoured ingredients for a main dish. High in fibre, iron, calcium, potassium, phosphorus and vitamins A, C and a whole host of essential amino acids, it is a worthy addition to the diet.

Amaranth leaves are also edible and the best time to harvest them for eating is in the spring and early summer when they are still tender and have a better flavour. They can be eaten raw or cooked like spinach in dishes. The leaves can be huge, so it is definitely worth using them in the kitchen as they will provide you with great quantities of greens.

MATERIA MEDICA

Astringent

GATHERING

Collect the flowering head as the flowers are opening. Leaves can be collected as and when required.

PREPARATIONS

- *Infusion* to calm and dry up excessive menstruation and diarrhoea. It can be used

externally as a skin wash for acne, skin wounds, eczema, psoriasis and hives.
• *Mouthwash* for ulcers and sore or bleeding gums.

None known.

Apple (Pyrus malus)

With over 2000 varieties of apple available there's plenty to choose from if you are thinking of trying to squeeze one in somewhere. Whether you have the opportunity to grow apples yourself, or just manage to find friends with a well stocked tree, they are an incredibly healthy addition to the diet. If you have no other source and need to buy all your apples it is important to buy organic as apples are one of the most heavily sprayed crops and non-organic ones are also often waxed (hard to remove under the tap) to make them shiny.

Containing magnesium, iron, potassium, vitamins B and C, they are literal powerhouses of health. One absolutely charming piece of folklore is that unicorns live beneath apples. (Cunningham 1985). I love the thought of that!

(see also crab apple p136)

MATERIA MEDICA

Antioxidant, diuretic, laxative

GATHERING

Collect the fruits as they ripen in autumn. They store well when individually wrapped in newspaper in a cool dark place, lasting easily throughout the winter. Don't forget to check regularly for rotting ones as just one could make the whole box go bad.

PREPARATIONS

• *Cider Vinegar* increases the alkalinity of the stomach, improving digestion and reducing gas. The presence of acetic acid and potassium helps activate friendly bacteria in the gastrointestinal tract. It helps break up mucous deposits, cleansing the liver and improving the efficiency of the other internal organs. It guards against and lowers high blood pressure by thinning and oxidizing the blood. It kills pathogenic micro-organisms within the intestines. The malic acid it contains has diuretic properties which help the kidneys expel uric acid, benefiting gouty conditions.

- **Compress** (cider vinegar) for arthritic joints.
- **Eat** (fruit) first peel and grate, then eat a single apple to stop diarrhoea, eat another if the first one doesn't work. Make the last thing you eat in the day a single apple eaten alone; the fibre will cleanse your gastrointestinal tract, alleviating constipation, whilst encouraging a healthy balance of intestinal flora. They are easy for the digestive system to process, are full of soluble fibre and help balance blood sugar levels and lower cholesterol, which helps guard against heart disease. They contain phosphates, required by the body for tissue building, which help improve levels of oxygenation, nourishing brain, nerves and muscles. They are cleansing to the body, making them ideal after over indulging, when convalescing and in times of stress. The pectin binds to toxins such as lead, mercury and other heavy metals, eliminating them through the bowel. The malic acid helps cleanse the liver, making it work more efficiently, whilst helping clear skin conditions such as acne that are rooted in a sluggish liver function. They help protect cells from damage and, in turn, guard against cancer, partly due to the action of the ellagic acid they contain, particularly useful for smokers as they block some of the damaging agents in tobacco smoke. They are rich in disease fighting flavonoids and quercetin, which helps protect your eyes against cataracts. They help support the respiratory system, improving coughs, helping to expel catarrh and generally improving lung function. They help your body expel uric acid, improving kidney stones, arthritis, rheumatism and gouty conditions. They help keep your teeth and gums healthy too, so
perhaps the old saying is true: 'An apple a day keeps the doctor away.'
- **Infusion** (dried peel) to ease rheumatic pains (Evert Hopman, 1991).
- **Juice** (fruit) drink 30 minutes before meals or before bed. Is therapeutic for anemic conditions. Drinking fresh juice will have the same function as eating, except it will contain less fibre. Juicing is a good way to get a large volume of apples into your system, and being sweet they are perfect to mix with less tasty juices.

CAUTIONS AND CONTRAINDICATIONS

Limit the amount of seeds you ingest as they contain hydrogen cyanide, which is poisonous in large quantities.

Asparagus (Asparagus officinalis)

It takes a few years and some attentive nurturing to get going, but as it's a perennial, and expensive to buy in the shops, it's worth the wait. Once it starts producing you will be provided with this yummy spring vegetable for years. It's the tips or spears that are commonly consumed and picking them encourages new ones to poke through, but do not harvest them excessively and exhaust the plant.

The spears are popular sautéd or steamed and served with butter and garlic, but I also enjoy grating the raw, fresh tender shoots into a salad or even just chomping on one whole. If you choose to cook them, the water they are cooked in or steamed over should be saved and drunk as it captures some of the beneficial properties. High in vitamins C, E and beta-carotene, they provide a nutritious and tasty springtime dish. When using them for their more medicinal properties it's preferable to juice them so that you can get enough into your system. A word of warning: consuming asparagus, even in relatively small quantities, makes your pee smell and can give it a greenish tint, which is quite alarming if you're not expecting it!

MATERIA MEDICA

Antibacterial, anti-inflammatory, diuretic, sedative

GATHERING

Collect the spears in late spring and early summer when they are still tender. Use fresh.

PREPARATIONS

- *Eat* (raw)/*Juice* as a kidney tonic. It contains asparagine which breaks down crystals of uric and oxalic acid in the kidneys and body. The diuretic properties will then help this flush through and out of the system. This action will ease and improve arthritic and rheumatic conditions and cystitis. It helps increase hormone production, stimulating the female reproductive system, whilst boosting libido. It can be taken as a tonic for those prone to anemia as it has a high folic acid content which ensures the production of plenty of red blood cells. It is also a laxative and a cardiac tonic.

CAUTIONS AND CONTRAINDICATIONS

Use with caution if you suffer from gout as the high purine content may aggravate your condition. Do not use if suffering from inflamed kidneys.

Beetroot (Beta vulgaris)

Grows with an attractive red veined leaf that, rather delightfully, the slugs and snails do not seem to have much interest in. The leaves can be eaten in salads, steamed or juiced, so there is very little waste from this plant. Both root and leaf contain an abundance of minerals including calcium, magnesium, iron, phosphorus, potassium, folic acid and vitamin C, helping them build and maintain a healthy, well functioning body.

The Medicine Garden

Preparing fresh beetroot will turn your fingers pink, and when you consume a large amount will turn your pee pink too! There is a multitude of ways to use them in the kitchen, from grating them raw into salads, steaming great chunks, making chutneys and pickling either slices or whole small ones. I even dehydrate thin slices into unfried 'crisps' for a healthy snack.

Juicing is the most efficient way to get a large amount in your system, but they are very strong so I would advise starting with just half of a small one mixed with other vegetables and building up slowly until you can take a whole medium sized one in a single juice which can still be mixed with other vegetables for their properties and tastes. If you juice too much you will soon learn of its laxative effects! The deep red colour gives a clue that beetroot works on the blood.

MATERIA MEDICA

Antiseptic, antioxidant, laxative

GATHERING

The seed can be planted directly in the ground from April and sown successively throughout the summer until July. It will take around 6-10 weeks from planting the seed until harvest unless you have chosen a long (as opposed to round) variety, which can take up to 18 weeks. It will normally tell you on the seed packet how long they will take, but you can of course just keep your eye on them and pull one up when it looks to be the size you require. However, leave them in too long and they will become woody, harder to juice and less pleasant to eat. If the foliage goes limp it is a sure sign that they are more than ready to be pulled up. You will normally be cropping from late summer potentially right through until early spring. They can be stored in a box of sand in a cool, dark, dry place such as a shed or garage. It is important to remove the foliage before storing by twisting off the tops.

PREPARATIONS

- *Eat* (raw)/*Juice* provides a fabulous blood tonic, cleansing and building the body, great to use while convalescing and otherwise trying to build yourself up. It stimulates the immune system and the high boron content stimulates the production of reproductive hormones, making it a valuable aphrodisiac. It helps restore the liver by cleansing, protecting and regenerating. It is one of the strongest ways to detox the liver, giving a rapid and thorough cleanse and an energy burst as it does so. It can be used to support the treatment of hepatitis, alcoholism and even some cancers. Part of its action is to stimulate the production and flow of bile. In addition it can help lower blood pressure.

HEALTHFUL COCKTAILS

Juice with carrot and cucumber for a kidney and gall bladder cleanse.

Do not use when suffering from an obstructed bile duct.

Black Currant (Ribes nigrum)

A lovely berry to grow, the bush is quite compact and, when in its prime, will literally drip with juicy black berries. Unlike its relation, the red currant, it will not need protection from birds. They seem to overlook the black currants, whereas they can strip a fully laden red currant bush within a day. The bushes lose vigour with age, so you will have to consider replacing them every 10 years or so. You will know when as the amount produced will go into a rapid decline. It's the deep purplish/black fruit skin, alongside the leaves, which contains the medicinal components. The vitamin C content of the berries is in fact much higher than that contained in oranges (when comparing on a weight to weight basis). The berries can be enjoyed fresh, combined into summer fruit mixes, made into jams or cooked fruit desserts. Children love to eat them and in this instance you don't necessarily need a spoonful of sugar to make the medicine go down! You will tend to

end up with a glut as they all become ripe within a few days, but they freeze well if you want to spread their tasty gifts throughout the year and don't have the time or inclination to process them into a syrup at the time of harvesting.

MATERIA MEDICA

Antibacterial, anti-inflammatory, antioxidant, diuretic, strengthens capillaries

GATHERING

Leaves are gathered throughout the growing season and used fresh, or dried for use in infusions. Fruits are picked during the summer when black and ripe (usually July). If picked early they will have a reddish glow, be harder to the touch and a little bitter to the taste. Each bush produces many small fruits hanging in clumps which can be removed with a comb, a fork or picked individually.

PREPARATIONS

- *Decoction* (berry) gently simmer the berries and add a teaspoon of honey per cup for a delicious and soothing brew for sore throats and chest infections.
- *Eat* (raw)/*Juice* (berry) for coughs (including whooping cough), colds and chest

complaints. The berries act as a tonic for the nervous system, improve the circulatory system, being both vasoprotective and strengthening to the capillaries, and will boost the immune system. These actions make them particularly beneficial in times of convalescence. They also help enhance the efficiency of the kidneys, ease colic and diarrhoea. The juice can be gently warmed and sipped to soothe and heal throat infections.

- *Gargle* (berry decoction) for sore throats.
- *Infusion* (leaf) this is a diuretic, stimulating the kidneys, improving rheumatism, gout and bladder stones. It also helps lower blood pressure, improve arteriosclerosis, reduce inflammations and is especially useful for sore throats.
- *Mouthwash* (berry decoction) for bleeding gums, ulcers and mouth infections.
- *Syrup* (berry) the high vitamin C content is well preserved in this form and can be used for sore throats, coughs and colds.

CAUTIONS AND CONTRAINDICATIONS

None known.

Borage (Borago officinalis)

There is an oil extracted from the flower seeds, known as starflower oil, which is full of brain feeding omegas and hormone balancing GLA (gamma-linolenic acid). Borage is also known as starflower because when you look at the downward pointing flowers from above, you will notice two separate, yet superimposed 5 pointed stars. The little blue flowers are quite beautiful and pull off easily, making them a fine one to munch when passing. Whenever I do so, I find myself chanting 'borage for courage.' I don't remember from whom I learned that, but it does somehow strengthen your heart as you repeat it. The flowers and chopped leaves can be used to decorate and flavour a jug of iced Pimms on a summer's afternoon. The flowers also make a pretty edible garnish on a summer dinner plate. Once they have flowered they will be difficult to rid from your plot as they are prolific self-seeders, but this is a good thing as they are highly attractive to bees who in turn will pollinate your veggies.

MATERIA MEDICA

Anti-inflammatory, diuretic, expectorant

GATHERING

Leaves and flowers are collected from late spring and throughout the summer and are used fresh. The stems and leaves are covered in fine hairs, so either harvest cautiously to avoid getting a few stuck in your fingers, or wear gloves. Both leaves and flowers can be dried, but do not store for more than a year as they will lose all their therapeutic properties by then.

PREPARATIONS

- *Compress* (leaf) for tired, swollen legs, feet and ankles that have spent all day standing. It will reduce swelling and help restore the circulation.
- *Eat* (flower) for the seeds which, high in essential fatty acids, help to regulate the hormonal system and lower blood pressure. On an emotional level they help cheer you up, alleviating anxiety, depression and easing feelings of melancholy and grief.
- *Eyebath* (leaf) to soothe red, irritated, inflamed eyes.
- *Gargle* (leaf) for a sore, infected throat.
- *Infusion* (leaf) has a cleansing, refreshing taste and will help loosen and clear phlegm and soothe coughs, bronchial infections and bronchitis. It can help reduce fevers, stimulate blood circulation and boost the activity of the kidneys. It helps reduce the symptoms of PMS and will increase the flow of breast milk in mothers. It helps balance the adrenal glands (also, interestingly, star shaped), small endocrine glands which sit above the kidneys and help us to process stress. Its cleansing properties will help clear skin conditions related to internal toxicity such as rashes and boils.
- *Mouthwash* (leaf) for mouth infections and ulcers.
- *Poultice* (leaf) for insect bites, stings, bruising, swellings, sprains and skin inflammations.

CAUTIONS AND CONTRAINDICATIONS

Do not consume to excess as it may cause liver damage (ie. Do not exceed 3 cups a day or use for a prolonged period). Avoid if you suffer liver problems.

Carrot
(Daucus carota sativa)

Carrot is a great vegetable to enjoy in a whole multitude of dishes. The domesticated varieties that are commonly grown at home and available to the consumer have a lower level of medicinal qualities than wild carrot, but are still useful nonetheless. It is certainly worth trying to get hold of some heritage seeds (see resources) for carrot as the older the variety and the closer to the wild original, the stronger the medicine will be. You will need relatively deep and stone free soil to get a good looking crop. If, like mine, your soil seems to grow new stones on a daily basis, then try growing them in stone free containers full of lovely rich compost. Carrots readily absorb chemicals through their leaves and skin when conventionally produced, so it would be preferable to consume organic ones which can be eaten unpeeled, more or less straight from the earth. Organic carrots have no residual toxic load and so are stronger medicinally, unhindered in their role of cleansing the liver and the blood. They are also particularly rich in vitamin A (beta-carotene), C & E. Beta carotene is very important in helping to prevent cancer. Carrot is excellent to include in your diet if you are pregnant or breast feeding as it helps promote the formation of healthy cells and the development of a strong immune system, giving your baby a great start in life.

MATERIA MEDICA

Antibiotic, antioxidant, antiseptic, diuretic

GATHERING

The whole plant (greens and roots) is harvested in late summer and can be stored in damp sand in a cold shed or cellar, but must be protected from frost and checked regularly to make sure none have rotted, which would in time spoil the lot. Despite the fact that carrot can be successfully stored for some time, it is best to use them as fresh as possible as the carotene content does start to decline once they have been picked.

PREPARATIONS

- *Eat* a plate of grated carrot to allay diarrhoea and paradoxically to ease a constipated bowel into action.
- *Infusion* can be made from the tops, even when they have maturing, seedy flower heads.
- *Juice* consume only 1-2 cups of fresh juice a day. If the carrots are organically home grown you may also juice the greens. Any pulp left in the juicer may be used to thicken soups and stews. Drinking carrot juice on its own will cause a spike followed by a crash in blood sugar levels, so it is advisable to mix it with less sweet juices to avoid this, however, the sweetness will be enjoyed by children, making this a sure way of getting them to consume some vegetables. It neutralises acidity in the blood, helping to cleanse and detoxify the blood and liver. This will initiate improvements in skin conditions that are related to a sluggish liver such as some cases of acne. It acts as a tonic to the liver, and by fortifying it, will help protect the liver against chemical pollutants encountered in the environment and diet. Carrots are high in carotenoids (including beta-carotene) which help prevent cancer, cardio-vascular disease and stroke. Vitamin A, which the body manufactures from the beta-carotene, not only strengthens the immune system but also promotes healthy cell growth, whilst the beta-carotene itself is highly antioxidant and will guard against cell damage caused by oxidation. The promotion of healthy cell growth will beneficially impact the respiratory tract lining, helping fight against respiratory infections and even lung cancer. Leukotriene (a hormone which is necessary for the body to create hay fever and asthma symptoms) production is hampered by the presence of carotenes, making it ideal in long term asthma and allergy prevention therapy. Carotenes are supportive of the eyes and carrots do indeed help you see in the dark, improving the condition of night blindness, protecting against cataracts, boosting weak vision, and protecting against macular degeneration. The juice provides a tonic for the nervous system, stimulates the

uterus, increases libido, soothes the digestive system and decreases wrinkles on the skin, having an anti-aging effect. The greens and roots, juiced together, are an effective diuretic, helping with bladder and kidney problems such as urinary stones and cystitis. It will also ease rheumatism and gout. The soluble fibre in the juice helps reduce cholesterol and treat atherosclerosis, although the greens provide a stronger juice than the root for achieving this, whilst also dilating the blood vessels, reducing high blood pressure and improving the condition of angina. In addition, when applied externally, undiluted juice will provide relief from insect bites, reducing both the level of pain and the amount of swelling.

- *Poultice* from grated raw carrot, for minor burns.

HEALTHFUL COCKTAILS

Juice with beetroot to cleanse and fortify the blood.

CAUTIONS AND CONTRAINDICATIONS

Excessive intake of juice can cause skin discolouration. Avoid drinking large amounts of carrot juice if suffering from liver disease.

Celery (Apium graveolens)

Celery can be found in the wild, usually growing in ditches. It is more bitter, pungent and stronger in its action than cultivated celery which, although a little weaker, still has a large number of beneficial medicinal uses. I consider it a hard one to cultivate at home, but that is just my personal experience. Whenever I buy celery I always shop around for the really leafy bunches, as I use the leaves as a herb, to flavour Thai dishes and salads. The seeds are the strongest part medicinally and will be what is used in any commercial preparations, however, the stem and the leaf, which I regularly juice, have the same, if a slightly weaker effect. Celery has a high potassium, phosphorus, iron, sodium, magnesium and calcium content.

MATERIA MEDICA

Antibacterial, anti-inflammatory, antimicrobial, antioxidant, antiviral, digestive, diuretic, relieves muscle spasms

GATHERING

Cut and use fresh as needed, when fully grown in autumn. The flavour becomes stronger after the first frosts, but will be damaged by repeat exposure or severe weather, so protect them in the ground by surrounding and covering them with a layer of straw.

PREPARATIONS

- *Juice* 3-4 stalks daily for 3 weeks, whilst monitoring your symptoms. If there is no improvement by this point discontinue regular use, as kidneys can become overstimulated and irritated by long term use. Being a powerful antioxidant and diuretic, celery juice helps boost the kidneys, making them more efficient at expelling waste and flushing out uric acid. These actions will improve rheumatic, arthritic and gouty conditions whilst helping to prevent the formation of bladder and kidney stones. The increase in urine flow, anti-inflammatory action and presence of apiol (a volatile oil with a mild antiseptic action) will soothe irritated bladder conditions and bladder infections. It is alkalizing to the entire system, relieving any symptoms of toxemia and acidosis, such as skin inflammations. The digestion will be improved, gas and indigestion relieved and stomach ulcers soothed. Containing coumarins its consumption will help guard against the development of cancer. It stimulates the uterus, reduces pre-menstrual water retention and acts as a sexual tonic for men. It is a mild sedative, calming the nerves, relieving anxiety and nervous stomach upset. It helps lower blood pressure by relaxing and widening the arteries which also improves angina. Drinking regularly will also lower cholesterol levels and is handy if you are following a low sodium diet as its high quantity of organic sodium will help your body retain its natural chemical balance. Electrolyte balance will also be maintained making it a great summer drink, helping keep you hydrated even if you regularly exert yourself and sweat a lot out in the sun.

CAUTIONS AND CONTRAINDICATIONS

Large quantities cause numbing of the tongue, usually a sign that you have had enough and it's time to stop. Avoid large doses if suffering kidney disease. Avoid medicinal doses during pregnancy.

Chilli Pepper (Capsicum annuum)

Rich in nutrients including iron, calcium, phosphorus, vitamins A, B complex and C. In fact chillies have more than six times the vitamin C content of oranges, weight for weight. The B vitamins help with food absorption and healthy functioning of the brain and nervous system, while vitamin C supports the immune and cardio-vascular system and helps the body detox.

A string of chillies in the kitchen has a great visual impact too, in fact in New Mexico strings and wreaths of large red chillies, called ristras, are sold for the decoration of front doors and homes. Chillies are the fruits of the chilli bush and they come in an amazing array of varieties, from mild to very spicy in flavour. Be careful which ones you choose as the really hot ones, such as habaneros and scotch bonnet, will blow the head off even the most hardened chilli lover. Add to salsas, dressings, guacamole or cook with them, although this will compromise their medicinal properties. To make a simple salsa just chop and mix chilli, onion, garlic, tomato, coriander and a squirt of lemon or lime - spicy but incredibly healthy, and it can't be beaten at the onset of a cold or flu.

One must beware as chillies are somewhat addictive! Your tolerance will rise rather sharply if you do start using them. They release endorphins in the brain, giving you a spurt of feel good factor a bit like high quality chocolate, and that in itself (chilli chocolate) is a synergy made in heaven which I definitely recommend trying if you haven't already.

MATERIA MEDICA

Antibacterial, antimicrobial, antiparasitic, antiseptic, pain relief, stimulates sweating

GATHERING

Collect fruit from the plant in late summer when red and use fresh. Hang up on strings to dry and use later. They can also be harvested when green and unripe and can be used fresh in this state. They will tend to ripen off the bush if collected when green, slowly going red. Red ones, left on the bush, will start to dry out if not picked when red and fleshy.

PREPARATIONS

- *Capsules* (maximum 3 a day) eating raw chillies can be a bit overwhelming and by cooking them you will compromise their healing properties and still have to deal with the spice. To avoid the spice but still benefit from the medicinal action, dry the chillies thoroughly, crush into a fine powder and put into capsules using no more than about ¼ teaspoon in each capsule (even if that leaves empty space), otherwise it may be too strong for your stomach. Consumed in this way it can be used for the same complaints as eating raw or drinking an infusion.
- *Eat* (raw) it contains capsaicin which stimulates the body to heal and cleanse. Chillies act most strongly on the cardio-vascular system, stimulating circulation, improving elasticity of the blood vessels, normalising blood pressure, helping to break down and prevent the formation of blood clots, lowering LDL (bad cholesterol) and consequently acting as a preventative against both heart attack and stroke. They are stimulating to the digestive system, improving circulation and increasing production of gastric juices and thus efficiency of digestion, increasing peristaltic action, relieving gas, and soothing the stomach. Regular intake of chillies also helps boost the metabolic rate. This is shown by the sweating that is induced by their consumption, so they could potentially be an aid to weight loss if used as part of a sensible, healthy eating and exercise plan. Eaten raw they will help expel parasites from the intestines. They boost circulation and increase perspiration, helping to break a fever, and aid with poor circulation, varicose veins and asthma. A single chilli contains the daily recommended amount of beta-carotene, so is potentially also protection against the development of cancer.
- *Infusion* you may want to experiment with quantity depending on the variety of chilli you are using. I find that half a teaspoon of dried and roughly crushed or 1 teaspoon of fresh chilli is enough for a stimulating, spicy brew. Maybe you will need to build up slowly and if you simply don't get on with the sensation at all, try the capsule approach instead. Sweetening will make the drink more palatable. Drink to stimulate circulation

and perspiration at the onset of colds and flu; it will relieve chills and sinus congestion.

- *Poultice* the chillies will irritate the area where the poultice is applied and this will increase blood supply and consequently decrease sensitivity to pain. Apply to sprains, neuralgia, lumbago, muscular pains and arthritis. Applied over the chest area it will relieve pleurisy.
- *Powder* Mix ¼ teaspoon of powdered chilli with warm water, a squirt of fresh lemon or lime and a tablespoon of maple syrup (the sweetness helps it go down). It provides a cleansing way to start the day and will give your circulation a boost at the onset of cold. Cayenne is the chilli most often used for this warming brew, but any hot pepper will do the same work.
- *Salve* will work like a poultice as a counter irritant, relieving pain from sprains, muscular aches, arthritis, lumbago, neuralgia and unbroken chilblains.

CAUTIONS AND CONTRAINDICATIONS

Always, always, wash hands thoroughly after handling chillies or you may have a painful surprise when you next go to rub your eyes, or anywhere else for that matter! Avoid contact with broken skin. Do not consume in excess. Do not use internally if suffering gastrointestinal problems.

Comfrey (Symphytum officinale)

This plant is quite invasive and hard to eradicate once established, but why would you want to? If it starts to get out of hand chop the leaves off and place directly in the compost where it will help accelerate the formation and improve the richness. It has a long flowering season starting in early spring, and its beautiful delicate little flowers seem to be on a conveyor belt, rotating forwards and upwards with new blooms as the older ones die off. Not just medicinal for the human body, being full of potassium and nitrogen, it's also nutritious for plants and can be easily made into a plant food for fruits and vegetables, eliminating the need to buy commercial tomato feed during the summer months. I also line my potato trenches with their leaves, which slowly feed the growing tubers as they break down underground.

The bees adore the flowers and will happily buzz around them as long as they are blooming. Comfrey contains constituents that, when used in the form of an extract, can cause liver damage. This has not been proven to be the case when the whole plant is used, however, it remains inadvisable to consume comfrey in large quantities. It can be eaten safely if not used to excess and the permaculture area of Glastonbury festival in fact sells, quite literally, millions of comfrey pakora to happy customers every year. The leaves can be added to salads or cooked as a spinach substitute. If you decide to eat comfrey it is best to only use the early fresh leaves that occur before flowering and stop when flowering starts as this will ensure that you don't consume too much and risk damaging your liver. Despite not being in vogue to take internally, externally used preparations are definitely worth keeping in your wild medicine first aid kit and are safe enough to use on babies. The medicinal qualities are easily absorbed through the skin, making this an easy way to stimulate the growth of new cells and enhance repair to the connective tissue and cartilage in the place where injury or problem lies.

MATERIA MEDICA

Antifungal, anti-inflammatory, astringent, expectorant

GATHERING

Leaves are more potent if collected early before flowering begins, but if you miss that narrow opportunity don't worry as I have found preparations made with leaves collected later in the growing season seem to work just as effectively. Leaves can be used fresh or dried and saved for later use.

PREPARATIONS

- *Bath* for bad bruising, sprains and over-strained muscles after a long hard day of manual labour.
- *Compress* on varicose veins, swellings, sprains, burns, cuts and sores.
- *Infusion* is a gentle remedy for diarrhoea and dysentery, soothing gastric and duodenal ulcers, colitis, IBS and reducing inflammation of the stomach lining. It will ease rheumatism, bronchial diseases and bleeding hemorrhoids.
- *Oil* for sprains, swellings, bruises, swollen joints, frozen shoulder and to improve the appearance of fresh scars.
- *Poultice* make a warm paste and use a piece of gauze to keep the plant matter from direct contact with an open wound. Use for varicose veins, swellings, sprains, burns, boils, cuts and bleeding wounds to stem the bleeding and speed the healing process. Use in an emergency where a fracture is suspected whilst waiting for the bone to be professionally set. It is particularly useful where there is a rib fracture which can't be bound by the hospital. Do not use on deep wounds as it increases the rate at which cells reproduce and may cause the surface to heal before the deeper wound, causing an abscess to form.
- *Salve* apply to healing bones after the cast has been removed. Also for acne, psoriasis, eczema, sores, boils, varicose veins, skin ulcers, hemorrhoids, bunions, sprains, rheumatism and arthritis.

CAUTIONS AND CONTRAINDICATIONS

The bristly foliage may irritate sensitive skin, so wear protective gloves whilst collecting. Restrict internal use to a maximum of 8 weeks. External use need not be restricted. Avoid ingestion if pregnant or breast feeding. Avoid ingestion if anaemic as its consumption can prevent iron absorption.

Cucumber (Cucumis sativa)

Cucumber is perhaps surprisingly a fruit, not a vegetable. It has a high water and low sugar content, making it a great fruit to mix with others in juices where its delicate lightness can dilute stronger flavours, making a drink more thirst quenching and refreshing. If you can't grow your own it is advisable to buy organic because, when conventionally grown, it is heavily sprayed and often waxed. It's a perfect snack, high in potassium, low in calories and with a satisfying crunch when eaten fresh from the vine and simply chomped on like an apple. The leaves are also edible so, as you remove the leaves from the growing plant to let the sun reach and ripen the fruits or to cut down the number of growing shoots, why not stick them in a salad or cook with them?

MATERIA MEDICA

Anti-inflammatory, antiparasitic, diuretic, laxative

GATHERING

Harvest in late summer when the fruit has grown to the size you require, but don't leave it too long or they will become rather bitter.

PREPARATIONS

- *Crush* whole pieces of the fruit in a blender and apply the mushy pulp to the skin for its cooling anti-inflammatory action on sunburn, minor burns, acne and otherwise irritated skin. Leave on for 30 minutes before rinsing off.
- *Eat* it is important to chew thoroughly to ensure the cellulose breaks down. It has a beneficial impact on stomach health, helping to maintain a healthy balance of intestinal flora whilst acting as a mild laxative and combating constipation. The fibre content also helps to regulate cholesterol levels. It helps dissolve uric acid and eliminate it via the kidneys and urinary system, breaking up kidney and bladder stones and relieving gout. The high potassium content will help balance high or low blood pressure and improve the flexibility of muscles. Eating the peel is beneficial to the skin, giving it a healthy glow whilst maintaining elasticity and reducing the formation of wrinkles (Harrod Buhner, 2003). Obviously the seeds are contained within the fruit and are eaten along with the skin and flesh, although some varieties I have grown end up with big and slightly hard seeds. Don't be tempted to discard these as they have health benefits in their own right. They are rich in oils, promote fertility and expel intestinal parasites.
- *Juice* to bring relief from arthritis, rheumatism and gouty conditions. It will break down bladder and kidney stones and soothes heartburn and gastritis. It can also be used on the skin, applied with cotton wool as a facial cleanser, or as a skin wash to soothe and cool skin irritations and sunburn.
- *Poultice* perhaps not strictly a poultice, but simply holding the peeled skin, wet side down, to the forehead will relieve headache.
- *Slice* and place over the eyes to cool, soothe, and rejuvenate. This will offer relief from conjunctivitis and tired, red, puffy eyes. Leave in place for 30 minutes before removing.

HEALTHFUL COCKTAILS

Juice with carrot to cleanse uric acid from the system and treat rheumatism.

CAUTIONS AND CONTRAINDICATIONS

Cucumber is a strong diuretic, so use it in moderation as excessive amounts may result in electrolyte imbalance caused by fluid loss.

Fig (Ficus carica)

Absolutely divine fresh from the tree when ripe and juicy and warmed by the sun. For that reason I understand why it had a place in the Garden of Eden, but why Adam and Eve choose to clothe their most private parts with it is a mystery as the milky sap can cause a minor skin reaction in some people and that is surely the last place you would want a red, sore patch of skin! They can be successfully grown in the UK against a sunny, south facing wall. If you do attempt to grow them you must contain the roots or the plant will concentrate on producing lots of foliage rather than fruits. This can be done by keeping it in a large pot. Dried figs, like their fresh counterparts, are high in calcium, potassium, iron and fibre and are readily available, which is useful for the times when they are out of season.

MATERIA MEDICA

Antibacterial, antioxidant, laxative

GATHERING

The fruits should be picked when ripe and consumed fresh or dried for later use.

PREPARATIONS

- *Crush* when the stems are broken a milky sap appears. This can be applied to warts.
- *Decoction* (made from dried figs, save the fruit and eat later) for constipation and catarrh in the nose and throat.
- *Eat* they are very soothing to inflamed tissues, especially the mucous membranes of the respiratory and digestive tracts. The high mucin and antioxidant content help clear toxins and excess mucous from the system, relieving catarrh of the nose, throat, and respiratory tracts. They are a natural laxative and the ficin content aids digestion. It helps kill harmful bacteria, allowing a good bacterial balance within the intestines. They are very sweet, providing energy for highly active people, whilst helping build up

convalescents. In addition the phosphorous content is beneficial to the nervous system and they are highly alkaline, benefiting the whole body.

- *Syrup* for constipated children, sore throats, asthma, coughs and bronchial infections.

CAUTIONS AND CONTRAINDICATIONS

None known.

Garlic (Allium sativum)

Something of a wonder remedy and extremely effective for a wide range of minor complaints and common ailments. If I had to choose only 5 plants that I could use in my medicine chest, this would be one of them. Garlic is widely used in cooking, but this is not particularly advisable before a date, unless you chew a bit of parsley straight after to banish the odour. It is mainly excreted through the lungs, which is why it gives your breath a bit of a whiff, but also why it is beneficial in many problems relating to the respiratory system. The leaves and flowers are also edible and can be harvested and eaten throughout the winter if the bulbs are left in the ground.

It is very simple to grow. Just break the bulb into cloves, taking care not to remove the papery covering on each one, place at a thumbs depth in the soil in late autumn and just wait for that clove to divide into a whole new bulb. The new bulb will be ready for harvest by mid to late summer. They need very little attention, just a bit of weeding and occasional water when it hasn't rained for a while.

MATERIA MEDICA

Antibacterial, antibiotic, antifungal, antimicrobial, antioxidant, antiparasitic, antiseptic, antiviral, expectorant, induces perspiration

GATHERING

Harvest the bulb when the leaves start to go brown and flop over. Dry on the ground for a couple of weeks before hanging up. If it flowers before the foliage dies back, pick off the flower or it will take vital energy from the maturing bulb. Garlic keeps for a long time when stored in a cool, dry, well ventilated place. It is commonly hung in plaits, but this is not as easy as it looks. The simple version is to just tie one bulb at a time down a hanging piece of string (as I do!).

PREPARATIONS

- *Crush* and rub over abscesses on the gums and under teeth.
- *Eat,* but to gain the maximum potential from garlic's healing properties you will need to eat it raw. Start with one clove a day and build up to three. It can be disguised by slicing thinly or dicing and adding to your meal as you serve it. Eating it whole is too strong for most people and, on an empty stomach, it may cause a few intense moments of nausea. It boosts your immune system and will enhance your state of well being. As an antiviral and antibacterial it is also a valuable remedy for colds, flu and viruses and will help you to sweat it out, lowering a fever. It helps the respiratory system fight and recover from coughs, whooping cough, bronchitis, chest infections, sinusitis, clear respiratory catarrh and improve asthmatic conditions. It cleans the blood, helping to remove heavy metals such as lead and mercury from the body, thereby protecting cells from damage caused by the presence of such toxins. It lowers blood pressure by dilating the blood vessels and preventing aggregation of platelets (clot formation), helping to guard against heart attack, stroke and thrombosis. Extremely good for heart and circulatory health, it also helps to lower cholesterol and increase HDLs (good cholesterol) and treats arteriosclerosis. It is also a great benefit when suffering gastrointestinal problems, relieving flatulence, indigestion and killing intestinal parasites whilst reducing yeast infections caused by Candida albicans overgrowth. It is actually one of the best plants to use for treating Candida as it will kill off the excess bacteria whilst re-establishing a healthy bacterial balance in the gut and killing off fungal infections such as thrush and athlete's foot that have crept in due to the Candida overgrowth. The beneficial effects on the bacterial flora in the gut also make it very useful to include after being prescribed a course of antibiotics which, by their nature, upset your body's natural balance. It helps fight the pain of menstrual cramps, arthritis, rheumatism, neuralgia and sciatica. It tones and gently improves the function of both the liver and kidneys. It is also being researched as a potential cancer inhibitor. If all that's not enough it also helps provide a natural deterrent to mosquitoes (whom it's said prefer the taste of sweet blood).
- *Juice* it can be used in juices, but this is not for the faint hearted! Only use one clove at a time and mix in with other juices to dilute the taste and make it a little more gentle on the stomach.
- *Oil* rub oil on sprains, aches, muscle pain, arthritis, neuralgia and sciatica, minor skin irritations and infections. It can also be rubbed on cold feet to encourage the circulation. Gently warm a teaspoonful and dribble into an ear to relieve earache and ear infections, but plug a little cotton wool lightly in your ear to stop it leaking back out, remove the cotton wool after an hour, by which time it should have been absorbed.
- *Plaster* place on your chest with a hot water bottle warming it from the other side. Leave in place for 30 minutes, but remove it sooner if it feels too hot or your skin is going red. This is to be used for coughs, but without the hot water bottle it can be placed over fungal infections or boils. It can also be placed on the soles of the feet to draw out toxins.
- *Rub* on the skin to clear up infected wounds, cuts, athletes foot, warts, thread worm and ring worm. You can hold it in place, but not for too long as it can irritate, burn and even blister if you do so.
- *Syrup* make using honey and take 3 teaspoons a day for sore throats, hoarseness,

asthma, coughs and other chest complaints.

CAUTIONS AND CONTRAINDICATIONS

Do not use in large doses if on blood thinning medication. Do not use medicinally if breast feeding as it will pass through the breast and may cause colic in nursing infants.

Kale (Brassica oleracea)

This is a particularly hardy vegetable, surviving in less than optimum soil conditions and suffering less at the hand of pests than other members of the brassica family, which makes it a good vegetable for the inexperienced gardener to attempt. It can happily be grown amongst flowers in a more ornamental bed where its foliage can add to the overall visual impact (until you eat it, that is). It has a higher nutritional value than most other greens, being high in calcium, iron, sodium, vitamin C, carotenes and chlorophyll. It contains more than 135mg calcium for every 100g of leaf (Patenaude, 2001), which means more per glass than cow's milk, with a higher digestibility too. The carotenes have anti-cancer properties, helping to guard against the development of cancer if consumed regularly. To gain the maximum nutritional value kale must be eaten raw or juiced. Eat young leaves raw, simply chopping finely and adding to salads. Older leaves will need to be cooked. Steaming will preserve more of the nutritional value than boiling, but juicing is perhaps an easier way to consume useful quantities.

MATERIA MEDICA

Antioxidant

GATHERING

The leaves and stem can be gathered all year round, but they become more tender and sweeter after the first frosts of winter.

PREPARATIONS

- *Juice* use one large leaf and its stem. If you are juicing an old leaf you may find it preferable to mix it with sweeter vegetables to improve the taste. It boosts the immune system and helps retain the balance of intestinal flora while the high fibre content helps reduce the risk of heart disease. Cancer has been connected to a lack of sulphur in the system, so the fact that kale contains a relatively large quantity, combined with the presence of carotenes, helps the body guard against the development of cancer.

CAUTIONS AND CONTRAINDICATIONS

None known.

Marigold (Calendula officinalis)

The flowers are a lovely rich orange, which breaks up all the greens on the allotment and provides fodder for insects. I pick the flowers and pull the petals off into the salad bowl. They can also be used as a poor man's saffron substitute in soups and rice dishes. The medicinal properties are concentrated on the underside of the flower head, and less so in the petals, so when drinking an infusion or making any other preparation be sure to include these in the mix. They are not very tasty which is why I don't include them in my food, but the tacky, bitter resins that ooze out of this part make a strong medicine. They are relatively long flowering, providing colour right through the summer and into autumn, when the first frosts tend to kill off any remaining stems. When you see a patch of them you will feel your heart lift up, and on an emotional level, Calendula can be used to bring a bit of sunshine in and lift a heavy heart.

MATERIA MEDICA

Antibacterial, antifungal, anti-inflammatory, antiparasitic, antiseptic, antiviral, astringent, diuretic, induces perspiration, relaxes spasms

GATHERING

Collect the flowers when they are fully open, any time during the flowering season, which typically lasts from May until October. Use fresh or dry the entire flower head at room temperature in an airy place. Don't be shy when harvesting as removing the flower heads will promote further flowering, but do let some of the flowers go to seed so that you end up with a perennial patch of these brightly coloured beauties.

PREPARATIONS

- *Compress* for skin inflammations, sprains and dislocations.
- *Crush* whole flower directly on wasp or bee stings for pain relief and to reduce the inflammation.
- *Douche* (with a strong infusion) for vaginal thrush.
- *Eyebath* for sore eyes and conjunctivitis.
- *Facial Steam* for its antibacterial effects on oily, pimply and acne prone skin.
- *Gargle* for tonsillitis, throat infections, gum infections and oral thrush.
- *Infusion* is stimulating to both the immune and lymphatic systems, helpful when trying to shake off a lingering infection, illness, swollen glands and glandular fever. It promotes sweating and, combined with its antiviral qualities, makes a good remedy at the onset of colds and flu. It also stimulates the liver and gall bladder and has an overall cleansing effect on the body which will improve chronic skin disorders such as eczema and acne. It has a soothing effect on the gastrointestinal lining, easing nausea, stomach disorders, colitis, Chron's disease, diverticulitis and both gastric and duodenal ulcers. Drink 5 times daily as part of a regime to overcome Candida overgrowth and also drink this quantity for a week before menstruation is due to alleviate painful periods. It also stimulates the uterus, promoting delayed menstruation and contractions during childbirth. The high lutein content helps protect the macular in

the eye from degeneration (the number one cause of blindness in over 40s). In addition it's a general remedy for nervous conditions. Make an extra strong infusion and use externally as a skin wash to dry up oozing wounds, to clean and heal minor burns, scalds, ulcers and eczema, for fungal infections including athlete's foot and ringworm.

- *Oil* rub on painful muscles and joints, stomach ache, dry damaged skin and rashes.
- *Salve* for chapped, cracked 'gardeners hands.' To promote healing in open and infected wounds, lacerations, cuts, scratches, grazes, chapped lips, ulcers and burns. Will soothe and reduce the inflammation on areas of sunburn, irritation, chaffing, nappy rash and hemorrhoids. Reduces discomfort and prevents further deterioration in varicose veins.
- *Tincture* can be diluted and used as a skin wash in the same way as a strong infusion. Internally it will also treat the same complaints as an infusion.

HEALTHFUL COCKTAILS

Infuse and mix with cold infused cleavers for lymph stagnation.

Infuse with marshmallow and meadowsweet to soothe ulcers.

Place in a bath with chamomile to soothe irritated skin conditions.

CAUTIONS AND CONTRAINDICATIONS

Use with caution if sensitive to the asteraceae family. Avoid internal use during pregnancy and breast feeding.

Nasturtium (Tropaeolum majus)

This flower is very easy to grow and eaten along with the leaves it has a delicious spicy flavour. It will flower from mid-summer right through the winter in mild and protected areas, but will be killed off by a hard frost. Some varieties have a trailing habit and can be planted to cascade down from pots, balconies, hanging baskets and other containers, which is ideal if your space is limited, but want your plants to be both delightfully edible and medicinal. It is a useful companion plant, which I grow amongst broad beans to divert the attention of black fly, but is a great addition anywhere. The leaves are high in vitamin C and sulphur.

To make tasty, spicy little salad bites, simply get some of the big leaves, fill them with whatever you have to hand; quinoa, goat's cheese, bean sprouts are all good choices. You may find yourself experimenting with different flavours and textures until you find one that really works for you. Once you are decided on the filling, just wrap the leaf around it and present the wrap like a dolma, decorating the plate with the flowers, which are edible too.

MATERIA MEDICA

Antibacterial, antibiotic, antifungal, antimicrobial, antiseptic, antiviral, diuretic,

expectorant

GATHERING

Flowers and leaves are collected and used fresh throughout the growing season.

PREPARATIONS

- *Eat* fresh on a regular basis, along with other dietary measures and herbal remedies, when trying to clear the system of either a Candida albicans overgrowth or a parasite infestation.
- *Facial Steam* for acne and pimples.
- *Foot bath* for athlete's foot.
- *Infusion* for bronchitis, respiratory tract infections and genito-urinary infections. It will loosen and help expel catarrh. Used externally as a skin wash it can be applied to minor skin infections, acne, pimples and wounds.
- *Juice* add 3-4 leaves to juices 3 times daily to ward off colds, flu, sinusitis, bronchitis, and generally help boost the function of the immune system.
- *Poultice* for skin wounds. Remove after 10 minutes as it contains mustard oil which may cause irritation or even burn if left on longer.
- *Tincture* for colds, flu, sinusitis and bronchitis.
- *Vinegar* take a large spoonful 3 times daily as soon as you feel a cold, flu or viral infection coming on. To increase its strength, add raw crushed garlic while you are infusing the vinegar. It can also be mixed with oil as a healthy salad dressing.

CAUTIONS AND CONTRAINDICATIONS

None known.

Onion (Allium cepa)

The leaves and flowers are edible along with the bulb, which is the normal section of this plant that you will see on your plate. Some people find its flavour very strong, especially when raw, but interestingly it is actually more digestible by the body in this form and is, of course, more medicinal. Rich in minerals, they contain calcium, magnesium, phosphorus, and quercetin. Never leave a cut onion uncovered as it will attract and absorb toxins.

Extremely easy to grow from sets, which are small bulbs you can plant directly into the ground. They can also be grown from seed, but this is slightly less reliable, and will involve some waste created by thinning out the seedlings. Once established, all you need do is keep them relatively weed free and water them when it's been hot. Other than that they will get on with it by themselves with rarely a problem.

MATERIA MEDICA

Antiasthmatic, antibiotic, antifungal, antimicrobial, antiseptic, blood pressure regulator, diuretic, expectorant, relaxes spasms

GATHERING

You can harvest throughout the growing season to use them fresh. The main harvest is when the tops have started to go yellow and flopped over. At this point move the foliage to one side, exposing as much of the bulb as possible to the sun. Slip a hand fork underneath to loosen its attachment to the earth slightly. Leave for approximately 2 weeks, then pull it up on a dry day, brushing off any remaining flecks of earth and leave outside for a few further days to dry (but bring them indoors if there's a threat of rain). Remove the tops and store in a cool, dry and well ventilated place. Hanging them works well, so the air can circulate. They will store over winter and, if timed well, they will run out just as your spring onions are ready the following year.

PREPARATIONS

- *Eat* (raw) a whole onion at the onset of a cold. I have never tried this myself, but made my friend Tony do it once. It looked like hard work, but he didn't complain about his cold again! It helps the intestinal tract to rid itself of parasites. The high iron content is good for treating anemia. It boosts the immune system, cleanses the blood and assists with digestion, relieving flatulence and colic. It contains various cancer fighting compounds including selenium, which also protects against stroke. Avoidance of stroke is also helped by the fact it has an inhibitory effect on platelets collecting together in clumps and forming blood clots. It helps lower blood pressure and cholesterol whilst raising HDL (high density lipoprotein/'good' cholesterol).
- *Plaster* place on the chest with a hot water bottle on top for coughs and on the forehead for sinus headaches.
- *Poultice* to draw something out from under the skin such as a splinter, a spike from a sea urchin or pus from a boil. Leave a slice in your mouth if suffering from toothache.
- *Rub* a cut edge on athlete's foot 2 times daily until it has cleared up and on cuts and acne where it will kill bacteria.
- *Syrup* made very simply by covering finely chopped onion with sugar or honey. After a day remove the onion, take the liquid by the teaspoon as needed and store in the fridge. You can also juice an onion, mix it with honey and store it in the fridge for a simple syrup. Take this to alleviate congestion, coughs, sore throats and colds.

HEALTHFUL COCKTAILS

Make into a syrup with thyme for a cough.

CAUTIONS AND CONTRAINDICATIONS

Excess consumption can cause gastrointestinal irritation. Do not consume if breast feeding as it may cause colic in your baby.

Pumpkin (Curcubita maxima)

Pumpkin grows as a trailing vine and can be grown around the feet of other taller vegetables such as sweetcorn and climbing beans. This is a traditional growing alliance in North America, where they are collectively known as the 'Three Sisters.' The flesh, seeds, leaves and flowers are all edible, the flowers making an incredibly showy piece of edible garnish. The seeds have a whitish outer sheath which must be removed before eating, however some varieties produce 'naked' seeds which are dark green and can be eaten as they are. They are best eaten raw and enjoyed for their nutty taste and high oil content. The seeds are highly nutritious, containing significant amounts of zinc, iron, calcium, magnesium and vitamin E (vital for healthy skin). Their properties provide a sexual tonic and prostate protection for men. The flesh is great steamed or made into soups or pies, but the fruit is probably most famous for being carved into scary faces and made into lanterns for the celebration of Halloween. Pumpkins can be used safely by pregnant women, children and those debilitated by disease.

MATERIA MEDICA

Antiparasitic, diuretic

GATHERING

The fruits are harvested when orange in autumn. The seeds are collected from the ripe fruit, separated from the pulp and spread out to dry. The husk does not need to be removed if using to grind into a paste or for decoctions, only if they are to be eaten. The whole fruits store well, even throughout the winter, if kept in a cool, dry place.

PREPARATIONS

- *Decoction* (seeds) for prostate problems and gout.
- *Eat* (seeds) it is preferable to grind the seeds before eating. This ensures they are broken down and not swallowed whole, making their nutritional and medicinal qualities available for absorption. You can use a coffee grinder or food processor to do this, however, if you grind more than you will eat straight away it is essential to refrigerate what is left, as once exposed to air, warmth and light, the oils they contain will rapidly go rancid, producing destructive free radicals. They are highly alkaline, which benefits the whole body and makes them an excellent choice for treating acidosis of the liver and blood. The high zinc content can slow prematurely greying hair. Being rich in magnesium makes them a valuable addition to the diet as most people are deficient in this mineral. Zinc and magnesium are both essential in the production of semen, making the seeds a worthy addition to the male diet, especially where there are fertility

problems, low sperm motility or low sperm count. The magnesium levels also benefit prostate problems and eating a handful of seeds each day will help to reduce an enlarged prostate. Eating seeds on a daily basis is also recommended for acne sufferers. They are soothing to bladder problems and may help guard against the formation of bladder and kidney stones. Eat seed paste for a whole day with no other food to expel tapeworm, round worm and other parasites, (pulp) to soothe an inflamed digestive tract. (flesh) to gain the maximum benefit eat raw. This is quite starchy, so don't try eating big chunks; either grate into a salad or a cooked meal that is ready to serve. It is full of beta-carotene which the body processes into vitamin A and this helps guard against the development of cancer, respiratory disease and heart problems.

- *Infusion* (flower) use 3 flowers per cup and drink for prostate problems.
- *Poultice* (pulp) for burns and use as a face pack for spots, pimples and acne, (seeds) grind into a paste and apply to minor wounds, burns and chapped skin.

CAUTIONS AND CONTRAINDICATIONS

None known.

Radish (Raphanus sativus)

Combining a strong flavour with plenty of bite, they are very popular in traditional salads, brightening up the bowl with a globe of pink. There are many varieties, most small and pink, but daikon is a long white kind that is popular in Asian cuisine. I prefer to grow daikon. The leaves have wobbly edges and, for the same effort, you get a much larger vegetable, which when left to seed gives you a new crop the following year. It is certainly worth letting one or two flower just to taste the flowers themselves as they have a serious kick to them. It's just a shame they're not a little larger.

Radish can be planted inbetween other things as it's relatively quick to grow and will be ready to harvest by the time the other crops fill out and cut off the supply of sunlight. They are rich in calcium, potassium, sulphur, beta-carotene, folic acid and vitamin C.

MATERIA MEDICA

Antibiotic, antibacterial, antifungal, digestive, expectorant

GATHERING

Harvest from early autumn onwards as needed and use fresh. It is best to sow every couple of weeks from late winter until late summer to ensure your harvest is spread over an equally long period.

PREPARATIONS

- *Eat* (1-3 daily, or an equivalent volume of daikon) helps improve digestion, reducing abdominal bloating, flatulence and relieving indigestion. They act on the urinary system, inhibiting the formation of bladder and kidney stones and gravel when consumed regularly and also help to break down any that have already formed. They help to break down fat deposits in the liver, gallstones and stimulate bile production, improving gall bladder function. When used on a regular basis they can also be used to alleviate both hyper and hypothyroidism by helping to normalise the production of thyroxine. Levels of calcitonin produced by the thyroid will also be normalised, which is important because it controls the quantity of calcium released into the blood and used during bone formation; levels too high, or low, will obviously have a knock on effect on the entire skeletal system. Radish will help dissolve excess mucous and ease bronchitis, sinusitis and sore throats.

- *Juice* (leaves) will have both a laxative and a diuretic effect, (root) can be diluted with other milder tasting juices and is used for the same complaints as eating the root raw.

HEALTHFUL COCKTAILS

Eat five dispersed throughout the day along with 3 cups of infused chamomile to dissolve kidney stones.

CAUTIONS AND CONTRAINDICATIONS

Eaten in excess radish can irritate the liver, kidney and gall bladder.

Raspberry (Rubus idaeus)

The small and yummy red fruits are rich in calcium, iron, potassium, magnesium and vitamin C. Both summer and autumn fruiting varieties exist, so if you plant a mixture you can have a ready source of fruit from early June well into October. If you enjoy raspberries you will save a fortune by growing your own as the plants are cheap to buy and within the first year you will have paid for them several times over with your abundant harvest. They are a delight to eat raw, but also freeze well and can be processed into jam or fancy deserts. Growing your own will also provide you with a ready supply of the leaves, a source of astringent tannins which tighten and tone the body's tissues.

MATERIA MEDICA

Fruit - antibacterial, anti-inflammatory, antioxidant, antiviral
Leaves - astringent

GATHERING

Collect the leaves throughout the growing season and use fresh or dry for later use in infusions. As always with flowering plants the potency of the medicine in the leaves is said to be stronger if collected before the plant flowers. I believe, however, that using fresh plant material is more potent. So, although I would recommend collecting what you need for out of season times before flowering and drying, if you do need to use it either during or after flowering and the plant still has fresh, usable leaves, use them first. Eat fresh, raw raspberries straight from the bush or freeze for use in winter.

PREPARATIONS

- *Eat* (fruit) to cleanse the system, clearing excess and accumulated mucous. The vitamin C ensures absorption of the iron contained in the fruits, so eat to combat anaemia. The array of minerals are beneficial for heart problems, fatigue, depression and during convalescence.
- *Eyebath* (leaves) for conjunctivitis.
- *Gargle* (leaves) for tonsillitis and mouth inflammation.
- *Infusion* (leaves) this is traditionally drunk during the last two months of pregnancy to help tone and strengthen the uterus in preparation for birth. It will also ease labour pains and may shorten labour. When drunk for the first month or so after delivery it will help the uterus tighten and return to normal, whilst enriching and encouraging the flow of breast milk. It will also ease menstrual cramps, regulate intermittent menses and reduce the symptoms of PMS. Sip slowly for throat infections to reduce swelling. Drink cold to treat diarrhoea, a safe remedy for children too.
- *Mouthwash* (leaves) for ulcers.

CAUTIONS AND CONTRAINDICATIONS

Do not take the leaf internally during the first 8 months of pregnancy.

Rocket (Eruca vesicaria subsp. sativa)

A popular salad plant that has a spicy bite to it. When grown in a sheltered position it will provide leaves throughout the winter months too. In fact it is best to grow it in a sheltered and somewhat shady position all year round, otherwise the bright sun will make the plants bolt and go prematurely to seed before any of the leaves reach a decent size. It is prone to attack by flea beetle, so if you are unlucky you will be eating rather perforated leaves. Luckily the flowers are also edible so, if you do get caught out by any of these pitfalls, at least you will still have something to eat. If you leave some to self-seed they will come back next year, providing you with a perennial patch.

The young leaves, although having a milder flavour, have the higher medicinal value, being high in antioxidants, but don't worry if you miss them as all the leaves are rich in iron and vitamin C, fortifying your system.

MATERIA MEDICA

Antibacterial, antioxidant, diuretic

GATHERING

Collect it throughout the growing season and use fresh.

PREPARATIONS

- *Eat* the leaves to help improve the digestion and give the lymphatic system a boost. The high vitamin C content ensures that the iron is absorbed, making them valuable in the diet of anyone who suffers from anaemia. The seed pods that develop after flowering are antibacterial, so eat a few along with other remedies when coming down with an infection.

CAUTIONS AND CONTRAINDICATIONS

None known.

Strawberry (Fragaria vesca/x ananassa)

The wild ones are ever so sweet, so you only need one or two and they will blow your mind! Although much smaller, the wild or alpine strawberries have greater nutritional properties, but, to get a decent bowlful you will need a cultivated variety. Once you have grown your own and eaten them super fresh, still full of the sun's warmth, you will never again buy the out of season imported ones, as they never acquire the same depth of flavour.

When the first one arrives it can become a ritual that you either share with your beloved, each carefully biting a half and savouring the moment, or potentially sneaking it for yourself and pretending the slugs got there first. Believe me, the guilt has never ruined this secret pleasure for me. Within a couple of weeks you will be collecting a bowlful every day with plenty to share. Depending on your levels of generosity, keep an eye on the ripening fruits as you are not the only one watching. Often you may find yourself going to pick them only to find a friendly neighbourhood slug or bird has beaten you to it, perhaps thinking it was doing you a favour by clearing away your excess and chomping a good half of the ripe berry in the process.

Strawberry plants only produce well for a few years, so make sure you let the runners grow. Once they have developed a decent root system, cover them with a little compost and cut the connection to the mother plant. This ensures you always have a supply of young, fresh, well fruiting plants. It is also sometimes necessary to cut some of the bigger leaves when they are fruiting to ensure that all the energy goes into the fruit and the sun is not obscured by the leaf, making them ripen more slowly. If you have no space and have to buy them, organic are far superior because strawberries tend to accumulate and store any pesticides and fertilizers that have been used during their growth.

The Medicine Garden

Strawberries have cleansing properties and can be used to make a face pack to freshen and rejuvenate a dull, dry complexion. Simply mash a bowl of fruits and apply them to the face, removing after 15-20 minutes. If you have sensitive skin it would be wise to do a patch test first. The luxuriant pleasure doesn't end there either. Having a June birthday I love to indulge in the extravagance of fresh, ripe strawberries sliced into a glass of champagne and refill it with champagne a number of times before munching the remaining boozy fruits. I obviously partake only to benefit from the high vitamin C content and the medicinal properties!

MATERIA MEDICA

Antibacterial, antioxidant, antiviral, astringent, digestive, diuretic, laxative

GATHERING

The fruits can be picked and eaten fresh when ripe, usually in June. The leaves are picked in early summer and dried for later use.

PREPARATIONS

- **Eat** (fruit) they are easily digested, but like all fruits they are best eaten alone and preferably 30 minutes before other foods. They clean the intestines and encourage a healthy balance of intestinal flora, while the insoluble fibres aid digestion. The fibre content also aids in the lowering of cholesterol levels and high blood pressure. Arthritis, rheumatism, gouty conditions, joint pains and kidney stones will also benefit from the fruit's cleansing effects. Eaten the morning after drinking alcohol they will relieve a hangover. The rich quantity of iron is easily absorbed due to the vitamin C content, making it a great remedy for both anaemia and fatigue. The vitamin C also helps the body fight infection. The folic acid content makes them especially good to eat if you are planning, and during the first three months of, pregnancy. They provide a tonic for the liver, blood and female reproductive system. They can also help ease diarrhoea and dysentery. Eaten regularly they can help guard against cancer as they contain ellargic acid which binds to cancer causing molecules, rendering them inert, whilst protecting genes from damage caused by pre-existing cancer cells.
- **Infusion** (leaf) for dysentery and to stimulate the liver.
- **Mouthwash** (leaf) for ulcers and mouth infections.
- **Poultice** (fruit) simply mash the fruit and apply to areas of sunburn to provide cooling and soothing relief. They can also be used in this way for pimples and spots.
- **Rub** (fruit) on the teeth, leaving in place for five minutes before rinsing off. This will improve any discolouration and remove plaque.

CAUTIONS AND CONTRAINDICATIONS

Do not take if allergic to aspirin.

Wormwood (Artemesia absinthium)

It has beautiful silvery grey foliage with wobbly edged, oily leaves growing to a similar size as a mature lavender or rosemary. It is a very pungent smelling herb. I can imagine how it would be too much for some people. It can be dried and burned as an incense which will help develop your psychic powers.

It was one of the ingredients of the original absinthe, which helped to inspire numerous artists and writers from the late 1700s until the early 1900s, including Van Gogh, with its psychedelic effects. Absinthe was apparently highly addictive and wormwood is no longer legal to use as an ingredient in the modern brews. In fact excessive use of wormwood can cause hallucinations and delusions and is toxic to both the liver and brain, so perhaps you can understand why. It is so toxic it will kill and rid the intestines of worms.

MATERIA MEDICA

Anti-inflammatory, antiseptic, cardiac stimulant, pain relief, reduces fever, relaxes spasms

GATHERING

The leaves and flowering tops can be collected in July and August. Hang them in bunches away from direct sunlight in a warm, well aerated space to dry.

PREPARATIONS

- *Compress* for bruises and sprains.
- *Infusion* prepare yourself as the taste is very bitter! It is important not to exceed 3 cups a day or to take it for longer than 7 consecutive days unless supervised by a professional herbal practitioner. It is calming to the nervous system, reducing anxiety and providing a soothing tonic during times of depression. It increases vitality, stimulating the digestive system, reducing flatulence and soothing gastritis. It will improve bad breath whose root lies in a sluggish digestive tract. It expels intestinal worms, specifically round and thread worms. It also stimulates and tones the uterus, liver and gall bladder, increasing the flow of bile. Additionally it can ease rheumatism.
- *Salve* for sores, bites, scabies, abscesses, bruises, sore muscles, sprains, rheumatic pains, and arthritic joints.
- *Tincture* be very careful with dosages. Do not exceed 5 drops daily and do not continue for longer than 7 consecutive days unless supervised by a herbal medicine practitioner. It can be handy to allay the nausea of travel sickness and will bring quick relief to indigestion.

CAUTIONS AND CONTRAINDICATIONS

Do not exceed the recommended doses and only use for short periods of time. Excess can cause nausea and damage to the nervous system. Avoid during pregnancy and if sensitive to the compositae family. Not for children!

Property Borders

In this section we shall explore those shrubs and trees that may be found at the bottom of your garden or betwixt you and your neighbour, perhaps adorning fences and walls. For me this is an exciting zone, away from the heavily managed areas close to the house. It's the place where wildness begins to creep in and it's in these hard to get to corners where the big boys rule, creating dark, dingy and damp micro-climates where spiders, squirrels and faerie folk tread a little freer. I've never had the pleasure of owning a property with a large amount of land, but the two homes I have owned have both backed on to a small woodland which has given the feeling of both space and wildness. Even in those homes in which I lived that had very small, neat fenced gardens there was something uncontrollable about the corners. They are the transition zones at the very end of your direct influence, and what lies beyond is no longer manipulated by you, but perhaps by a neighbour or the local authority.

Beech (Fagus sylvatica)

Beech makes great hedges. It is thick and tall, giving a great degree of privacy once established. It has such wonderful and brilliant electric green leaves which dominate the woodland in early spring when the bluebells and wild garlic lay carpets of contrasting colour beneath it. In autumn, too, they delight on those crisp blue sky days with their deep, now coppery leaves which hold tight to the branch long after many other a leaf has fallen. Beech is no longer widely used medicinally, however, they are still popular with squirrels, so if you want to collect some of the edible nuts (masts) you will have to beat these furry rivals to them. The masts ripen around September and October when the shells will open, politely letting you know that they're ready. You will need to remove the hairy fluff that coats each mast within the shell before you eat them, which can be quite a laborious process, but is worth it, even if you only eat a few just for the flavour or to keep you going on an autumnal woodland walk. You could also take the masts home and roast them before eating for a different twist. They are not the most tasty of nuts but they are rich in oils which will help you build up a winter layer of fat (if you need any help, that is!). The young, newly emerging spring leaves are also edible. I usually munch on a few as a snack whilst collecting wild garlic, however, they make a fine addition to the salad bowl during that distinctly meagre time of year. They have a light tang, but within a couple of weeks of opening they lose this and become a bit tough and are no longer pleasurably palatable.

MATERIA MEDICA

Antiseptic, anti-inflammatory

GATHERING

The leaves are used and can be gathered from when they open in April until they begin to change colour in the autumn.

PREPARATIONS

- *Poultice* on swellings and sprains (Paterson, 1996).
- *Salve* on swellings and sprains.

CAUTIONS AND CONTRAINDICATIONS

Don't eat too many masts or you will get an upset stomach.

Birch (Betula pendula)

Betula pendula is commonly known as silver birch for its fine white, or perhaps silvery, trunks whose bark peels easily in layers, like thin sheets of paper. One of my fire lighting tricks, if I have some birch wood available, is to peel off some of the bark and place it under my stack of kindling. It fizzes and sparks, burning for a long time and igniting the fire without a fuss. It's a guaranteed and foolproof way to light a fire. The leaves and bark contain salicylates which have pain relieving and anti-inflammatory properties and are, in fact, the active ingredients in Aspirin. Birch is used for purification and cleansing, acting specifically on the blood.

MATERIA MEDICA

Anti-inflammatory, antiseptic, astringent, diuretic, laxative, pain relief

GATHERING

The leaves are best used fresh and can be collected either when in bud in spring or fully opened during the summer months. Bark is collected as needed throughout the growing season. Never remove a ring of bark from around the trunk as this will kill the tree. It is best to peel the bark from smaller branches or in patches to save damaging the trunk and the integrity of the tree itself. Both leaves and bark can be dried at room temperature out of direct sunlight for later use.

PREPARATIONS

- *Bath* (bark) a strong bark decoction can be added to the bath to dry and heal moist skin irritations.
- *Decoction* (bark) apply as a skin wash for pain relief and to aid the healing of stubborn sores, open wounds, burns and skin irritations.
- *Infusion* (leaf) the diuretic properties reduce the levels of uric acid in the body, benefiting joint problems such as arthritis and gout. Being naturally rich in potassium the use of birch will not deplete the body of this vital mineral as artificial diuretics often do. Partly for this reason it is safe to use regularly as a preventative measure against gout symptoms. It will also aid kidney and bladder disorders including urinary tract infections, water retention, cystitis, kidney stones, urinary gravel and stones. Rheumatism will also be eased, as will skin conditions relating to internal toxicity

including some cases of psoriasis and eczema. By increasing perspiration it reduces fever and can also be used for the treatment of inflammatory bacterial diseases including those where spasms or cramps are present. In addition it has deworming properties.

- *Juice* (leaf) a handful of leaves can be diluted with water or added to other fruit or vegetable juices twice daily and will have the same, but stronger, actions as an infusion.
- *Mouthwash* (leaf) for mouth ulcers and sores.
- *Oil* (leaf) for psoriasis and rheumatism.
- *Poultice* (bark) probably the most simple way to use birch is to get a section of the bark and apply the inner side, still damp after removal from the tree, directly to painful and aching muscles, where it will provide quick and effective pain relief and (leaf) on painful, arthritic, inflamed joints.
- *Tincture* (leaf buds) as a laxative which will improve the tone of the bowel and ease constipation (Evert Hopman, 1991).

CAUTIONS AND CONTRAINDICATIONS

Use with caution if sensitive to aspirin.

Ginkgo (Ginkgo biloba)

Often planted by roadsides as it is tolerant of pollution, especially sulphur dioxide, and so growth and the health of the tree will not be adversely affected by reduced air quality. I have one in a pot and consequently it is still rather small, despite now being over 10 years old. It is a great tree once mature with a lovely shape and ample branches that you can easily climb or hang a swing from (although not if grown in a pot!). The leaves are unique and quite different from any other deciduous leaves, being thick with narrow, straight, pronounced ribs and almost frilly. The shape could perhaps be likened to a cross section of a brain.

MATERIA MEDICA

Anti-inflammatory, antioxidant

GATHERING

Leaves are picked as they change colour in autumn. The leaf can be dried for infusions or fresh leaves made into a tincture.

PREPARATIONS

(***Start by drinking*** just 2 cups a day and increase slowly, or take 2-4ml of tincture daily. You will need to use it for a minimum of 6 weeks to see any improvement, however, it is safe for long term use).

• *Infusion* or *Tincture* for dilating blood vessels and stimulating circulation. This will improve oxygen delivery in the brain, promoting clear thinking, improving mental function, memory and alertness. Useful with Alzheimer's and senile dementia sufferers, general confusion in the elderly and aiding in stroke recovery. Circulation to the limbs is improved, helping with varicose veins, cold extremities and other circulatory complaints. Also potentially offering relief from tinnitus by improving circulation in the ear. It may slow or even reverse macular degeneration and generally guard against vision deterioration caused by compromised circulation in the retina. In addition to dilating the blood vessels it also helps regulate nitric oxide, a free radical produced in the body, that in excess will hamper circulation by affecting the muscle tone in blood vessels. Blood flow will also be improved to the reproductive organs and greater blood flow to the penis can help men overcome impotence and increase libido. Gingko thins the blood, helps lower cholesterol and reduces the risk of heart disease (Conway, 2001). It decreases the effects of environmental and chemical pollution, helping protect against premature aging. In addition, it dilates the bronchial tubes, easing chest tightness and wheezing in asthmatic conditions and allergic inflammatory responses. Dizziness resulting from vertigo can also be eased with the long term use of ginkgo.

CAUTIONS AND CONTRAINDICATIONS

Excess may cause headaches, diarrhoea and vomiting. Stop usage at least 48 hours before any surgery, due to its anti-blood clotting effects. Do not use if on anti-coagulant , anti- platelet or other medication for circulatory conditions.

Holly (Ilex aquifolium)

Traditionally considered magically protective against evil spirits, and with their sharp, stiff pointy leaves and red berries, (red being nature's danger signal), you can see why. Although rarely used in medicine at present they are still found growing in many places, from churchyards to woodlands across the country. The red berries provide winter forage for birds and form a traditional part of Christmas decorations. For the last few years I have dressed my house on winter solstice with a combination of holly, ivy, yew and mistletoe which transforms it instantly and looks great, with the added bonus of not costing a thing and being totally biodegradable.

MATERIA MEDICA

Diuretic, promotes perspiration

GATHERING

Leaves are collected in May or June and can be used fresh or dried for later use.

PREPARATIONS

• *Infusion* for catarrh, pleurisy, coughs, colds, flu. It encourages sweating, thus lowering fevers. It also relieves rheumatic pains.

CAUTIONS AND CONTRAINDICATIONS

Do not eat the berries as they are poisonous, being both emetic and purgative. Avoid during pregnancy.

Honeysuckle (Lonicera periclymenum)

Another plant that has fallen out of common use for its medicinal qualities. It is, however, a beautiful and easy to grow climber that, with the help of a trellis, will easily cover a wall or fence within a couple of years with beautiful flowers which range from pink to peach in colour. The flowers have a delicate perfume and I remember from early childhood finding the delight of beheading a honeysuckle flower to suck the sweet juice out from its base. Fresh flowers crushed on the forehead are said to heighten psychic powers.

MATERIA MEDICA

Antiseptic, diuretic, expectorant, laxative

GATHERING

They flower from June until late summer. The flowers hold the strongest medicine and are collected early in the morning before they have fully opened. They are dried in the shade.

PREPARATIONS

• *Syrup* relieves spasms, so is useful for respiratory problems, coughs and asthma.

HEALTHFUL COCKTAILS

Syrup made with thyme for coughs.

Salve made with calendula for skin infections.

CAUTIONS AND CONTRAINDICATIONS

The berries are poisonous. Excess causes vomiting, so do not exceed recommended dosages.

Hops (Humulus lupulus)

With lovely, vibrant large green leaves appearing in spring, this is another climber that, despite dying back in winter, will provide vigorous and dense cover for unsightly walls and fences as long as it gets some sun. The leaves and shoots can be eaten as a vegetable in early spring (though no later than May) and can be chopped into a salad or fried. The flowers are a little plain but have begun to gain popularity as environmentally friendly and totally biodegradable confetti for weddings. It is very rare, but I actually suffer with a skin irritation that comes from handling hops; I end up with huge welts on my forearms. I have been reassured that this only occurs in about 1 person in every 3000 (Hilton, 2007), however, if that person is you it is very irritating and unpleasant, so I would recommend proceeding with caution by wearing gardening gloves and long sleeves when collecting and handling.

MATERIA MEDICA

Antimicrobial, digestive, diuretic, sedative

GATHERING

Collect flowers (or strobiles, to give them their botanically correct name) in September and dry.

PREPARATIONS

- *Infusion* brewing for more than a few moments will make it taste rather bitter, so keep your eye on the time when infusing. A cup drunk half a hour before eating will aid the digestion by encouraging the secretion of digestive juices. It will also improve appetite, reduce flatulence, colic and ease IBS. It soothes muscle spasms, relieving gas and cramps. It also soothes the nerves, easing irritability, tension headaches, anxiety and over stimulated nervous conditions. When drunk before bed it helps induce restful sleep. In addition it stimulates menstruation.

- *Sleep pillow* will bring restful sleep for infants, children and adults alike.

CAUTIONS AND CONTRAINDICATIONS

Avoid if suffering depression due to their sedative qualities. Avoid during pregnancy and whilst breast feeding.

Ivy (Hedera helix)

Ivy grows well in the shadows, covering ground, wall and tree trunks alike. The waxy leaves are most often heart shaped when young and, as they grow, provide a dense shelter for birds and other wildlife. It does not seem to be adversely affected by a harsh trim every now and then, but if you don't do this it may start to smother everything in its path. Once trimmed you can save the more woody parts as, once dried they burn exceptionally well, providing good kindling if you have an open fire or wood burner.

Ivy is poisonous and will cause diarrhoea and vomiting if taken internally. It is important to use it only externally! Qualified practitioners may use it internally for various complaints ranging from gout and rheumatic pains to whooping cough and bronchitis, but the dosages are very precise and it is not worth experimenting on yourself for fear of encountering the adverse effects.

MATERIA MEDICA

Antibacterial, anti-inflammatory, expectorant, lowers fever, relaxes spasms, pain relief

GATHERING

Leaves are picked as needed throughout the year and used fresh.

PREPARATIONS

- *Decoction* to be used externally only. It provides a cooling skin wash for eczema, minor burns, impetigo, scabies and cellulitis.
- *Poultice* for boils, corns, warts and painful joints.

- *Vinegar* to be used externally as a wash for boils, corns, warts and painful joints.

CAUTIONS AND CONTRAINDICATIONS

Do not take internally!

Jasmine (Jasminum officinale)

What a delightful perfume jasmine provides on a warm summer's evening. There can be nothing more pleasurable to the nose than the heady scent of jasmine on the breeze, especially if it comes unexpectedly whilst passing someone's garden. It climbs well and can be trained up a fence, trellis or even over a little love seat in the garden. The flowers can vary from pinkish, through cream to white, while the foliage can be either golden or dark green, making it visually versatile and able to fit in with most designs or colour schemes.

MATERIA MEDICA

Sedative

GATHERING

The flowers can be collected shortly after opening on summer mornings and placed directly into oil for preservation or dried for infusions.

PREPARATIONS

- *Compress* for nervous headaches.
- *Infusion* drink just one cup a day before bed for relieving nerves, anxiety and promoting restful sleep.
- *Oil* use to rub on or massage the body for relief from depression, tension, stress and nervousness. It will promote relaxation, causing tense muscles to soften whilst providing pain relief . When rubbed on the chest it will also relieve a nervous cough.

CAUTIONS AND CONTRAINDICATIONS

None known.

Lime (Tilia europaea)

Also known as Linden blossom, the large, mild tasting leaves can be used to replace regular lettuce in the salad bowl until mid-summer, a very low input way to get healthy summer greens on your table. Don't park your car under one when it's flowering though, as aphids feed heavily on the rising sap within the tree and excrete a sticky residue that will end up all over your bonnet. It's a mild and calming medicine, safe to use with children. I always call it by the Latin name, Tilia. It is such a pretty, gentle name and for me it captures the essence of its energy, like a beautiful young woman taking your head on her lap and stroking your hair and brow until your worries have gone, and you, feeling safe and protected, fall into a long and peaceful sleep.

MATERIA MEDICA

Digestive, induces sweating, relaxes spasms, sedative

GATHERING

Flowers and the attached light brown bracts should be collected just after the flowers have opened in mid-summer on a dry day. Dry in the shade. Don't store for more than a year as they may develop narcotic qualities.

PREPARATIONS

- **Baths** are very relaxing and great for use in cases of hysteria and for babies having trouble sleeping. Will also provide relief from rheumatic pain.
- **Foot bath** for agitation, restlessness, tension headaches and insomnia. Works well for over excited children.
- **Infusion** drink as often as is required. It will induce sweating, break a fever, and stimulate the immune system. It is great at the onset of colds and flu. It lowers blood pressure and cholesterol, relaxes the arteries, encouraging good circulation and dissolves hard deposits in the arteries, thereby helping safeguard against heart disease. It eases palpitations and calms the system, making it a great remedy for nervous tension, anxiety and insomnia. It calms nervous and hyperactive children. It helps alleviate headaches and migraine, irritability and pre-menstrual symptoms. Relaxing to the stomach, it eases indigestion, IBS and nervous stomach disorders and soothes coughs, sinus problems and helps bring up catarrh. It can also be used for urinary infections.
- **Sleep pillows** very calming for anxious, nervous adults, hyperactive children and babies who don't sleep well.
- **Syrup** for coughs and colds.

HEALTHFUL COCKTAILS

Sleep pillows also work well with either lavender, chamomile, hops or any combination of these.

Infuse with hawthorn for raised blood pressure, elder for feverish colds, yarrow at the onset of a cold or flu, hops for nervous tension and feverfew for menstrual problems.

CAUTIONS AND CONTRAINDICATIONS

Avoid prolonged, excessive use.

Mallow (Malva sylvestris)

Mallow grows well on waste land such as underused allotments and by the side of rail tracks. It self-seeds readily so, although you may not have planted it, if you have any neglected areas in you garden you may well find one. Mallow has large pink flowers and is attractive. It has similar, although inferior, properties to the marshmallow (See page 172), however, common mallow is readily abundant, whereas marshmallow is becoming increasingly rare. You may have difficulty getting permission to harvest marshmallow when you do find it, but as common mallow grows as a weed and is widespread, people will most likely be more than happy for you to take some. The leaves and flowers are both edible and can be eaten raw in salads, although I would recommend cutting the leaves rather finely as they can be quite tough. The leaves are, however, good to eat as they have a high mineral and vitamin C content.

MATERIA MEDICA

Anti-inflammatory, astringent, expectorant, laxative, soothes tissues

GATHERING

The leaves can be collected in spring and the flowers throughout the summer and into the autumn. Both are either used fresh or dried. Using the leaves or flowers fresh will have a more potent effect than using them dried.

PREPARATIONS

- *Bath* for boils, minor burns, weeping eczema and abscesses.
- *Compress* for boils, minor burns, abscesses and insect bites.
- *Gargle* for throat inflammation, tonsillitis.
- *Infusion* as an expectorant it helps rid the lungs and respiratory tract of excess mucous and catarrh, soothing inflamed and irritated tissues. It is especially useful for coughs, bronchitis, asthma and emphysema. Also for throat infections, laryngitis, stomach ulcers and to assist in recovery from gastritis.
- *Mouthwash* for inflammation of gums and mouth.
- *Poultice* for sores, cuts, bruises, ulcers, burns, insect bites, skin inflammation, rashes, swollen glands and swollen injuries.

CAUTIONS AND CONTRAINDICATIONS

Excessive usage may cause nausea and diarrhoea

Mulberry (Morus nigra)

Oh, how lucky you are if you have access to this the most delicate of fruits. At the herb nursery where I used to work we were blessed with a mature mulberry, and every August

I used to punctuate my day with trips to the shade of this beautiful tree in search of a few more of the juicy fruits as they ripened. They have few reported medicinal uses, except in China where it is used widely within the frame work of traditional Chinese medicine, treating both deficiency and excess in the different elements. The best medicinal use I have found so far is the broad, deep smile the sight of a mulberry tree laden with ripe fruit will bring to my face and the ensuing bliss as I well and truly stain my fingers whilst munching on a handful. Another plus point is that they are nutritious, being high in iron, calcium and other minerals.

MATERIA MEDICA

(Leaves) antibacterial, antioxidant, diuretic, expectorant
(Fruit) antioxidant, immuno-stimulant, mild laxative

GATHERING

The leaves are collected after frost in the autumn and can be dried or used fresh. Collect the fruits when nearly ripe and still bitter to the taste. They can be dried but are very juicy and so I think it's best to eat them or juice them immediately, or process into a syrup on the day of picking.

PREPARATIONS

- *Eat* (fruit) for the high vitamin C content, to stimulate the immune system, to relieve tinnitus, as a kidney tonic and for urinary incontinence.
- *Infusion* (leaf) for colds, flu, stomach ulcers and to cleanse the blood.
- *Syrup* (fruit) for sore throats, restorative after illness including recovery from colds and flu. Also for constipation in the elderly.

CAUTIONS AND CONTRAINDICATIONS

None known.

Passion Flower (Passiflora incarnata)

One of the most intricate and beautiful flowers I know and a great climber with abundant flowers when it's happy with its site and has had a few years growth behind it. Whilst spending time with a medicine man in Kenya we came across a large stand of passiflora in the forest. He enthusiastically collected some leaves for me to use with an epileptic girl I was working with at home. He uses it for treating epilepsy due to its anti-spasmodic effect, although I wouldn't recommend self-medicating for this. It is always best to check with your health care professional first. The leaves and flowers can be eaten in salads or cooked as a vegetable (Fern, 1997), although I could never bring myself to take such a flower and expose it to the heat of a steamer, thereby destroying its beauty. It is a non-addictive sedative with no 'hangover' and is gentle enough to be used safely for children. I use it alongside mugwort, chamomile and skullcap in an infusion to be drunk before bed for the enhancement of dreams.

MATERIA MEDICA

Anti-inflammatory, relaxant, relaxes spasms, sedative

GATHERING

The leaves are collected before the flowers bloom, from May to July, or when there is fruit on the vine. Dry them in the shade in a place with adequate airflow as they have a high water content.

PREPARATIONS

- *Infusion* for calming anxiety, nervous tension, palpitations, trembling, muscular tension, extreme emotional upset, hysteria, and hyperactivity. To relieve insomnia when falling asleep is impossible due to worry and turning situations over and over in your mind. It can help reduce muscular aches and pain related to neuralgia, shingles and headache. It can lower blood pressure and help in cases of exhaustion, PMS (premenstrual syndrome) and general irritability. It can relax intestinal spasms, especially those caused by anxiety, including IBS and nervous indigestion. It will relieve cases of asthma where there is associated tension. It can also be a great relief to those suffering the symptoms of Parkinson's disease.

HEALTHFUL COCKTAILS

Infuse with chamomile and drink mid-evening for a gentle, sleep inducing tea.

CAUTIONS AND CONTRAINDICATIONS

It may have adverse interactions with medication taken for sedation, depression or anxiety. As with all plant remedies, check with your health care professional before use if you are already taking prescribed medications. Avoid during pregnancy.

Plum (Prunus domestica)

The fruit is edible, juicy and delicious. If they fall to the floor they will quickly go mouldy and are a favourite of wasps, so you would do well to keep on top during the fruiting season, checking for wind falls daily. The tree can be quite vigorous, sending up suckers all over the garden. You must be vigilant for these, cutting them back when they appear so that all the energy goes into creating big, juicy fruits rather than new trees.

MATERIA MEDICA

Laxative

GATHERING

The fruits are collected as they ripen from August to September. They can be eaten fresh or preserved by freezing (with the stones removed). You could attempt to make your own prunes by drying them whole on a rack, but protect them from flies with muslin. They should be ready after 3 weeks. Alternatively, if you have a dehydrator, remove the stones and put them in at 41°C (you could also do this on a tray in the oven). They will take longer than 24 hours at this temperature, but it is worth keeping it that low to allow the enzymes to remain intact.

PREPARATIONS

- **Eat** (fruit) for their high energy content and as a tonic for the nervous system and (prunes) as a gentle laxative and bowel stimulant, especially useful for those with nervous or frail bowel function. They are a rich source of iron, so are also worth adding to the diet if suffering from anaemia. If they are too dried out, rehydrate by soaking in water for a few hours.

CAUTIONS AND CONTRAINDICATIONS

They are rich in oxalic acid, so eat in moderation, especially as excess can cause stomach ache and diarrhoea.

Quince (Chaenomeles speciosa)

Quince has bright crimson flowers in early spring and beautiful golden yellow fruits in the autumn. The tree itself is quite small and so will easily fit in your garden. The fruits are the best bit, especially when you cut one from side to side where the seeds are. It has a great geometry to it but is quite a dry, tart fruit when eaten raw. It is traditionally processed into jams, jellies and added to apple pies.

MATERIA MEDICA

Anti-inflammatory, relieves spasms, circulatory and digestive stimulant

GATHERING

The fruits are gathered when ripe in autumn and used fresh or dried for decoctions.

The Medicine Garden

PREPARATIONS

- **Decoction** to relieve stomach cramps, muscular cramps, rheumatism, arthritis and lower limbs that are painful, weak or swollen.
- **Juice** to relieve nausea, gas and vomiting.
- **Syrup** for diarrhoea.

CAUTIONS AND CONTRAINDICATIONS

None known.

Rowan/Mountain Ash (Sorbus aucuparia)

The bright orange berries are loved by birds and are also edible for humans, but they are bitter and rather unpleasant despite their high vitamin A and C content. To make them more palatable they have traditionally been made into a jelly. Rowan have been known in folklore as trees which protect against witchcraft and enchantment, and have been viewed as magical across many cultures for thousands of years. They don't become too big for a garden and will attract birds, whilst keeping the baddies at bay.

MATERIA MEDICA

Antibiotic

GATHERING

Collect the fruits when ripe from August to November, although if they are not harvested by you or the birds they can hang on the tree until January. Dry the berries to preserve them.

PREPARATIONS

- **Decoction** as a laxative. Use as a skin wash for hemorrhoids.
- **Gargle** use either fresh juice or a decoction and gargle for sore throats, inflamed tonsils, hoarseness and inflamed mucous membranes.
- **Juice** use just a small handful at a time as a mild laxative. To improve the flavour add some sweet fruits.

CAUTIONS AND CONTRAINDICATIONS

The seeds are poisonous, so do not use in excess as they will cause stomach upsets.

Walnut (Juglans regia)

Most people will be familiar with these nuts, often the hardest one to crack in a winter nut bowl. I always found the flavour a bit strong and bitter until I had the ultimate pleasure of eating a fresh one, and what a difference! A milder taste with a texture more like a chestnut with much more moisture in it than the typical dried ones you can buy. Once out of the shell the nuts look a bit like brains. It is an attractive tree to grow, but beware as it puts out chemicals from the roots which inhibit the growth of other plants in its vicinity, most notably other walnuts, although this should not be a problem if you are only intending to grow one.

MATERIA MEDICA

Anti-inflammatory, antiparasitic , antiseptic, antiviral, astringent, expectorant, germicidal, laxative, soothes irritated tissue

GATHERING

To get green rind (husks), collect from July onwards as they become ripe around October or November. Separate into husks, shells and nuts. The rind does stain your fingers with a kind of orange tobacco colour, but don't worry, it's not permanent. The leaves can be picked throughout the growing season and used fresh or dried.

PREPARATIONS

- *Crush* (leaves) on skin as an insect repellent (Fern, 1997).
- *Decoction* (husks) for diarrhoea and anaemia.
- *Gargle* (husks) mixed with a teaspoon of honey for sore throats.
- *Infusion* (leaves) for chronic coughs, asthma, constipation, urinary and kidney stones. Also drunk for inflammatory skin conditions, including acne and psoriasis and as a skin wash for eczema and herpes. It can also be drunk to restore vigour after a lengthy or lingering illness.
- *Mouthwash* (leaves) for mouth sores and ulcers.
- *Powder* (leaves) for moist skin conditions, weeping eczema and bleeding wounds.
- *Salve* (husks) for skin irritations, minor burns, dry eczema and flesh wounds.

CAUTIONS AND CONTRAINDICATIONS

None known.

Witch Hazel (Hamamelis virginiana)

Not a tree you will often see in the wild here, as they are not native. I am growing one in a large container, but if I had more space I would liberate it and grow it directly in the earth. They have the most beautiful yellow dangly flowers in early spring, a bit like mini-ribbons or streamers. Commercial preparations are made from steam distilling the twigs and combining them with alcohol. This is not something you could do at home, leaving the preparations you can make somewhat limited in their actions by comparison. However, it is always fun to try and rewarding to experiment for yourself and see how useful these home preparations actually are, despite being less potent.

MATERIA MEDICA

Antibacterial, anti-inflammatory, astringent, pain relief

GATHERING

Collect the leaves from early to mid-summer. They can be used fresh or dried.

PREPARATIONS

- *Compress* to stem bleeding, for bruising and varicose veins.
- *Eyewash* for conjunctivitis.
- *Gargle* for sore throats and tonsillitis.
- *Infusion* used externally as a skin wash for pimples (especially on oily skin) and wet eczema. Also apply directly to the skin to reduce swelling and soothe insect bites, stings and sunburn.
- *Mouthwash* for bleeding gums and ulcers.
- *Poultice* for abscesses, boils and painful swellings.
- *Salve* for hemorrhoids, varicose veins, minor cuts, scrapes and bruises.

HEALTHFUL COCKTAILS

Combine in a salve with arnica for anti-inflammatory relief from bruises.

CAUTIONS AND CONTRAINDICATIONS

Avoid taking internally as it may cause liver damage.

Hedgerows

Hedgerows are part of our national heritage and have been used for millenia to demarcate the borders of fields or one's property in rural areas and as stock proof barriers to keep animals safely on one's land. The older the hedgerow, the richer it is, containing a more diverse range of species, making them havens for wildlife and full of rich pickings for the wild food or medicine forager. At one point it seemed that we would lose our ancient hedgerows. After the Second World War, as agriculture became more industrialised, financial incentives were given to remove them, ensuring that we would have enough space to be self-sufficient in food crops. New machinery was developed that could not maneouvre in small spaces, making huge fields necessary. Fortunately it seems, with the global rise in environmental consciousness, that we have somehow turned a corner and they are now back in vogue (Phew!!!). There are now government grants available for the planting and protection of these valuable resources. Acting as wildlife corridors between the ever decreasing islands that are our natural spaces, they are more important now than ever. I can often be found, basket in hand, perusing my local hedgerows for the season's riches.

Blackberry (Rubus fruticosus)

Also known as brambles, blackberries are probably the most well known and most oft collected hedgerow fruit. The juicy black berries can be eaten fresh from the plant. They are high in fibre so beware, as eating an excessive amount or under ripe fruits can give you an upset stomach. High in antioxidants, minerals and vitamin C, they will strengthen your immune system, cleanse your blood and promote tissue repair. Normally they arrive with such abundance that you may want to preserve some. I usually freeze plenty to ensure a berry supply for smoothies later in the year thus avoiding the need to purchase over priced inferior quality supermarket berries. It is also popular as an addition to other autumn fruits such as apples in winter crumbles. Alternatively you can soak them in sugar and vodka and have a bottle of blackberry liqueur ready for Christmas. Don't forget to reuse the blackberries once they have been drained from the vodka as they make a great accompaniment to ice-cream, or you could even attempt to make a boozy sorbet if you are feeling creative.

MATERIA MEDICA

Antibacterial, anti-inflammatory, astringent

GATHERING

Collect the leaf from March until it starts flowering. They can be dried and stored for later use. The fruits are collected as they ripen. This is ongoing from August until early October. The roots can be lifted in summer and their bark peeled, dried and saved, whilst the roots themselves should be discarded.

PREPARATIONS

- *Chew* (fresh leaf) for mouth ulcers.
- *Eat* (fruits) for their antioxidant effects to cleanse the blood.
- *Gargle* (leaf infusion) for sore throats.
- *Infusion* (leaf) for diarrhoea, dysentery, cystitis. It can be used externally as a skin wash for eczema, insect bites and minor burns.
- *Mouthwash* (leaf infusion) for mouth ulcers and inflamed gums.
- *Syrup* (fruits & root bark) for sore throats, coughs, colds and flu.

CAUTIONS AND CONTRAINDICATIONS

None known.

Blackthorn (Prunus spinosa)

Many years ago whilst walking with my aunt and uncle, we found a huge bounty of sloes (blackthorn fruit) which we collected for the purpose of making sloe gin. Items of clothing were duly removed to provide containers in which to carry them home. That was my first conscious acknowledgment of blackthorn, which had been unknown to me until that point. Now I appreciate this dark, bitter little fellow has many other uses alongside its ability to combine well with gin and make people merry! However, thus said, it does the merry making well, as you cannot avoid a huge smile crossing your lips when you see its branches heavily laden with spring blossom.

MATERIA MEDICA

Anti-inflammatory, diuretic, laxative, relaxes spasms

GATHERING

Pick the fruits after the first frosts as the skin will be softer and more permeable for making syrup and decoctions. Fruits can be dried and stored for later use. Leaves can be collected throughout the summer, although earlier leaves will be more tender. They can also be dried and stored for later use. The flowers appear from mid-April and must be collected as they open and used fresh.

PREPARATIONS

- *Decoction* (fruits) as a tonic to stimulate the metabolism and clean the blood. Can help ease allergies and prostate problems.
- *Gargle* (leaf) for sore, inflamed throat, tonsillitis and laryngitis.
- *Infusion* (flowers) for stomach problems including dyspepsia, colic, relaxing spasms and diarrhoea. Paradoxically it's also a mild laxative. It can be used as a tonic to cleanse and decongest the digestive system and boost circulation. Its diuretic properties help clear kidney and bladder disorders, bloating and fluid retention. It also soothes upper

respiratory tract infections.
- *Mouthwash* (fruits) for mouth infections and inflammations.
- *Salve* (fruits) for minor skin inflammations and eczema.
- *Syrup* (fruits) high in vitamin C. It's helpful for bronchial conditions, colds, catarrh and inflammation of the throat.

CAUTIONS AND CONTRAINDICATIONS

Avoid if pregnant or breast feeding.

Burdock (Arctium lappa)

Probably best known as a carbonated drink when combined with dandelion, although you would be unlikely to find much trace of either in any commercial brand. Interestingly the tiny hooks on the burrs provided the inspiration behind the invention of Velcro. It is quite versatile as a vegetable. The leaf stalks, young stalks and roots can all be eaten raw in salads or lightly cooked once the surface layers have been removed. Containing high levels of iron, niacin, inulin and vitamin C, they are beneficial to the lungs, gall bladder and liver.

MATERIA MEDICA

Antibacterial, antifungal, anti-inflammatory, astringent, diuretic, pain relief

GATHERING

Leaves are collected in the summer before flowering and can be dried. Roots are best lifted during their first summer or they will begin to rot. They are hard to dry as the high oil content means they go rancid quickly, so it is often best to preserve them as either a tincture or a syrup.

PREPARATIONS

- *Chew* (root) and hold on the gums to relieve toothache.
- *Decoction* (root) for coughs, colds and catarrh. It cleanses the blood and so is useful where there are skin conditions resulting from internal toxicity such as eczema, psoriasis, boils and sores (Brown, 1995). It eases cystitis, increases urination, reduces urinary tract inflammation and is cleansing for the kidneys, and lymphatic system. It contains inulin, a carbohydrate that strengthens the liver. It's a laxative and can ease minor stomach disorders (Mindell, 2000) and is also mildly sedative (Poulnin, 1992) and can relieve sciatica. It helps eliminate a build up of uric acid and so can help alleviate gout, arthritis and rheumatism. It is also used to promote perspiration and adversely to reduce excessive sweating (Wood, 1997). It is a useful remedy for skin irritations such as burns, minor wounds, measles, acne and eczema when applied externally. Using the decoction as a skin wash its antifungal properties help clear up ringworm, herpes and athlete's foot.
- *Infusion* (leaves) this is not used internally, but rather as a skin wash for skin

inflammation and irritations.
- *Mouthwash* (root) for ulcers.
- *Poultice* (leaf) for gout and bruising.
- *Salve* (root) for hemorrhoids.
- *Syrup* (root) and *Tincture* (root) can both be used internally to achieve the same actions as the decoction. The tincture can also be used as a skin wash. Add a teaspoon to an espresso cup full of water. If this does not have the desired effect, add another teaspoon of tincture to the water.

HEALTHFUL COCKTAILS

Add a teaspoon of root syrup to an infusion of dandelion leaves to cleanse and strengthen the urinary system and kidneys. Drinking this mix will also ease many skin conditions, especially those caused to by a sluggish liver and a toxic system.

CAUTIONS AND CONTRAINDICATIONS

Use with caution if sensitive to asteraceae family. Avoid during pregnancy.

Cleavers (Galium aparine)

You may not think you know cleavers, but every child does, and so too does every gardener. It is quite a satisfying plant to remove when it's growing in unwanted places, as the slightest tug will bring you an enormous clump, turning what seemed like a big weeding job into just a few moments of work. At this point, however, instead of incinerating or composting, I implore you to stick some in a pint glass and make an overnight cold infusion. It is not the most wonderful of tastes, but is so much better than simply discarding this powerhouse of goodness.

It is edible. I once tried it cut finely in a bowl of roasted, salted peanuts which was enough to disguise the texture, but the iodised salt and roasted fat probably undid all the good that the cleavers themselves had imparted. It can be boiled if you are determined to eat it and don't like the sandpaper like texture, but in so doing you would lose a lot of its qualities, including a great deal of its high vitamin C content.

It's a mood lightener too. For example, throwing it at the backs of random friends whilst out walking can provide hours of light entertainment. You can snigger to yourself for the entirety of the walk as they stroll along ignorant that they are carrying a substantial clump of foliage around on their back - rather childish maybe, but you've got to get your kicks somehow.... Its common name, 'sticky willie,' also makes me chuckle, but thats probably my cheeky childish part popping up yet again, and this plant certainly seems to bring that youthful cheekiness out in me.

MATERIA MEDICA

Astringent, diuretic, induces perspiration, lymphatic tonic

GATHERING

The whole plant is used. It has a very shallow root system that will readily come out, but the roots will need a rinse to clean off sticky soil particles. It is most potent when used fresh, although it is possible to dry cleavers. It's really a spring plant and so is best used then, when bright, fresh and growing vigorously. If you do choose to use it after June it would be worth making some preparations earlier in the year using fresh spring growth as by that time it will have become woody, started to dry out and will no longer be good to harvest.

PREPARATIONS

- *Cold Infusion* fill a pint glass with cleavers. Literally stuff them in, cover with cold water
  and leave overnight. In the morning place the plant matter in the compost, then drink the mild tasting yellowy green infusion. Repeat this daily for two weeks for a powerful lymphatic flush and to jump start your lymph system for spring. It can also be drunk freely during a fever to help you sweat, whilst rehydrating you and boosting your system into a detox that should help fight the infection. This is also a great way to disguise herbal medicine for a feverish child suffering from swollen glands. Either mix with a cordial or fruit juice. If your child has no fever but does have swollen glands you can heat it slightly and mix it with lemon and honey.
- *Infusion* for urinary infections, stones, gravel and cystitis. It's a liver and blood cleanser and will improve hepatitis and skin conditions that are aggravated or caused by internal toxicity such as eczema and dry psoriasis. By inducing perspiration it will act to cool the body during fever. It lowers blood pressure and acts on the nervous system, bringing calm where there is hysteria and anxiety, whilst promoting restful sleep. It's a mild laxative and through its diuretic properties will ease arthritis and kidney problems. It is probably best known as a lymphatic flush and is indeed one of the best tonics for the lymph system. By supporting and cleansing the lymphatic system it will relieve and improve the condition of complaints relating to the glandular system, including glandular fever, swollen glands, tonsillitis, adenoid problems and irritated and swollen prostrate. It can even help treat lymphatic cancer. It helps reduce the symptoms of chronic fatigue syndrome, otherwise known as ME (myalgic encephalomyelitis). It helps reduce cysts too. As an external skin wash it can relieve and help heal sores, wounds, sunburn, ulcers and psoriasis.
- *Juice* can also be used for a lymphatic flush. It would be just as effective if not more so than a cold infusion. It is a concentrated way to get the medicinal values that you would be seeking from a regular infusion. Drink it as part of a spring cleanse to revitalise and fortify yourself ready for summer. Flavourwise you will most probably want to dilute it

either with water, juiced fruits or vegetables.
- *Oil* for eczema, psoriasis, skin inflammations and sores.
- *Poultice* for wounds, ulcers and abraded or weeping skin.

HEALTHFUL COCKTAILS

Combine with red clover and make a salve for eczema and psoriasis, for use only where the skin remains unbroken.

CAUTIONS AND CONTRAINDICATIONS

Due to the strength of cleavers as a diuretic it is advised that diabetics use it with caution. Having type 1 diabetes myself i don't understand why, as i find there is nothing my body likes more than a spring cleanse to clear out all the residue that the artificial insulin leaves in my body. However, i would advise diabetics to use their own discretion on that one. Avoid using alongside other diuretics.

Crab Apple (Malus sylvestris)

This is the wild relation of the domesticated apple. The fruit is rather sour and is consequentially most often overlooked by humans and left for songbirds and other wildlife. However, high in vitamin C, it is great to incorporate into the diet or medicine chest. My granny always used to make crab apple jelly, which I loved. It has a large quantity of naturally occurring pectin and hence lends itself to this kind of processing. It helps neutralise uric acid and reduce excess stomach acid which is why it is also made into a sauce to aid in the digestion of meats such as pork.

MATERIA MEDICA

Antioxidant, anti-inflammatory

GATHERING

Collect the flowers as they come into full bloom in mid-March. Collect the fruits as they ripen in autumn.

PREPARATIONS

- *Juice* (fruit) the seeds actually contain small amounts of cyanide which is beneficial to the digestion in small doses. The juice is very cleansing and mildly laxative. It contains malic acid which supports the kidneys in clearing uric acid, so eases gout. It also has a cleansing effect on the liver and the high phosphate content builds tissues. This makes it very useful in periods of convalescence, especially as it also helps transform a negative mental state. It also helps to break down gall stones, and ease diarrhoea, dysentery, colds and coughs.

- *Poultice* (fruit) for drawing splinters, wounds, boils and abscesses.
- *Vinegar* (flowers) cover flowers with vinegar and shake daily for 3 weeks. Strain and repeat the process for a strong and effective remedy for bee and wasp stings. Dip cotton wool in the vinegar and hold on the sting for at least 10 minutes. Repeat for up to 30 minutes and there will be no remaining pain or swelling (Roberts, 2000).

HEALTHFUL COCKTAILS

(All juice combinations from Evert Hopmann, 1991)
Juice with celery, beetroot and carrot to clear skin and loosen catarrh.

Juice with cucumber to improve kidney function and benefit intestine, lungs and skin.

Juice with horseradish and garlic to help rid skin of ulcers, boils, acne, abscesses, psoriasis and eczema. This cocktail will also reduce lung inflammation and loosen catarrh.

CAUTIONS AND CONTRAINDICATIONS

Do not consume excessive amounts or for a prolonged period due to the cyanide content of the seeds.

Elder (Sambucus nigra)

Dark, dark berries, rich in vitamins A and C, which stain your fingers deep purple if you crush them as you pick. I love putting a handful of the berries with raspberries and other late summer fruits with water in the blender for an antioxidant blast of vitamins and flavour. The individual flowers are small but appear in clusters that remind me of huge dinner plates, flat and white and just waiting to be brushed so they can sprinkle their yellow pollen generously on passers by, but beware not to get a nose full or you will sneeze yourself into next week! A light summery taste, the flowers can be eaten raw. I like to munch them straight from the bush as I pass by. The clusters of flowers become smaller as the bush gets older, but a lot of hedgerows are radically cut back in autumn or spring and this creates new growth and larger clusters of flowers. If the only clusters you are finding are small ones, look for an area that is more heavily managed and the size of the flower clusters should be much larger.

A friend of mine once made some magnificent elderflower champagne, although I believe it was rather sticky work as one or two bottles exploded in her garage. This tasty flower has been made into numerous different cordials and sparkling drinks. All the ones I've tried have been quite delightful. Both the flowers and berries are tasty, which is lucky as, being safe to use on children, tasting good will help the medicine go down!

The Medicine Garden

MATERIA MEDICA

Antibacterial, antioxidant, anti-inflammatory, antiviral, diuretic, expectorant, pain relief

GATHERING

The flower heads are collected when fully open, usually throughout May and June. They should never be washed as they are covered in fine, dusty health giving pollen. Simply pick off any insects and dry them whole away from sunlight, or use fresh. The berries are collected when ripe, from late summer until early autumn (August until October approx.). Leaves are collected as and when needed throughout the growing season and used fresh.

PREPARATIONS

- *Bath* (flowers) for bruises, sprains, swollen glands, sore muscles, stiffness and rheumatic pains.
- *Compress* (flowers) use lukewarm over closed eyes for a few minutes to soothe sore, irritated eyes. It can also be used on chilblains and other skin irritations including boils and skin ulcers for its pain relieving and soothing action.
- *Crush* (leaf) rub over skin as an emergency insect and midge repellent (Fern, 1997).
- *Decoction* (berries) for its decongestant properties to clear phlegm and catarrh, soothe coughs and congested colds. It also eases sinusitis, neuralgia, sciatica, calms anxiety and soothes frayed nerves. It's a remedy for both constipation and diarrhoea and it acts as a blood builder which helps control anaemia. It helps guard against hay fever and will relieve both headache and migraine. It reduces inflammation, easing arthritis and rheumatic aches. It also lowers fever and so is particularly useful at the onset of colds, flu, and other viral infections and feverish illnesses.
- *Eyebath* (flowers) for conjunctivitis, use twice a day (Conway, 2001).
- *Footbath* (flowers) for coughs and fevers in children (Conway, 2001).
- *Gargle* (berries) for sore throats.
- *Infusion* (flowers) has an anti-inflammatory, anti-allergy, immuno-stimulating action and is soothing on the mucous membranes. These qualities make it an ideal remedy for arthritis, ear infections, sinusitis, catarrh, colds, flu, respiratory tract infections and hay fever. Let the infusion cool completely and drink to relieve night sweats. In addition, when applied cold it can be used as a soothing, cooling, skin wash for sunburn.
- *Poultice* (flowers) to relieve pain and reduce inflammation in cases of rheumatism and arthritis.
- *Salve* (flowers) for burns and wounds.
- *Syrup* (berries) juice the fresh berries and combine 10 parts juice to 1 part honey and keep in the fridge. A more traditional style syrup can also be made from a decoction of dried berries. This is great to use at the onset of a cold, flu or fever to promote sweating and bring the fever out. It also tastes great and will sweeten up other medicinal teas when feeling full of cold and rather low.
- *Tincture* (flowers) to promote sweating at the onset of cold, flu or fever, and as an expectorant for bronchitis and pneumonia. You can place a few drops directly on your nipple if you are breast feeding a feverish infant which will help bring the fever out (Evert Hopman, 1991).

• *Vinegar* (berries) take a teaspoon at a time for asthmatic conditions.

HEALTHFUL COCKTAILS

Add a teaspoon of syrup to an infusion of wood betony or meadowsweet for headaches or migraine.

Infuse flowers with lemonbalm to promote sweating in a summer flu and for its expectorant qualities when suffering from a cough.

Infuse with nettle and drink regularly over the course of a couple of weeks to fend off hay fever. Start this treatment as soon as it starts to flower.

Decoct berries with ginger and add a squirt of fresh lemon to fend off a cold.

Make a syrup from the berries combined with thyme for coughs with fever.

CAUTIONS AND CONTRAINDICATIONS

Avoid during pregnancy and breast feeding.

Hawthorn (Crataegus oxyacantha)

A personal favourite, I love the heavily blossomed branches in late spring and the deep red berries of autumn. In between times the leaves can be eaten fresh and raw as a spring tonic and are known in folk tales as 'bread and cheese,' but precisely why I am unsure as they taste nothing like either. The flowers provide a tasty spring nibble whilst I normally munch lightly on the berries whilst gathering the autumn harvest. The berries are a cardiac tonic and have a very interesting quality; they are known as an adaptogen, which in this circumstance means they either stimulate or depress heart function according to the individual's need.

MATERIA MEDICA

Digestive, diuretic, sedative, heart tonic

GATHERING

Flowers can be collected from May through June and are used fresh. Leaves are collected during the spring before they become too dark and tough and can also be used fresh. Berries, or haws, are collected when they reach a ripe, dark red in late September and throughout October. They can be laid out on newspaper to dry thoroughly.

PREPARATIONS

- *Decoction* (berries) to dilate blood vessels which helps improve circulation, warming you up on a cold winter's day and increasing the supply of blood and oxygen to the heart. It's a sedative and drunk before bed for insomnia. Also used for diarrhoea, dysentery and kidney inflammation. It contains antioxidants which may help prevent damage from free radicals, implicated in premature aging and the development of certain cancers. It may help reduce cholesterol and can be used as a skin wash for acne. The main use, however, is as a heart tonic, helping with palpitations, arteriosclerosis, angina pectoris, heart failure (where the heart is not strong enough and symptoms such as shortness of breath and fatigue are experienced), arrhythmia (irregular heart beat) and in cases of both high and low blood pressure.
- *Gargle* (berries) for sore throats.
- *Poultice* (flower) to draw out a splinter.
- *Tincture* (berries) mash the berries throughly first. You can make a double infused tincture (see preparations for instructions). This will ensure you get a strong tincture with the maximum medicinal qualities. It may help lower LDL (bad cholesterol) and will work on all the same complaints as a decoction.

HEALTHFUL COCKTAILS

Infuse the leaves with rose petals when suffering grief following the loss of a loved one. It will strengthen the heart and help it to open again.

Infuse leaves with ginkgo to improve micro-circulation and hence memory (Brown, 1995).

Decoct berries with valerian root to lower high blood pressure and regulate irregular heartbeat.

CAUTIONS CONTRAINDICATIONS

Avoid during pregnancy and breast feeding. Never self diagnose. Always get advice from a healthcare professional if using for heart or blood pressure, especially if already undergoing drug treatment.

Horseradish (Armoracia rusticana)

Fresh leaves can be eaten raw in salads, but for a more intense flavour sensation grate the fresh root into salads and dressings. It is most well known as horseradish sauce, a popular accompaniment to beef. If you plan to grow it at home it's best to use a large pot as it will freely spread and take over large areas if planted directly in the soil. However, be sure to have either a big enough pot or harvest regularly to avoid having your pot crack and shatter like ours did, under the strength of the growing root. It's a healthy addition to the diet, having a higher vitamin C content, weight for weight, than an orange.

MATERIA MEDICA

Antioxidant, antibacterial, digestive, expectorant

GATHERING

Collect whole pieces of root in autumn. Don't dry them, but store in damp sand as you would a big crop of carrots. Leaves can be collected throughout the growing season as needed.

PREPARATIONS

- *Gargle* (root) with a teaspoon of honey for sore throats.
- *Infusion* (grated root) as a tonic for the liver and spleen. It aids digestion and eases wind. It soothes bronchitis, congested lung and chest conditions, whilst loosening mucous and treating respiratory tract infections. It eases sore throats, sinusitis, arthritis, gout, urinary tract infections and sciatica. It also increases perspiration and helps sweat out colds and flu.
- *Juice* (root) for allergies and especially for hay fever, (leaf) apply to cuts, burns and chilblains (Lipp, 1996).
- *Oil* (root) rub on chest to alleviate chest complaints.
- *Poultice* (root) for arthritis, rheumatism, sciatica, infected wounds and place on the chest for bronchitis. Leave in place for a maximum of 10 minutes or it may burn the skin, causing blistering, (wilted leaf) hold directly in place for toothache and facial neuralgia.
- *Syrup* (grated root in honey) for coughs and asthma.
- *Vinegar* (root) mixed with honey for hoarseness. Warm a couple of teaspoons in water and drink to promote sweating during colds and flu. Mix 3-4 tablespoons with honey daily for rheumatism. Whist making, remove the lid every few days to release gasses that will build up within the brew.

CAUTIONS AND CONTRAINDICATIONS

Excess causes vomiting. Do not use if suffering from stomach ulcers or thyroid problems.

Jack in the Hedge/ Hedge Garlic (Alliaria petiolata)

There is a hint of garlic in these lovely fresh spring leaves that arrive any time from February onwards and usually begin flowering in May. They simply shout 'eat me, eat me!' every time I pass their beautiful, vibrant green leaves. I am currently trying to cultivate some in my back garden due to sheer laziness as they are already abundant enough along local lanes and hedgerows. The two which arrived in my garden are presently out of bounds for eating until they become more prolific as they are said to self-sow readily. They are a triumph in the foragers basket, adding a truly great flavour to spring salads. It is one of the earliest appearing greens, making it all the more valuable and filling my plate during the 'hungry gap' (the time when there is little fresh produce available from the vegetable garden).

MATERIA MEDICA

Anti-inflammatory, antiseptic, expectorant, promotes perspiration

GATHERING

Leaves and stems can be collected throughout the spring and early summer and used fresh, juiced or dried for later.

PREPARATIONS

- *Eat* as a strengthening and toning digestive tonic.
- *Infusion* to soothe and heal respiratory tract infections, bronchitis and asthma. It will also promote perspiration, helping to break a fever.
- *Oil* apply by rubbing on the chest after very gently heating to bring relief from respiratory tract infections.
- *Poultice* to promote healing and clear infections, especially used for wounds and ulcers. To relieve the itchiness of bites and stings. To bring relief from gout, rheumatism and neuralgia.

CAUTIONS AND CONTRAINDICATIONS

None known.

Stinging Nettle (Urtica dioica)

There is nothing like the all pervading smell of fresh nettle as you walk down a green lane in spring time. It smells deep and rich and has many layers to it. I think you could almost extract medicine from the smell of this little beauty alone. Nettle is a bit of a wonder herb,

being incredibly nutritious and medicinal and with a wide range of other uses from fabric dye to plant feed and even making paper. Like hemp it is a real option for sustainable fabrics of the future as it grows prolifically with no need for encouragement and has incredibly strong fibres. I have seen it coated with aphids, but only rarely, and have never noticed any pest damage, so there would be no need to use chemicals, even if growing on a large scale.

Many people cook with it. I like to throw it in the blender and make a super powered green smoothie, or simply juice it. It makes a lovely pesto and is commonly made into soup. It is so well charged with minerals that ingesting it will strengthen and support the whole body. It contains iron, potassium, vitamins A, C, and many trace minerals. It has a deeply nourishing flavour, almost like soup or even blood and more so the longer you leave it to brew.

I cultivate a patch in the back garden, always harvesting the tips and only pulling out bits when it starts to get a bit unruly and tries to take over the entire bed. Even then I just sling it in the compost where it acts as an accelerator. Nettle is never wasted or discarded in my home. It does spread by creeping rhizomes, so you will have to keep an eye out for it popping up a foot or more away from your controlled patch if you choose to grow it.

It was the Romans who brought nettle to the UK specifically to help improve their circulation in these cold lands by self-flagellating with it, or so it is said. I haven't tried that myself, preferring to wear a jumper, but the stings are also reputedly useful when applied to arthritic joints where they apparently ease pain due to the fact they are a counter irritant, so feel free to have a go!

Butterflies love it, which can only be a bonus for all of us. The flowering heads are dangling and delightful and worthy of close inspection with a magnifier. You can actually collect and eat the seed. They are high in omegas and are beneficial to menopausal women. If you toast them lightly they add a great crunch to salads. I find it interesting that the seeds will help fortify women going through menopause, whilst the root will aid men with prostate problems.

An old love once told me that if you have a firm grasp when pulling them up you won't get stung, but that simply isn't true (well he was a Scorpio, maybe it was an in joke?). I recommend always protecting your hands with gloves when harvesting or you will get stung. Boiling, steaming, soaking, drying and blending will all disarm the sting.

MATERIA MEDICA

Antihistamine, anti-inflammatory, astringent, diuretic

GATHERING

Leaves appear from March onward, but should only be collected for internal use until June when they start to flower and build up oxalate crystals, becoming a bit grainy. They are best used fresh, but can be dried for later use. Always collect them wearing gloves, and even then handle carefully as I have been known to receive an almighty sting even through thick, tough gardening gloves. Roots are at their best for collection in June and July.

The Medicine Garden

PREPARATIONS

- *Cold Infusion/ Infusion* (leaves) use either hot or cold water. If you use cold water you must leave for several hours, preferably overnight. Even if using hot water leave for as long as possible. If you prefer to drink it hot, pour it into a flask to infuse so that it can be left for some time whilst remaining warm or gently warm up the cold infusion when you are ready to drink it. You can, of course, drink after just 10-15 minutes as you would with most infusions, but if you do experiment with leaving it longer you will soon appreciate why this is valuable as the flavour becomes so much richer and deeper as it pulls more and more good stuff out from the leaves. It encourages the body to expel uric acid, easing gout, rheumatism and arthritic conditions. By supporting the kidneys it also helps relieve kidney stones. An effective blood and liver cleanser, it is valuable to use when on a detox or cleanse. The high vitamin C content ensures the iron will be absorbed, making it a valuable remedy for anaemia. It is a tonic, strengthening and vitalizing the system, boosting convalescents and those suffering weakness or debility. It can support the body when going through times of change, especially for women upon reaching puberty and again at menopause. It dries up excessive bleeding within the body, including excessive menstruation, frequent nose bleeds, hemorrhoids, and blood found in the urine and stools. It acts on the lungs, relieving asthma, bronchitis and congestion. It helps improve the appearance and severity of both childhood and nervous eczema. As a natural antihistamine it is useful in reducing both allergy and hay fever symptoms. Start drinking one month before your hay fever symptoms usually appear and this will reduce the mucous membrane hyperactivity and inflammation that occurs with hay fever, resulting in a greater quantity of pollen needed to cause a reaction. It lowers blood sugar levels, blood pressure and elevated heart rate whilst encouraging the flow of breast milk. Nettle has relatively large quantities of the essential amino acid tryptophan. This cannot be produced by the body and so must be sourced from the diet. The presence of tryptophan is essential for the formation of seratonin, a hormone generated in the brain and essentially a feel good hormone. When your body is in balance and manufacturing adequate quantities you will naturally feel good as it helps regulate sleep, appetite, mediates moods, relieves anxiety and inhibits pain. As such it can be used as a mild natural antidepressant to gently lift the spirits. As I suggested earlier, nettle really is a wonder herb.
- *Compress* (leaves) for burns. A strong infusion/fresh sap/juice on a tissue and inserted in the nostril will stop a nose bleed.
- *Crush* (stem) rub the juicy sap on stings and bites to relieve pain and inflammation. Paradoxically it's also a remedy for its own stings.
- *Decoction* (root) being diuretic the roots will help ease kidney problems and water retention. It inhibits the production of certain enzymes which contribute to the enlargement of the prostate gland, reducing prostate enlargement and relieving problems associated with urination that accompany prostate enlargement.
- *Eat* (seeds) to ease the changes accompanying menopause.
- *Juice* (leaves) mix with a teaspoon of honey to relieve asthmatic conditions. It can be applied to the skin to soothe and heal eczema.
- *Powder* (leaves) use as a snuff, inhaling a pinch to stop nose bleeds. If you find it hard to inhale, just pack the nostril with powder.
- *Syrup* (root) for whooping cough and inflamed throats (Lipp, 1996).

- *Tincture* (root) for prostate problems and coughs, (leaf) you can either tincture in the traditional way or if you have a high quality leaf juicer you can juice fresh leaves and combine with brandy at a ratio of 3 parts juice to 2 parts brandy, but you must use a strength of 40% vol or higher. If you make the juice version you will be able to use it straight away, without the usual 3 week wait. Either way you make it, it can be used for the same complaints as an infusion. The juice tincture (liquid extract) will have the strongest action.

HEALTHFUL COCKTAILS

Infuse the leaf with fennel to improve the quality and increase the quantity of breast milk.

CAUTIONS AND CONTRAINDICATIONS

Use with caution if pregnant or breast feeding.

Yellow Dock (Rumex crispus)

High in vitamin C and quite pleasant to eat, it was once used to treat scurvy. The almost fibreless leaves can be eaten fresh in salads or cooked as a spinach replacement in recipes, or even blended with olive oil, Parmesan cheese and pine nuts to make pesto. It can be eaten all year round, although the younger leaves appearing in spring and early summer are the most tasty. Dock is probably the most widely known folk remedy, as there must hardly be a small child in the land who has not at one point fallen foul of a nettle and then had their dad lovingly crush up dock and rub it on to take the sting away.

MATERIA MEDICA

Astringent, diuretic, digestive, supports liver function

GATHERING

Roots can be collected from late summer through to early autumn, then split down the middle lengthways and left to dry. Leaves are picked throughout the growing season and used fresh.

PREPARATIONS

- *Crush* (leaf) on nettle stings.
- *Decoction* (root) to cleanse and detoxify the system and improve liver function. Acting on the urinary system it eases cystitis, urinary tract infections, water retention, urinary stones and gravel. It eases constipation, acting as a laxative and relieving skin conditions that are related to a sluggish bowel or liver. Promoting the flow of bile it acts as a blood cleanser and helps in cases of gout, arthritis and rheumatism. It can be used in the spring as a cleanser, stimulating congested lymph. It helps the body absorb iron, so is ideal to use when taking iron supplements for anaemic conditions. Additionally,

it works on the female reproductive system, normalizing menstruation, especially heavy flow, painful periods and helps heal fibroids.

- *Gargle* (root) for laryngitis.
- *Mouthwash* (root) for ulcers.
- *Poultice* (steamed leaves) apply to arthritic joints, rheumatic pains and skin complaints such as psoriasis and eczema.
- *Syrup* (root) for bronchitis, asthma and upper respiratory tract infections.
- *Tincture* (root) used for the same complaints as a decoction.

HEALTHFUL COCKTAILS

Combine leaves with calendula flowers in a facial steam for acne.

Infuse with cleavers for a lymph flush.

Infuse with dandelion to stimulate a sluggish liver.

CAUTIONS AND CONTRAINDICATIONS

Use in moderation because it contains high levels of oxalic acid and an excess causes vomiting. Use with caution if suffering from ibs. Avoid during pregnancy, breast feeding and if suffering from kidney stones or liver disease.

In the Woods

Woodland truly expresses the season. There is no mistaking that when the branches are bare, and underfoot there is a decomposing brown carpet together with a lingering damp, earthy smell in the air that it is mid-winter. Springtime is so exciting, with buds pregnant with the promise of life, lysergic green beech leaves and a carpet of bluebells or wild garlic and birds filling the air with song. Summer brings sparkling shafts of light breaking through the thick, cool canopy to the ground below. Autumn is a carnival of reds, oranges, yellows and browns with a crispness to the air and a snapping of old twigs underfoot. The woods provide a year round haven from the noise and stresses of daily life, ever full of sensory delights and good medicine foraging.

Angelica (Angelica archangelica)

The tall feminine form of Angelica has similar properties to its American cousin (Angelica atropurpurea) which, according to Grieve, is inferior, although I have heard to the contrary from people who use it frequently and as one of their key medicines. If you have access to both I would recommend trying both and forming your own conclusions, although if you only have access to one the argument is immaterial as you can only use that to which you have access. The name implies an angel, an archangel perhaps, so use of this plant could be thought of as putting yourself in the care of an angelic being who may offer spiritual protection. Bees and wasps seem to go crazy for the flower heads, so beware if you are thinking of growing this and have a fear of stings, although the rest of your garden would of course benefit considerably.

MATERIA MEDICA

Antibacterial, antifungal, anti-inflammatory, digestive, diuretic, expectorant

GATHERING

Leaves are collected during spring and early summer, before flowering commences. Removing flower heads before they bloom will extend the collecting season and potentially the life of the plant, but you would miss out on the beneficial insects the flowers attract. Roots are collected in the autumn of their first year and can be dried for later use.

PREPARATIONS

- *Decoction* (root)/*Infusion* (leaves) is especially warming to the system, but unlike other warming remedies will not irritate the lining of the intestines or stomach. It stimulates digestion, relieving flatulence, colic, indigestion and gastric ulcers. Calming nerves and muscle tension, it's a stimulatory tonic for the nervous system, easing symptoms of chronic fatigue. It stimulates the lungs and relaxes spasms, so can be used for coughs, bronchitis, pleurisy and catarrh. As a woman's tonic it helps ease the transition into menopause, premenstrual symptoms, painful menstruation and helps bring on delayed menstruation. It nourishes the blood and stimulates the circulation. It helps bring out a fever so is particularly useful during colds and flu, especially when a cough is also present. As a diuretic it induces urination and is helpful in cases of cystitis and other urinary tract infections.

- *Gargle* for sore throats.
- *Poultice* for rheumatic pains and neuralgia.
- *Powder* (root) and apply directly to athlete's foot.
- *Syrup* (root) for coughs and congestion.

HEALTHFUL COCKTAILS

Decoct the root with ginger to ease nausea accompanying migraine.

Infuse with crushed fennel seeds to calm the digestion.

Infuse with mugwort for relief from menopausal and premenstrual symptoms.

Infuse with mullein for coughs.

CAUTIONS AND CONTRAINDICATIONS

Use with caution as it may cause skin sensitivity to sunlight. Also use with caution if you are diabetic as its action causes an increase of sugar in the urine, do not use if monitoring sugars simply with urine test strips rather than blood. Avoid during pregnancy and breast feeding.

Hazel (Corylus avellana)

Hazel produces edible, hard shelled nuts also known as filberts and cob nuts. Nuts can be gathered as the leaves on the tree turn to their autumn shade, or as they fall to the floor, but be quick if you wish to collect some as you will be competing with squirrels getting their winter supplies together. The nuts are rich in phosphorus, potassium, magnesium, copper and protein, so it's worth trying to find at least a few handfuls from the woods to nibble on. Old legend holds hazel in high regard as a tree of divine wisdom, perhaps connected to the fact that hazel is used for divining sticks to find water and lost objects by those open to the more magical arts.

MATERIA MEDICA

Antiparasitic, increases sweating

GATHERING

The leaves are gathered in spring.

PREPARATIONS

- *Infusion* for diarrhoea, coughs, varicose veins and bruising. There is a substance in the leaves that supports collagen, making the infusion useful when elasticity needs to be restored, especially in the lungs, improving the condition of both emphysema and pulmonary fibrosis.

CAUTIONS AND CONTRAINDICATIONS

None known.

Lungwort (Pulmonaria officinalis)

The characteristic leaves dotted with white are hard to miss once you know what you are looking for. The first time I ate the leaves was several years ago, and now I look out for them in early spring when there's not much else around to fill my wild salad bowl. High in vitamin C they are great to eat as the leaves begin to increase in size and the hardest days of winter have become confined to memory. Disliked by both slugs and snails, it survives well even in damp and shady woodland areas.

MATERIA MEDICA

Anti-inflammatory, expectorant

GATHERING

Leaves can be collected from early spring until early autumn, when they begin to die back for winter.

PREPARATIONS

- *Eyebath* for inflamed and tired eyes (Brown, 1995).
- *Gargle* for sore throats.
- *Infusion* for coughs, catarrh, bronchitis and laryngitis.

CAUTIONS AND CONTRAINDICATIONS

Use with caution as lungwort can act as a skin irritant or allergen in some. Avoid during pregnancy, breast feeding, if you have a low blood platelet count, a history of digestive tract bleeding or are currently on blood thinning medication.

Primrose (Primula vulgaris)

Moths pollinate them at night, whilst by day they are loved by bees, butterflies and faeries. This early blast of colour in the woodlands and hedgerows is enough to cheer anyone up. The flowers and young leaves can be added to salads, bringing spring directly onto your dinner plate.

MATERIA MEDICA

Anti-inflammatory, expectorant, pain relief, relaxes spasms

GATHERING

The whole plant, including the roots, can be collected during spring whilst it's flowering, usually in April and May.

PREPARATIONS

- *Bath* for relaxation and to lighten one's mood, bringing the sense of hope and joy that comes with spring.
- *Decoction* (roots) for nervous headaches, respiratory tract infections, coughs and bronchitis.
- *Infusion* (leaves and flowers) for anxiety, nervous disorders, insomnia and to relax the mind. It eases rheumatic pains and gout.
- *Poultice* (leaves and flowers) for minor wounds and joint pains.
- *Salve* (leaves and flowers) for minor wounds.
- *Tincture* (leaves and flowers) for its sedative and cheery qualities.

HEALTHFUL COCKTAILS

Infuse with lungwort and/or thyme for coughs.

Infuse with wood betony for nervous tension.

Infuse with chamomile to bring restful sleep.

CAUTIONS AND CONTRAINDICATIONS

Avoid during pregnancy, whilst using blood thinning drugs or if you suffer from a sensitivity to aspirin.

Ramsons/Wild Garlic (Allium ursinum)

This has to be one of my favourite plants for a simple but effective home remedy. The woodlands where I live fill with their aroma and become a sea of white flowers every spring time. They are so prolific I can collect all I need for a year's worth of cold remedy and enough to fill my plate all week and not even make an impression. The leaves and flowers are both edible and have a great garlicky bite to them. In the kitchen they are pretty versatile and used in salads, pesto, nettle soup or even as a replacement for spinach. The flowers alone make a very attractive and tasty garnish. Medicinally it shares most of the properties of cultivated garlic.

MATERIA MEDICA

Antiseptic, antioxidant

GATHERING

Leaves can be collected from February until they die back and flowers from late March until early June.

PREPARATIONS

- *Infusion* (or eat fresh) for high blood pressure, to improve circulation, reduce cholesterol and as a blood cleanser.
- *Vinegar* chop the leaf finely and cover with organic cider vinegar. Shake daily for 3 weeks then strain through muslin, squeezing the last of the goodies out of the leaf matter which you can then compost. Keep the vinegar in a glass jar in the fridge. It will last until next year's crop appears. This is my first resource for a cold. Do a small shot of this and it will send shivers down your spine as it sends the cold packing. Tasty enough to combine with olive oil and make into a salad dressing if you think the whole family needs an immune system boost.

CAUTIONS AND CONTRAINDICATIONS

None known.

Sweet Cicely (Myrrhis odorata)

The flowers have a slight pinkish tinge and a sweet aniseed flavour. They, like the leaves, can be eaten raw in salads or with sour fruits as a mild sweetener and are often used when cooking sour fruits such as rhubarb to take the tart edge off. Sweet cicely is recommended for diabetics or anyone who is trying to cut down on refined sugar from their diets, but still has a bit of a sweet tooth.

MATERIA MEDICA

Antiseptic, digestive, expectorant

GATHERING

Leaves can be collected throughout the growing season, which extends from early spring right into winter. The leaves lose potency rapidly once picked and therefore should not be dried for later use. The root can be dried and is best collected in autumn.

PREPARATIONS

- *Eyebath* (leaves) for sore eyes.
- *Infusion* (leaves) for coughs and minor digestive complaints.
- *Poultice* (roots) for boils and wounds.
- *Syrup* (roots) for coughs and minor digestive complaints.

CAUTIONS AND CONTRAINDICATIONS

None known.

Wood Betony (Stachys officinalis)

My first guided meditation to a plant was to wood betony. I found myself immersed in a beautiful scene, languishing in a flower filled meadow at a woodland edge. A beautiful woman dressed in a white, flowing dress led me into the woods where she told me that wood betony would like me to learn its song and sing to it. The meditation made a great impression on me and I will always have a special place in my heart for this little woodland dweller. It is one to be loved.

MATERIA MEDICA

Antiseptic, astringent, digestive, diuretic

GATHERING

Collect the leaves in spring and early summer before flowering. Dry them in the sunlight.

PREPARATIONS

- *Gargle* for sore throats.
- *Infusion* is soothing to the stomach and digestive tract, easing gas, burning, discomfort, colic, gastritis and nervous digestive upsets. It is famed for its use against headache and migraine. It's a de-stressing tonic for the nervous system, relaxing tension whilst easing anxiety, panic attacks, insomnia and bestowing a feeling of 'groundedness.' It is useful in lung complaints, coughs, phlegm, catarrh and sinusitis. It can help painful menstruation, normalise irregular menstruation and ease menopausal symptoms. It's a vasodilator, which means it can help improve circulation, lower blood pressure and even improve circulation around the brain, slowing loss of memory and other deteriorations in brain function relating to micro-circulation. It brings relief to sufferers of facial neuralgia and is a liver and gall bladder tonic. Externally a strong infusion can be used as a wash for wounds and skin ulcers.
- *Mouthwash* for gum inflammation, toothache and mouth ulcers.
- *Oil* rubbed gently over bruising and joint pains.
- *Poultice* for wounds.
- *Tincture* acts on the same conditions as an infusion.

HEALTHFUL COCKTAILS

Infuse with skullcap for nervous headaches (Hoffman, 1996).

Infuse with elderflower for sinus headaches.

CAUTIONS AND CONTRAINDICATIONS

Use in moderation as excess causes diarrhoea and vomiting. Avoid during pregnancy.

By The River

What a pleasure it is at any time of year to walk alongside banks of fresh flowing water; it is so cooling and refreshing to do so on a hot summer's day, timelessly watching water, boatmen and dragonflies skating and glinting as flashes of colour on the shady riverside. There's a peace, a great calmness, that descends despite the often frantic activity and the constant spiraling flow. Perhaps because it's movement with a purpose, its destination ultimately the ocean, yet eventually returning back to the river through the natural process of evaporation and the release of juicy, fat raindrops. The complete cycle is somehow poetic, the energy expended so full of life and invigoration. Rivers are a great place to spend time absorbing this most organic and dynamic of energies, a place to recharge and yet relax, perhaps one of nature's great paradoxes. But what a treat to forage for wild medicine in this environment.

Celandine, Greater (Chelidonium majus)

Not to be confused with lesser celandine, which is also known as pilewort. Pilewort, as the name suggests, is a great remedy for hemorrhoids. Greater celandine has a large number of uses, including everything from gall stones to whooping cough, but it is very toxic, so use by oneself at home must be restricted to external complaints, where it can be applied directly to the skin.

A member of the poppy family, its bright yellow flowers appear in May and continue flowering all summer long. The subject of myth and legend, this sacred plant was known to the ancients as 'alchemists' gold.'

MATERIA MEDICA

Antibacterial, anti-inflammatory, antioxidant, diuretic, pain relief, promotes sweating, relaxes spasms

GATHERING

The whole aerial part of the plant is used and should be collected whilst the small clusters of flowers are open, from late spring to late summer. Dry as quickly as possible in the shade.

PREPARATIONS

- *Infusion* not to be taken internally but used directly on the skin as a wash to relieve eczema and other sore, inflamed skin conditions.
- *Rub* the fresh orangey-yellow sap from a freshly broken stem onto warts daily. Allow the sap to dry on the warts and they should be gone in around a week. The same treatment can be given to verrucas.
- *Tincture* again not to be taken internally, but mix a dropper full in an egg cup of water and apply to sore patches of eczema with a piece of cotton wool. You can also apply a

few drops undiluted onto warts and verrucas when you don't have access to the fresh stems, although using fresh stems will remove them more quickly.

CAUTIONS AND CONTRAINDICATIONS

It contains toxic alkaloids, making it unsafe to use internally by anyone except those professionally trained. Be careful not to get sap on unintended parts as it will stain.

Horsetail (Equisetum arvense)

A prolific plant and one dominant on many shady river banks. It is very sociable, loving to reproduce into infinity, so if you are thinking of introducing this plant into your cultivated space, do it with extreme caution as you may find yourself with more than you bargained for. Having said that it can be used not only medicinally but also to improve the strength and vitality of hair, skin and nails, and as such is a handy natural beauty product. Although it has antiseptic properties, it is not strong enough to clear infections by itself and must be used alongside other herbs such as sage, rosemary or thyme to do so.

MATERIA MEDICA

Antiseptic, anti-inflammatory, astringent, diuretic

GATHERING

The green stems are collected in early summer after the fruiting stems have died back. The stems are then crushed to allow any water in the joints to drain before drying them in small bunches.

PREPARATIONS

- *Baths* for sprains, rheumatic pains, joint pains and eczema.
- *Compress* on wounds to staunch bleeding.
- *Infusion* nourishes our bodies, enriching blood with high levels of minerals, specifically calcium and silica which work to build and regenerate bones (useful in the treatment and prevention of osteoporosis) and tissue, especially cartilage. It increases levels of calcium absorption which strengthens brittle nails and hair. It eliminates excess oils from hair and skin. It helps break down hardened deposits and as such can help treat arthritis, gout, cysts, arteriosclerosis, kidney and urinary stones. It can help relieve the symptoms of an enlarged prostate. It strengthens the urinary system and, by promoting urination, relieves water retention.
- *Mouthwash* for ulcers.
- *Poultice* on wounds to staunch bleeding.

CAUTIONS AND CONTRAINDICATIONS

Do not use for longer than 6 consecutive weeks. It is not suitable for the very young and very old or whilst planning or during pregnancy. Avoid if suffering from impaired heart or kidney function (Vaughan & Judd, 2003).

Meadowsweet (Filipendula ulmaria)

Meadowsweet, as its name suggests, has a lovely sweet smell and taste. The leaves can be added to sauces and soups and is used to sweeten when cooking tart fruits. The flowers are a beautiful addition to a summer fruit salad, especially if you are using fruits that need a little added sweetness. Known as nature's antacid, it's great for digestion, protecting and soothing the mucous membranes of the digestive tract. It can be used safely with children, who will especially love to eat the flowers. It contains salicylic acid, the active ingredient in Aspirin, but unlike the manufactured pills, using meadowsweet internally will not irritate the stomach and gastrointestinal tract, but will actually soothe and protect them.

MATERIA MEDICA

Antibacterial, anti-inflammatory, diuretic, pain relief, reduces fevers

GATHERING

The whole of the aerial part is used. It is best collected when the flowering begins in June, although it does flower until August, so keep checking for fresh flower heads. The plant can be hung upside down to dry in a well ventilated place and saved for later use.

PREPARATIONS

- **Bath** for sores and skin rashes. Also for relaxation, to bring a sense of peaceful bliss.
- **Compress** for arthritis.
- **Eyebath** for itchy, sore, inflamed eyes and conjunctivitis.
- **Infusion** acts to protect and heal tissue, especially in the digestive tract, soothing hyperacidity, heartburn, wind, colic, flatulence, gastritis, peptic ulcers, nausea, diahorroea and dysentery. It provides pain relief, specifically in hot, swollen joints, arthritis, rheumatic conditions, neuralgia and headaches. As a diuretic it eases water retention, cystitis, kidney and bladder problems. It brings out a fever and is helpful

when suffering from colds or flu. In addition it's a great relaxant during times of depression, soothing tension and easing one into a peaceful sleep.

- *Tincture* will have the same effect as drinking the infusion, but it is more potent in this form and will act more quickly.

HEALTHFUL COCKTAILS

Infuse with yarrow, peppermint and mix in some elderberry syrup for colds and flu in children.

CAUTIONS AND CONTRAINDICATIONS

Use with caution if asthmatic. Avoid during pregnancy and whilst breast feeding. Do not use if sensitive to aspirin.

Sweet Flag (Acorus calamus)

It grows in the shallows along the water's edge and flowers only rarely. Interestingly it was an ingredient in absinthe, a mildly psychoactive tipple which became popular in the 1790s, and may unwittingly have been instrumental in the conception of some of the great artworks of the impressionist period, as the artists were known to consume the beverage quite liberally. Although recently absinthe has seen a revival, the ingredients have changed to something a little less incongruous to the modern paradigm. In the past it was widely used in medicine by various different native North American tribes. It was also more popular in the UK at one time, but has been found to contain potentially carcinogenic constituents and as a result has not only fallen out of vogue, but is actually now the subject of legal restrictions in some countries.

As it lives in wetlands the roots are saturated with water and shrink to a third of the original size when dried. The result is that it has a great capacity for absorbing fluids and is often used specifically for this reason, helping to remove excess mucous from the body.

MATERIA MEDICA

Digestive, expectorant, relaxes spasms

GATHERING

Collect the root in either late autumn or early spring. The preferred age for collection is around 2 or 3 years. Choose a piece of root that is firm as when they get too old they go somewhat flaccid, as do iris roots. Halve the root along its length and leave to dry out of direct sunlight.

The Medicine Garden

PREPARATIONS

- *Chew* for toothache and dyspepsia.
- *Compress* for rheumatic pains and neuralgia.
- *Decoction* it's a gastrointestinal tonic easing flatulence, stomach cramps, indigestion, gastritis, gastric ulcer, stimulates the appetite and helps expel intestinal parasites. It's also a nerve tonic, calming nerves and clearing a stressed and muddled head. Its expectorant qualities help remove mucous and phlegm from the lungs and respiratory tracts, easing bronchitis and sinusitis.
- *Tincture* can be made from the macerated root and then used to clear the same conditions as the decoction.

CAUTIONS AND CONTRAINDICATIONS

Stick to dosage guidelines as an excess causes vomiting. Avoid during pregnancy and whilst breast feeding.

Watercress (Nasturtium officinale)

Amazingly watercress is actually recommended during pregnancy and breast feeding. It is very rich in minerals, notably sulphur, iron, iodine, calcium and phosphorus. It is also high in vitamins A and C and is often eaten as a spring tonic. You will gain most benefit by eating it raw as the heat of cooking will destroy the digestive enzymes (as with most plants). It is also a source of vitamin B17, the lack of which has been implicated in the development of cancer by Edward Griffin in his book 'World Without Cancer; The story of B17.' It is also highly alkalanizing, which is the body's optimum state for healthy functioning as an acidic system is associated with the development of a great number of conditions and diseases.

It can easily be grown from a bunch bought at the grocer's as they often come with fine white root hairs still attached. Simply place the bunch in water that you change daily until the roots grow a little, when they can be transplanted into a pond. They like slow moving water, so if attempting to grow at home it's best if your pond has a pump or a water feature which circulates the water.

MATERIA MEDICA

Antibacterial, antibiotic, antioxidant, digestive, diuretic, expectorant

GATHERING

Collect the leaves throughout the growing season. Cutting back the foliage for use encourages new growth. Do not collect from the wild unless you are sure the waterway is unpolluted and free of 'run off' coming from fields filled with grazing livestock, as this may contain parasites. Do not preserve by drying the leaf as it loses its potency rapidly.

PREPARATIONS

- *Crush* on infected wounds.
- *Juice* a small bunch 3 times daily, always with other vegetables or fruits as it is very strong. It's a blood cleanser and the high sulphur content helps with cell building and protein absorption. It will clear minor skin problems, brighten bloodshot, dull eyes and give you an energy boost if you have been feeling lethargic. It will help clear mucous and catarrh, easing bronchitis. It will help break up deposits, so is useful if suffering from gout, kidney or bladder stones and some cases of rheumatism. It can be applied directly to acne and other skin irritations. The high iron content helps when suffering from anaemia.
- *Infusion* as a liver tonic. It has the same properties and uses as juice, but has a milder action.

CAUTIONS AND CONTRAINDICATIONS

Do not use for prolonged periods of time. Avoid if suffering kidney inflammation or gastrointestinal ulcers.

Watermint (Mentha aquatica)

A member of the mint family that grows at the edge of water bodies. It can be collected and used in the same ways as Peppermint (see page 37). Never collect it from water that you suspect may be polluted. I always look for a sprig when filling my water bottle from a spring as it adds a lovely hint of flavour and is quite invigorating. If there is no spring but some watermint I then just pick a couple of leaves to chew whilst enjoying my walk along the riverside.

Willow (Salix alba)

Flexible, graceful and fast growing, willow has many practical uses, for example around the base of an outside compost loo as it will happily take up all the excess nutrients in the deposits left behind. It actually loves such nutrients and can be found breaking open sewers

to get to the treasures inside. The bark contains salicin, which is converted into salicylic acid by the digestive system (Conway, 2001). This is the active ingredient in commercial Aspirin. Fortunately, unlike the commercial drug, it will not irritate the stomach lining as it contains tannins which are beneficial to the digestive system (Mindell, 2000).

MATERIA MEDICA

Anti-inflammatory, antiseptic, astringent, pain relief

GATHERING

Bark is removed and dried from spring and throughout the summer months. It is incredibly important never to remove a ring of bark from around the trunk as this will kill the tree. Luckily, as willow is often coppiced or pollarded, you will easily find thin whips which you can cut right back to the main stem or ground and then strip the bark and dry it. Alternatively, cut back new shoots, the bigger the better, and strip them, but remember to leave the bark intact on the main trunk. In fact, if you cut a branch too many you can just put it back in the soil and it should set root and grow into a new tree. The stripped stems can be dried and used as kindling, leaving no waste. It is best to store the bark in large pieces as breaking it down will create more surface area to oxidize and consequently deteriorate. You can crush it or powder it just before use to ensure maximum shelf life.

PREPARATIONS

- *Decoction* drink only one cup throughout the day in teaspoon portions (Evert Hopman, 1991). Use to ease the pain from neuralgia, headaches and menstruation. It lowers fevers and treats diarrhoea and heartburn. It is especially useful for pain relief and connective tissue inflammation in cases of rheumatism, arthritis and gout. It can be used externally as a skin wash for burns, sores and wounds.
- *Gargle* for sore throats and gums.
- *Infusion* powder the bark before adding to hot water. You can then avoid having to simmer the bark as you would for a decoction. Wether you choose to make an infusion or decoction, it will have the same action.
- *Tincture* has the same uses as decoctions and infusions. It may be more convenient to crush and tincture it once the bark has dried rather than store large sections or, alternatively, have to powder sections frequently.

CAUTIONS AND CONTRAINDICATIONS

Avoid if pregnant, breast feeding, taking or sensitive to aspirin.

Meadow

The thought of a sunny meadow full of wild flowers and alive with the buzzing of bees and the colourful flicker of passing butterflies makes me feel so warm inside. You just want to be there, skipping through the tall grass and maybe even rolling down a flower strewn hillside, giggling with glee. Meadows are at their best in mid-summer when you can sit or lay back peacefully, watching the clouds go by on a long July evening. I cannot think of a summer meadow without smiling, so what better place to go and forage for medicines, stringing it out, even taking all day to fill your basket with flowery delights to lift your spirits and remind you of summer when feeling under the weather later in the year.

Cowslip (Primula veris)

The leaves are rich in vitamin C, beta-carotene, potassium, calcium and sodium. In addition they contain salicylates which detoxify and strengthen the immune system whilst lowering cholesterol. Leaves are available fresh from early spring until around October and can be eaten raw or added to cooked dishes in place of other greens such as spinach. However, it would be a shame to cook them as in doing so you lose so many of the nutritional qualities. The flowers can also be eaten brightening up a plate with their fresh yellow colour.

MATERIA MEDICA

Antioxidant, anti-inflammatory, expectorant, relaxes spasms, sedative

GATHERING

Cowslip has a short flowering season, generally just throughout April and May. This is when they can be collected and used fresh or dried for later use. To preserve the medicinal qualities the flowers must be dried in the shade. Roots can be lifted in the spring and dried for decoctions or made into tinctures.

PREPARATIONS

- *Bath* (flower) for tense muscles and as a general relaxant for body and mind.
- *Compress* (root decoction) for arthritic pain.
- *Decoction* (root) as an expectorant for bronchitis and coughs.
- *Infusion* (flower) to relieve muscle spasms, cramp, arthritic and rheumatic pain. Cowslip acts therapeutically on the nerves and so can be used for easing stress, tension, nervous excitement, nervous headache, nightmares and insomnia. Its expectorant qualities are useful for bronchitis, catarrh, dry cough and whooping cough. It reduces fever and can be used for colds and chills. In addition it eases asthma and stimulates lactation in nursing mothers. Externally it can be used as a skin wash for sunburn.
- *Oil* (flower) rub on bruises.
- *Poultice* (flower) for wounds.
- *Syrup* (flower) for coughs, bronchitis, catarrh and asthma.

- *Tincture* (root) for arthritis, insomnia and anxiety.

HEALTHFUL COCKTAILS

Infuse with wood betony for headaches.

Infuse with chamomile for anxiety.

Infuse with mugwort for insomnia.

CAUTIONS AND CONTRAINDICATIONS

Avoid during pregnancy, if allergic to aspirin or using anti-coagulant drugs.

Milk Thistle (Silybum marianum)

Not so easy to collect if you are using it for anything more than the occasional hangover due to the quantity of seed needed. You can buy seed in bulk (see suppliers) and make your own preparations whilst setting aside a corner of your garden in which to grow milk thistle if you are determined, or just want them around for the spiritual connection to such a generous plant. My introduction to the amazing benefits of milk thistle was through a friend who was suffering from Hepatitis C. She was incredibly sick for several years, but after undergoing a range of therapies including intensive use of milk thistle, is now totally clear of the disease and is raising a young family. It is, however, important to remember never to self-diagnose, and if you are suffering from a chronic disease, always seek the advice of a qualified healthcare professional.

MATERIA MEDICA

Antioxidant, anti-inflammatory, liver tonic

GATHERING

The seeds ripen between August and October and can be collected by cutting off the mature seed heads and storing in a warm place away from direct sunlight. After a few days simply tap the heads over a bit of newspaper to catch the seeds as they fall.

PREPARATIONS

- *Infusion* the main active ingredient, silymarin, is not easily soluble in water so the best preparation to use is a tincture. If you are trying to avoid alcohol you can make an infusion by really crushing the seeds as much as possible and leaving them to infuse for at least 20 minutes. This will, however, not act as strongly on the system as a tincture.
- *Poultice* (pulverised seed) for skin ulcers and varicose veins.
- *Tincture* milk thistle is a great liver tonic. It protects the liver against toxins, regenerates liver cells and enhances overall liver function. It is great to use where the liver is overloaded by toxins, be they from smoking, alcohol, drugs, or chemicals in the work

place or environment. It helps minimize the adverse effects of chemotherapy on the liver. Useful in cases of liver damage and disease, especially inflammatory diseases such as hepatitis C. It eases skin conditions that relate to a stagnant liver which include some cases of eczema, psoriasis, acne, and dermatitis. Also used for gall bladder disease and to stimulate bile production. In addition it is a blood cleanser, mild laxative and increases milk production in nursing mothers.

CAUTIONS AND CONTRAINDICATIONS

Do not use if you have previously suffered hormone related cancers. Use with caution if you have a sensitivity to the asteraceae family. If you are already undergoing drug therapy of some kind, please consult with your healthcare professional before using milk thistle as it may affect your liver's ability to absorb the drugs. Use of milk thistle may intensify the action of hypoglycemic drugs (drugs that lower blood sugar levels), so be aware and check your blood sugar levels regularly.

Mugwort (Artemesia vulgaris)

One of my major plant allies, we have worked together for several years now, mainly working with clients on a spiritual level. It is used in Plant Spirit Medicine (see resources), where it is regarded with particular reverence due to its ability to make shifts in the spiritual realm and remove unwanted presences and emotional blockages. It is used in a similar way by some Acupuncturists and practitioners of other Traditional Chinese Medicine based therapies, in the form of moxibustion, where the leaf is rolled and gently smoulders as it's held over certain points along the body's energy lines (meridians) to move stagnant energy. Burning the leaf as an incense will cleanse spaces and has a sedative effect. Well known for its ability to enhance dreams by aiding their recall, but also by facilitating astral projection and lucid dreaming, it is often sewn into small pillows and placed by one's head whilst sleeping. Very much a doorway to the invisible world.

MATERIA MEDICA

Antibacterial, antiseptic, anti-inflammatory, digestive, sedative

GATHERING

Leaves and stems are collected before flowering which occurs from July to September as this is when it's most potent. Hang the stems upside down in small bunches in a warm, well ventilated place away from direct sunlight to dry and preserve for later use.

PREPARATIONS

- *Bath* to ease stress, aid relaxation and for aches in muscles and joints.
- *Gargle* for sore throats.
- *Infusion* (maximum of 2 cups a day) as a digestive stimulant easing dyspepsia, flatulence, bloating and to assist the expulsion of intestinal parasites. It's a nerve tonic

easing stress, tension, depression, nervousness and bringing a sense of calm. It stimulates the uterus and can help normalise menstruation and smooth the changes that come with menopause. It helps improve poor circulation. Externally it can be used as a skin wash for fungal infections and sores on the skin.

• *Poultice* for infections.

CAUTIONS AND CONTRAINDICATIONS

Avoid during pregnancy, whilst breast feeding, if suffering uterine inflammation or pelvic infection. Use with caution if you have a sensitivity to the asteraceae family. Do not use for longer than 6 consecutive days.

Mullein (Verbascum thapsus)

Mullein is a bright yellow flower on a tall flower spike. There is something a little prehistoric about it. I can imagine it dotting the plains as the dinosaurs blundered past millions of years ago. I have seen it in meadows and on roadsides from the uplands of Kenya to the high altitude desert of New Mexico, where its generous, soft leaves are reportedly used as an emergency source of toilet paper!

MATERIA MEDICA

Antiseptic, antibiotic, anti-inflammatory, expectorant, diuretic, pain relief

GATHERING

Collect the leaves from plants in their first year (before the flower spikes arrive) and flowers in the summer months. Dry in a shady place and do not use if they turn brown. Separate the individual flowers from the spikes before drying.

PREPARATIONS

• *Facial Steam* (leaves and flowers) for asthma, coughs, congestion and sore throats.
• *Infusion* (leaves) for nervous tension, insomnia and to promote courage. It clears congestion, promotes healing and soothes irritation, especially in chest complaints. Also for urinary tract infections and to relieve stomach cramps and diarrhoea. Always strain the infusion through a fine mesh to avoid swallowing the fine hairs that can be tickly and irritating.
• *Oil* (flowers in olive oil) for direct application to skin inflammations, wounds, boils, sores, chilblains, hemorrhoids, varicose veins, bruises, sprains, swollen joints, arthritis and rheumatic pains. Rubbed on the chest it will provide relief for chest congestion and bronchial inflammation. It can also be warmed slightly and dribbled in the ear to bring relief from earache and infection. Mullein makes a great triple infused oil (see preparations chapter). This would be almost impossible to buy, and makes an incredibly powerful medicine.
• *Syrup* (leaves and flowers) to soothe and lubricate dry coughs, whooping cough,

bronchitis, laryngitis, tonsillitis, sore throat, catarrh and to loosen phlegm in the upper respiratory tract.

HEALTHFUL COCKTAILS

Infuse and mix with syrup made from marshmallow leaf for coughs.

Infuse with thyme for coughs.

Make an infused oil with yarrow and garlic for earache.

CAUTIONS AND CONTRAINDICATIONS

None known.

St. John's Wort (Hypericum perforatum)

It has gained popularity in recent times and is now known as nature's Prozac. It's a worthy plant to view up close, through a magnifier if you have one. The leaves are covered in pin prick perforations and the flowers laced with red dots. The red dots are oil glands and are what gives preparations made from St. John's wort a red colour. They are both, of course, also visible with the naked eye. The perforations are not only what gave it the second part of its Latin name, but also a way of knowing you have identified the plant correctly. It usually flowers around mid-summer's day, somehow managing to hold the energy of that time of year, washing away the winter blues and easing the symptoms of seasonal affective disorder (SAD) at the opposite end of the sun's annual dance.

It will grow on sunny banks, but doesn't mind a bit of shade either. I currently grow it in my garden because I couldn't find enough in the wild locally to feel comfortable about harvesting. It happily shares a space with my lovingly nurtured nettle and grows to about the same height.

Matthew Wood has made the interesting connection that, metaphysically, St. John's wort acts on the solar plexus (also yellow). This energy point is connected to self-esteem, emotional blockages and trauma. By using St. John's wort and working on the solar plexus it helps one trust gut level instincts, giving people the strength and courage to deal with their lives, specifically helping to work through issues relating to fear and periods of depression.

MATERIA MEDICA

Antibacterial, anti-inflammatory, antiseptic, antiviral, astringent, expectorant, diuretic, nerve tonic, pain relief, sedative

GATHERING

The flowers are cut as they begin to open, usually in late June.

The Medicine Garden

PREPARATIONS

- **Compress** for wounds, sprains, bruises and swellings.
- **Infusion** if taking for depression use for at least a month before expecting results. It can help treat mild to moderate depression, SAD, nervous tension, anxiety, excitability, insomnia and will smooth the emotions during menopause and pre-menstrually. It also eases premenstrual cramps. Beneficial to the circulation, it promotes wound healing and will fight off viral infections and colds. It helps remove mucous from the lungs and the intestines, treating coughs, strengthening digestion and decongesting the liver. The diuretic properties help wash out toxins and, combined with its anti-inflammatory action, will ease rheumatic pains, arthritis and gout. It also brings relief to sciatica and shingles.
- **Oil** as the flowers infuse, the oil will become red and the redder the better. You can do a double or even triple infusion (see preparations section for instructions) if the flowers are abundantly available for long enough. Apply to bruises, swellings, sprains, burns and sunburn. Massage gently onto aches, stiffness, rheumatism, gout and areas of poor circulation. Using the oil on the limbs after suffering a stroke will help a greater level of sensitivity to return. Use after surgery or injury on the skin over areas where there has been internal trauma and nerve damage. It also helps relieve back pain, neuralgia and sciatica. Rubbed on the temples it will relieve headache (Peterson, 1995). The hypericum acts as a preservative, meaning the oil should last indefinitely.
- **Tincture** like the oil, the tincture will also go red as the hypericin infuses into the liquid. The tincture may be more convenient than infusions if being used for depression as it will need to be used regularly over quite some time. It can be used for the same complaints as the infusion.
- **Salve** for wounds, sores, bruises, sprains, varicose veins, sciatica, neuralgia, tennis elbow and mild burns.

HEALTHFUL COCKTAILS

Infuse with hops and valerian for insomnia.

Infuse with lavender and lemonbalm for depression.

Infuse with passionflower for anxiety.

Make a salve with comfrey for joint problems.

CAUTIONS AND CONTRAINDICATIONS

Harmful if eaten, it is a skin allergen in sunlight and, if taken internally one may become photo-sensitive, so be extra careful of burning in the sun when using. As always, if you are already taking prescribed medication, check with a healthcare professional before using as it is not to be taken alongside some drugs, although it can be used externally whilst undergoing drug therapy. Avoid during pregnancy and breast feeding. Not to be taken by children.

Moorland

My experience of moorlands is of walking into driving rain, heading almost horizontally and with malice straight for my eyes, and blinding me every time I lift my bowed head to see where I'm going. Although not always burdened by such extreme conditions it is a tough and harsh landscape that produces equally tough and hardy little plants. As they cling to the earth through the extremes of the seasons, unprotected by an upper canopy of lush trees or shrubs, their strong personalities are reflected in the strength of their medicine.

Bilberry (Vaccinium myrtillus)

I had never even heard of bilberries until I went to visit my partner's parents in Yorkshire where we spent a whole afternoon filling container after container with this small and delicate fruit. Picking them is quite addictive as each bush is so heavily laden. Time just seems to stand still as you enter into an altered state where just you and the delicious berry seem to exist. They can be eaten raw as they come or in smoothies and are popular sweetened and baked in pies and jams.

MATERIA MEDICA

Antioxidant, antiseptic, diuretic, digestive, improves circulation

GATHERING

The berries are picked when ripe from July through to September. They squash easily when picking, so it's good to dry, freeze or otherwise process them as soon as you get home. Interestingly, fresh fruits are laxative whereas dried fruits are anti-diarrhoeal, so you may want to freeze some and dry others. The leaves are picked in spring and dried for decoctions.

PREPARATIONS

- *Infusion* (fruit) improves blood supply in veins and capillaries helping skin, eyes and the nervous system. This boost in micro-circulation helps prevent effects which are frequently associated with aging. The improvement in circulation is partially due to its blood thinning effect and can help in cases of varicose veins and thread veins. In addition drinking this brew will help protect the body from free radical damage which is implicated in the development of cancer and cardio-vascular disease. It helps boost night vision and the regeneration of visual purple (the bit that causes the bleached effect you get after looking into a bright light). It's also useful for urinary complaints, water retention, anaemia and assists in reducing levels of cholesterol, helping to prevent hardening of the arteries.
- *Decoction* (leaves) for gastrointestinal complaints and lowering blood sugar levels.
- *Mouthwash* (dried fruit) for gum and mouth inflammations.
- *Syrup* (dried fruit) for diarrhoea and dysentery.

CAUTIONS AND CONTRAINDICATIONS

Exercise caution if taking other blood thinning drugs.

Heather (Calluna vulgaris)

Commonly found in widespread swathes on moorland, colouring the landscape like a purple carpet throughout the summer months. It is associated with luck and sold in bunches by gypsy folk to bestow that magical quality. Whenever we drove to Scotland on family holidays we always came back with a large sprig of heather tied to the front grill of the car to protect us on our journey home.

MATERIA MEDICA

Astringent, anti-infammatory, antiseptic, diuretic, induces perspiration, mildly sedative

GATHERING

The flowering shoots are cut in summer during August and September when they are fully open. The flowers can be dried for later use, but this must be done out of direct light.

PREPARATIONS

- *Bath* for rheumatic pains.
- *Infusion* for coughs, colds, diarrhoea, cystitis, kidney infections and urinary tract infections. It is a gentle remedy for insomnia, depression and nervous exhaustion. It alleviates arthritis and rheumatism by reducing joint and bone inflammation. In addition it strengthens the heart and detoxifies by cleansing the blood.
- *Oil* rub gently on rheumatic pains and arthritic joints.
- *Salve* apply directly to rheumatic pains and arthritic joints.

CAUTIONS AND CONTRAINDICATIONS

Not recommended for prolonged use.

Tormentil (Potentilla erecta)

Quite a low growing shrub, this is lovely in the garden and brings bright little yellow flowers to moorland areas from June till September.

MATERIA MEDICA

Antiallergenic, antibiotic, antiseptic, astringent, immuno-stimulant

GATHERING

The whole plant, including the finely chopped root, is used in preparations. Roots can be lifted in autumn or spring. Wash and cut them into small pieces before drying. The aerial part of the plant is cut in summer and can be used fresh or dried.

PREPARATIONS

- *Douche* for vaginal discharge.
- *Eyebath* use a weak infusion for conjunctivitis (Mabey, 1991).
- *Gargle* for sore throats, laryngitis and pharyngitis.
- *Infusion* is cooling, soothing and promotes healing, especially in the gastrointestinal tract, where it treats gastritis, diarrhoea, enteritis, colitis, Chron's disease, diverticulitis and peptic ulcers. In addition it promotes restful sleep. Externally it can be applied as a skin wash to weeping sores, abrasions, infected wounds, ulcers, burns, sunburn and shingles.
- *Mouthwash* for bleeding gums and mouth ulcers.
- *Poultice* for cuts, wounds, sores and ulcers.
- *Salve* for hemorrhoids and also to speed the healing of wounds, sores and cuts.

CAUTIONS AND CONTRAINDICATIONS

Exercise caution when applying topically as it contains strong tannins which can cause scarring. Always patch test first and use sparingly.

By The Coast

There is nothing like a day at the coast, whether you are wandering along a cliff path with the sun shining, or enjoying the moody dark skies and crashing waves of a powerful winter storm on the beach. It's a place where you can feel the wild forces of nature at work. I love to visit the coast at any time of year and I in fact prefer the winter months when I get the beach to myself and can feel the wind blowing the cobwebs from my mind. It can be incredibly invigorating. Anything that grows in the coastal zone knows the wildness of these harsh, windy, salty winters and hot summers, where being trampled by the bucket and spade wielding masses becomes just another part of the challenge. The plants here are strong, often with very deep roots and a level of versatility beyond that of most inland dwelling plants. Translate that to strength of spirit and you know immediately that using these plants will ground you in a multitude of situations.

Bladder Wrack (Fucus vesiculosus)

This seaweed is found growing on submerged rocks close to the shoreline and is often washed up on beaches. It has bubbles on its strands that can be popped if it has dried a bit in the sun, which sometimes comically squirt out water, providing hours of entertainment! Full of nutrients, it's frequently used as a plant food and soil conditioner. Simply take a handful and spread it thinly, directly onto your beds. Not just a mineral boost for plants and soils, it also contains iodine, potassium, magnesium, zinc, iron, calcium and vitamin B12, so can be a great addition to your own diet too. You can steam it and serve with sea food or salads, but I find it very salty and prefer to dry, then crumble and sprinkle it on my favourite foods. It should be used as an occasional treat, maybe once a week, as the iodine levels are rather high to consume on a daily basis.

MATERIA MEDICA

Antibiotic, mineral boost

GATHERING

Collect in summer when the nutrient content is highest. Always be sure that the area you are collecting from is not polluted. Only collect pieces that are still attached to rocks and submerged, as any that have washed up will have started to degrade, and most often will have a cloud of flies in residence doing their business. Cut the stems and take the upper part, leaving a length still attached to the rock which will allow it to regrow. Dry in the sun to preserve, protect from flies and turn frequently.

PREPARATIONS

- *Compress* for sprains, bruises, rheumatic pains and arthritis (Mabey, 1988).
- *Infusion* to restore depleted minerals, for rheumatism, to control weight gained as a symptom of under active thyroid and to treat goiter present as a result of low iodine levels (under active thyroid). Consumption of bladder wrack stimulates the thyroid, so it is important not to use it in cases of over active thyroid.
- *Poultice* for arthritis (Mabey, 1988). It is great to use as an emergency poultice if you suffer bruising or a sprain whilst on the beach and should serve to ease your injury whilst you struggle home.

CAUTIONS AND CONTRAINDICATIONS

Exercise caution if using blood thinning drugs as it has a mild blood thinning action. If you start using bladder wrack and find yourself with new and unexplained symptoms, go and get checked by a physician as it may be the seaweed has been subjected to pollution and is contaminated with low levels of heavy metals. Do not use if suffering from an over active thyroid. Avoid during pregnancy, whilst breast feeding and if on a low salt diet.

Marshmallow (Althaea officinalis)

A pretty, sweet, soothing flower found along the banks of tidal rivers, salt marshes and backing beaches. Although the flowers themselves are not used in any medicinal preparations, they can be eaten raw, added to either a fruit or savory salad, or just as a tickle of sweet sunshine as you eat a few single flowers in passing. Dried sections of root can be given to teething infants to soothe the pain and inflammation that comes with a sharp tooth cutting its way through tender and delicate gums. Just as the actions of marshmallow soothe our bodies internally, their presence and use can also soothe us emotionally, smoothing off the ragged edges of irritation and annoyance in our day to day lives.

The Medicine Garden

MATERIA MEDICA

Antibacterial, anti-inflammatory, expectorant, pain relief

GATHERING

Leaves are collected in late summer. Roots are collected in autumn as the flowers and leaves die back.

PREPARATIONS

- *Chew* (dried root) for teething pains (Brown, 1995).
- *Decoction* (root) for inflammatory bowel disease such as Chron's disease and ulcerative colitis, acid indigestion, heartburn and pain relief for peptic ulcers. The mashed root can also be left in cold water overnight. It will become very slimey and must be strained before being gently warmed and taken by the spoonful to soothe and protectively coat irritated intestines.
- *Eyebath* for inflamed eyes.
- *Gargle* (leaf infusion) for sore throats.
- *Infusion* (leaf) for urinary tract inflammations, cystitis and as a kidney cleanse. It soothes inflammation and irritations in the bronchial tubes and lungs, so is great for bronchitis, coughs, catarrh, and to loosen phlegm. It also boosts the immune system.
- *Mouthwash* (root decoction) for mouth and gum inflammation.
- *Poultice* (root) for abscesses, boils, ulcers, skin infections and varicose veins. (applied hot) for inflammation and bruises and (leaves) to draw out a splinter.
- *Salve* (root) for skin ulcers, rashes, wounds.
- *Syrup* (leaves) for sore throats, coughs, bronchitis, chest and urinary complaints and (root) for inflammation of the gastrointestinal tract and digestive irritations.

HEALTHFUL COCKTAILS

Mix syrup (root) with an infusion of flowers from pot marigold (Calendula) for digestive complaints.

CAUTIONS AND CONTRAINDICATIONS

To be used with caution if on drug therapy as marshmallow coats and lines your stomach and intestines with slime and, consequentially, may affect the absorption of medications.

Sea Buckthorn (Hippophae rhamnoides)

Found on permanent sand dunes and cliffs, this tough and thorny fellow is known for its ability to stabilize soils and has been used for that property in areas of huge soil loss over large parts of Asia. I had my first interaction with sea buckthorn during a dream one night. I could see bronze coloured fruits and small leaves on a shrubby bush and kept hearing the name over and over. The next morning I ran straight to my herb book where I found it listed and read about it. My boyfriend had awoken that morning with a sore throat and the onset of a cold, so I popped down to the health store for a few provisions to get him through. The first shelf I turned to had sea buckthorn syrup at eye level! It tasted delicious and I'm sure its high vitamin (A, C & E) content helped speed him back to full health.

MATERIA MEDICA

Antioxidant, antimicrobial, anti-inflammatory

GATHERING

It starts fruiting in August and should be picked before the first frost, although it does continue fruiting well into winter. The fruits can be dried, frozen or used fresh.

PREPARATIONS

- *Infusion* (mashed fruit) for intestinal problems, diarrhoea, liver detox, rheumatism and to help fight off colds and flu.
- *Juice* the flavour is rather sharp, so it is good to juice with sweet fruits such as apple. It is used to soothe and heal gastric and duodenal ulcers. Limit the dosage to one handful of fruits a day.
- *Syrup* making sea buckthorn syrup is very simple; just mix equal parts of fresh juice and honey, warm gently over some boiling water, allow to cool and keep in the fridge. This is a great tonic for convalescents, and for the early stages of colds and flu as it boosts the immune system. Just take a spoonful as needed.

CAUTIONS AND CONTRAINDICATIONS

None known.

Sea Holly (Eryngium maritimum)

Found along sandy shorelines, once spotted it is never forgotten as it has a quite unique steely blue foliage and spiny flower. It dries well and can be used for a bit of something different in dried flower arrangements. It was one of my favourites in my days at the herb nursery, just because of its strange and beautiful appearance.

MATERIA MEDICA

Anti-inflammatory, diuretic, expectorant

GATHERING

The roots are collected after flowering in autumn and then dried.

PREPARATIONS

- *Decoction* for urinary tract infections, cystitis and kidney stones.
- *Syrup* for long standing coughs.

CAUTIONS AND CONTRAINDICATIONS

None known.

Endnote

Whilst undertaking research for this book, whenever I found myself processing something emotionally or physically, the plant I began working with next was the one to counteract that state or condition. Suprising? Not really. Our plant brothers are possibly more intelligent than we give them credit for. It is said that a remedy will start growing in one's vicinity 6 months before you start needing to use it.....and why not? If I am feeling a little down hearted, or under the weather in one way or another, why shouldn't the beautiful plants I am writing about come to the rescue time and again. You just have to open up to it and be observant, and you might just be amazed at the number of ways the plant world is trying to communicate with you...

Exercises For Befriending The Plant People

The plants you notice most strongly, those you cannot pass without taking in a deep lungful of their aroma or without a smile bursting onto your lips: these are the ones that hold the strongest and most significant medicine for you. I encourage you to sit with them. Spend time again and again with them, they are calling you. You may want to try these simple steps to help enhance and deepen your relationship with these plants, allowing with practice and time for them to become true friends and allies:

1)   Sit with the plant, introduce yourself and ask that it shares its secrets or its medicine with you. You are asking the plant to give you something, so it is respectful to reciprocate and give something of yourself in exchange, perhaps a pinch of tobacco (traditional in the Americas) or simply a hair from your head.

2)   Plants live at a much slower pace than we humans, so to slow yourself take 30 minutes to simply draw what you see. You will find the momentum and urgency of your day peeling off as you begin to make acute observations and see the minutiae that you have never noticed before.

3)   As you draw, a feeling will descend upon you; you may even feel that you have entered a kind of dream state. Be aware of how you are feeling, both physically and emotionally, and note it down.

4)   Use all your senses; touch the plant, smell it, ask its permission and, if you feel that the answer is yes, then taste a small piece.

5)   Use your heart to extend love to the plant, much as you would on seeing a beautiful sleeping baby.

6)   Throughout the process be aware of any and all sensations you are experiencing and write them down.

7)   When your time is up, thank the plant before you leave.

8)   Later, review what you have written and, most importantly, how you felt. Then look up the 'uses' of that plant in a book. You will be surprised how your feelings mirror what science or millenia of folk tales have found out about that plant.

It may take some practice but in time you will come to trust what you are feeling, what the plant is telling you. This way of finding out about a plant can be extremely personal, yet somehow the more personal it feels, the more universal it becomes. It is original knowledge and once you trust nature to be your friend and guide, it cannot be argued with.

This way of communicating with plants is where the magic of wild medicine truly begins. If you are interested in this way of working with plants and would like to learn more, please visit my website www.gatewaystoeden.com where you'll find more information and the opportunity to attend one of my regular workshops on the subject.

Quick Remedy Finder For Common Ailments

ACNE ✦ amaranth, basil, burdock, carrot, comfrey, coriander, cucumber, dandelion, echinacea, hawthorn, iris, lady's mantle, marigold (calendula), milk thistle, nasturtium, onion, pansy, peppermint, plantain, pumpkin, walnut, watercress

ANAEMIA ✦ asparagus, bilberry, dandelion, elder, elecampane, onion, parsley, plum, raspberry, rocket, stinging nettle, strawberry, walnut, watercress

ANGINA PECTORIS ✦ carrot, celery, hawthorn

ANXIETY ✦ basil, borage, celery, cleavers, cowslip, elder, evening primrose, hops, hyssop, jasmine, lavender, lime, marigold (French), marjoram, passionflower, periwinkle, primrose, St. John's wort, skullcap, stinging nettle, valerian, wood betony, wormwood

ARTHRITIS ✦ apple, arnica, asparagus, birch, bladder wrack, burdock, catmint, celery, chickweed, chilli pepper, cleavers, clover (red), comfrey, cowslip, cucumber, elder, evening primrose, feverfew, garlic, ginger, golden rod, heather, horseradish, horsetail, iris, lady's mantle, marjoram, meadowsweet, mullein, pansy, parsley, quince, rose, rosemary, St. John's wort, speedwell, stinging nettle, strawberry, sunflower, thyme, willow, wormwood, yellow dock

ASTHMA ✦ carrot, chilli pepper, cowslip, crocus, elder, elecampane, evening primrose, feverfew, figs, garlic, ginkgo, honeysuckle, horseradish, hyssop, Jack in the hedge, mallow, mullein, parsley, passionflower, plantain, stinging nettle, sunflower, thyme, violet, walnut, yellow dock

ATHLETE'S FOOT ✦ angelica, echinacea, garlic, lavender, marigold (calendula), mugwort, nasturtium, thyme

BITES AND STINGS ✦ basil, blackberry, borage, carrot, chamomile, clover (red), crab apple, dandelion, echinacea, feverfew, golden rod, ground elder, houseleek, hollyhock, Jack in the hedge, lemonbalm, mallow, marigold (calendula), peppermint, plantain, sage, stinging nettle, witch hazel, wormwood, yellow dock

BRONCHITIS ✦ angelica, balloon flower, borage, catmint, cowslip, elder, evening primrose, feverfew, garlic, hollyhock, horseradish, hyssop, Jack in the hedge, lungwort, mallow, marshmallow, mullein, nasturtium, plantain, primrose, radish, stinging nettle, sunflower, sweet flag, thyme, violet, watercress, yellow dock

BRUISES ✦ arnica, bay, bladder wrack, borage, burdock, catmint, chervil, comfrey, cowslip, daisy, dandelion, elder, geranium, hazel, hyssop, lavender, mallow, marshmallow, mullein, plantain, St. John's wort, selfheal, thyme, witch hazel, wood betony, wormwood

MINOR BURNS ✦ blackberry, burdock, carrot, chamomile, comfrey, cucumber, daisy, elder, giant hyssop, ginger, horseradish, houseleek, ivy, lady's mantle, mallow, marigold (calendula), plantain, pumpkin, St. John's wort, selfheal, stinging nettle, tormentil, walnut, willow

CIRCULATION ✦ angelica, bilberry, black currant, blackthorn, borage, chilli pepper, coriander, crocus, garlic, gentian (yellow), ginger, ginkgo, hawthorn, lime, mugwort, parsley, ramsons, rosemary, St. John's wort, wood betony

COLDS ✦ angelica, balloon flower, basil, bay, bergamot, blackberry, black currant, blackthorn, burdock, catmint, chamomile, cowslip, crab apple, crocus, dill, echinacea, elder, garlic, giant hyssop, ginger, heather, holly, hollyhock, horseradish, lemonbalm, lime, marigold (calendula), marjoram, meadowsweet, mulberry, nasturtium, onion, peppermint, ramsons, rose, rosemary, sage, St. John's wort, sea buckthorn, sunflower, thyme, yarrow

COLD SORES ✦ lavender, lemonbalm

COLIC ✦ angelica, bay, black currant, blackthorn, catmint, daisy, dill, fennel, feverfew, geranium, hollyhock, hops, hyssop, lavender, lovage, marigold (French), marjoram, meadowsweet, onion, wood betony

CONJUNCTIVITIS ✦ chervil, coriander, cucumber, elder, fennel, marigold (calendula), meadowsweet, tormentil, witch hazel

COUGHS ✦ angelica, apple, balloon flower, blackberry, black currant, borage, burdock, chickweed, clover (red), cowslip, crab apple, crocus, daisy, echinacea, elder, elecampane, evening primrose, fennel, figs, garlic, giant hyssop, ginger, golden rod, hazel, heather, holly, hollyhock, honeysuckle, horseradish, hyssop, jasmine, lime, lovage, lungwort, mallow, marjoram, marshmallow, mullein, onion, pansy, plantain, primrose, rock rose, sage, St. John's wort, sea holly, speedwell, stinging nettle, sunflower, sweet cicely, thyme, valerian, violet, walnut, wood betony

CUTS GRAZES SCRAPES ✦ chickweed, comfrey, echinacea, garlic, geranium, horseradish, hyssop, lady's mantle, lavender, mallow, marigold (calendula), onion, periwinkle, selfheal, speedwell, thyme, tormentil, witch hazel, yarrow

CYSTITIS ✦ angelica, asparagus, birch, blackberry, burdock, carnation, carrot, cleavers, golden rod, heather, horsetail, lovage, pansy, parsley, plantain, marshmallow, meadowsweet, sea holly, yarrow, yellow dock

DEPRESSION ✦ borage, catmint, chervil, crocus, feverfew, heather, jasmine, lavender,

The Medicine Garden

lemonbalm, meadowsweet, mugwort, raspberry, rose, rosemary, St. John's wort, skullcap, stinging nettle, wormwood

DERMATITIS ✦ milk thistle, peppermint

DIARRHOEA ✦ amaranth, bilberry, blackberry, black currant, blackthorn, catmint, comfrey, crab apple, daisy, elder, elecampane, gentian (yellow), geranium, golden rod, hawthorn, hazel, heather, hollyhock, meadowsweet, mullein, plantain, quince, rock rose, sea buckthorn, sunflower, tormentil, willow, yarrow

DIVERTICULITIS ✦ chamomile, hollyhock, marigold (calendula), tormentil

ECZEMA ✦ amaranth, birch, blackberry, blackthorn, burdock, carnation, celandine (greater), chamomile, chervil, chickweed, cleavers, clover (red), comfrey, dandelion, elecampane, evening primrose, geranium, golden rod, horsetail, ivy, lady's mantle, mallow, marigold (calendula), milk thistle, pansy, peppermint, plantain, speedwell, stinging nettle, valerian, violet, walnut, witch hazel, yellow dock

FEVER ✦ angelica, basil, bergamot, birch, borage, carnation, chilli pepper, cleavers, coriander, cowslip, echinacea, elder, garlic, giant hyssop, golden rod, holly, hyssop, Jack in the hedge, Jacob's ladder, lemonbalm, lime, meadowsweet, pansy, speedwell, sunflower, willow, yarrow

FIBROIDS ✦ iris, lady's mantle, yellow dock

FLU ✦ angelica, basil, bay, blackberry, catmint, chamomile, dill, echinacea, elder, garlic, ginger, holly, horseradish, hyssop, lemonbalm, lime, marigold (calendula), marjoram, meadowsweet, mulberry, nasturtium, peppermint, rosemary, sage, sea buckthorn, violet, yarrow

GASTROENTERITIS ✦ basil, geranium, peppermint

GOUT ✦ apple, birch, black currant, burdock, carrot, celery, clover (red), crab apple, cucumber, dandelion, ground elder, horseradish, horsetail, Jack in the hedge, lady's mantle, pansy, primrose, pumpkin, St. John's wort, stinging nettle, strawberry, watercress, willow, yellow dock

HAY FEVER ✦ carrot, chamomile, coriander, elder, elecampane, horseradish, marjoram, plantain, stinging nettle

HEADACHE ✦ basil, clover (red), cowslip, cucumber, elder, evening primrose, hops, houseleek, Jacob's ladder, lavender, lemonbalm, lime, marjoram, meadowsweet, passionflower, peppermint, primrose, rose, rosemary, St. John's wort, selfheal, skullcap, thyme, valerian, violet, willow, wood betony

HEMORRHOIDS ✦ burdock, catmint, chickweed, comfrey, geranium, ground elder, marigold (calendula), mullein, periwinkle, rowan, selfheal, stinging nettle, tormentil, witch hazel, yarrow

HYPERTENSION ✦ black currant, borage, carrot, celery, chervil, chilli pepper, cucumber, dandelion, garlic, ginger, hawthorn, lime, onion, passionflower, periwinkle, ramsons, strawberry, valerian, wood betony, yarrow

IBS ✦ chickweed, comfrey, hollyhock, hops, lime, passionflower, peppermint, plantain

INSOMNIA ✦ basil, bergamot, catmint, cowslip, crocus, dandelion, evening primrose, hawthorn, heather, hops, jasmin, lavender, lime, marjoram, mullein, passionflower, periwinkle, primrose, St. John's wort, skullcap, valerian, violet, wood betony

MENOPAUSE ✦ angelica, clover (red), dandelion, fennel, lady's mantle, lemonbalm, mugwort, rose, sage, St. John's wort, stinging nettle

MENSTRUATION DELAYED ✦ angelica, asparagus, carnation, crocus, elecampane, feverfew, gentian (yellow), golden rod, hops, marigold (calendula), mugwort, raspberry, rose, skullcap, wood betony

MENSTRUATION EXCESSIVE ✦ amaranth, geranium, lady's mantle, periwinkle, plantain, rock rose, selfheal, stinging nettle, yarrow, yellow dock

MENSTRUATION PAINFUL ✦ angelica, chamomile, crocus, garlic, lovage, marigold (calendula), marjoram, rose, St. John's wort, valerian, willow, wood betony, yellow dock

MIGRAINE ✦ basil, elder, feverfew, iris, lime, rose, valerian, wood betony

NAUSEA ✦ basil, bergamot, chamomile, coriander, dill, gentian (yellow), ginger, iris, marigold (calendula), meadowsweet, peppermint, quince, wormwood

NERVOUS TENSION ✦ bergamot, chamomile, cleavers, cowslip, crocus, hops, hyssop, Jacob's ladder, jasmine, lemonbalm, lime, meadowsweet, mugwort, mullein, pansy, passionflower, periwinkle, primrose, rose, St. John's wort, skullcap, sweet flag, valerian, wood betony, wormwood

NEURALGIA ✦ angelica, chilli pepper, coriander, elder, garlic, horseradish, Jack in the hedge, meadowsweet, passionflower, St. John's wort, skullcap, sweet flag, valerian, willow, wood betony

PMS AND PMT ✦ angelica, borage, evening primrose, lady's mantle, lime, passionflower, raspberry, St. John's wort, skullcap, wood betony, yarrow

The Medicine Garden

PROSTATE ✦ blackthorn, cleavers, fennel, horsetail, pumpkin, stinging nettle

PSORIASIS ✦ amaranth, birch, burdock, chamomile, chickweed, cleavers, clover (red), comfrey, dandelion, echinacea, iris, milk thistle, pansy, walnut, yellow dock

RASHES ✦ borage, chickweed, coriander, clover (red), evening primrose, hollyhock, lavender, mallow, marigold (calendula), marshmallow, meadowsweet, pansy, plantain, thyme, violet

RHEUMATISM ✦ angelica, apple, arnica, asparagus, bay, bergamot, birch, black currant, bladder wrack, burdock, carrot, catmint, celery, chervil, chickweed, comfrey, coriander, cowslip, cucumber, dandelion, elder, evening primrose, fennel, feverfew, garlic, ginger, golden rod, heather, holly, horseradish, horsetail, hyssop, iris, Jack in the hedge, lavender, lime, marjoram, meadowsweet, mullein, pansy, parsley, peppermint, primrose, quince, rosemary, St. John's wort, sea buckthorn, speedwell, stinging nettle, strawberry, sunflower, sweet flag, thyme, watercress, willow, wormwood, yellow dock

SCIATICA ✦ burdock, elder, garlic, ground elder, horseradish, St. John's wort, skullcap

SINUSITIS ✦ chamomile, elder, garlic, golden rod, horseradish, lime, marjoram, nasturtium, peppermint, plantain, radish, sweet flag, wood betony

SKIN IRRITATIONS ✦ birch, blackthorn, borage, burdock, carnation, celandine (greater), celery, chickweed, cleavers, clover (red), coriander, cucumber, elder, elecampane, evening primrose, garlic, hollyhock, houseleek, iris, Jacob's ladder, lovage, mallow, marigold (calendula), marshmallow, mugwort, mullein, nasturtium, pansy, periwinkle, rose, sage, selfheal, speedwell, thyme, tormentil, valerian, violet, walnut, watercress, willow, yarrow

SPRAINS ✦ arnica, bay, beech, bladder wrack, borage, chilli pepper, comfrey, elder, garlic, ginger, horsetail, lavender, marigold (calendula), marjoram, mullein, plantain, St. John's wort, selfheal, wormwood

STRESS ✦ chamomile, clover (red), cowslip, jasmine, mugwort, rosemary, skullcap. valerian

SUNBURN ✦ chamomile, cleavers, cowslip, cucumber, elder, houseleek, St. John's wort, strawberry, tormentil, witch hazel

TONSILITIS ✦ balloon flower, blackthorn, cleavers, echinacea, mallow, marigold (calendula), mullein, periwinkle, raspberry, rowan, sage, thyme, witch hazel

ULCERS MOUTH ✦ amaranth, basil, birch, blackberry, black currant, borage, burdock, geranium, golden rod, horsetail, lady's mantle, periwinkle, raspberry, sage, selfheal, strawberry, tormentil, walnut, witch hazel, wood betony, yellow dock

ULCERS SKIN ✦ chickweed, cleavers, comfrey, elder, golden rod, Jack in the hedge, mallow, marigold (calenula), marshmallow, milk thistle , plantain, tormentil, violet, wood betony

WHOOPING COUGH ✦ clover (red), cowslip, elecampane, evening primrose, garlic, golden rod, mullein, pansy, plantain, stinging nettle, sunflower, thyme

WOUNDS ✦ amaranth, burdock, chickweed, cleavers, comfrey, cowslip, crab apple, daisy, echinacea, elder, garlic, golden rod, hollyhock, horseradish, horsetail, hyssop, Jack in the hedge, lady's mantle, marigold (calendula), marshmallow, mullein, nasturtium, parsley, plantain, primrose, pumpkin, rose, St John's wort, selfheal, speedwell, sweet cicely, tormentil, walnut, watercress, willow, wood betony, yarrow

Resources

Heritage Seeds

It is often hard to find open pollinated, non-hybridized, heritage seeds, so in the UK the best way to get more information and a few packets of seeds as part of your annual membership is by joining Garden Organics' Heritage Seed Library.

Garden Organic
Coventry
Warwickshire
CV8 3LG 0247 630 3517 or membership hotline 0247 630 8210
www.gardenorganic.org.uk/hsl/ enquiry@gardenorganic.org.uk
Alternatively, look for the old boys at the allotments who may religiously still save their seed and be using varieties passed down through generations of their family. They are often most generous with their knowledge and resources, being happy to pass it on.

Permaculture

Permaculture is a design system that observes and mimics nature to develop sustainable systems that produce food, energy and a healthy, well balanced environment. It incorporates the ethics of earth care, people care and fair shares. To learn more either subscribe to Permaculture Magazine, which is a fantastic and interesting quarterly publication, or contact the Permaculture Association.

Permaculture Magazine

The Sustainability Centre
East Meon
Hampshire
GU32 1HR 01730 823 311
www.permaculture.co.uk info@permaculture.co.uk

BCM Permaculture Association
London
WC1N 3XX 0845 458 1805
www.permaculture.org.uk office@permaculture.org.uk

Plant Spirit Medicine

A form of healing that draws on the healing power of plant spirits to restore balance in an individual. It combines shamanism and Five Element Chinese Medicine to diagnose and heal with the ancient wisdom and energy of individual plant spirits. To find out more or to locate a practitioner in your area visit www.plantspiritmedicine.co.uk .

SUPPLIERS

These are a few of the suppliers I use for buying organic herbs, base oils, beeswax, glass bottles and jars.

www.organicherbtrading.com

www.spiceworld.uk.com

www.starchild-international.com

www.ebottles.co.uk (only supplying bottles and jars, but with a great choice and they are especially useful if you want to buy a large quantity).

For capsules, supplying both gelatin and vegicaps, try www.baldwins.co.uk .

For a good range of juicers than can deal with leaves, try www.fresh-network.com/acatalog/juicers.html

Obviously there are many more suppliers out there, but these are just the ones I am familiar with.

Glossary

ACIDOSIS an excess hydrogen-ion concentration, an abnormally high acidity (pH less than 7.3), of the blood and other tissues.

ANAESTHETIC a substance that produces a temporary partial, or total, loss of sensation, specifically the feeling of pain.

ANTIBACTERIAL a substance that destroys or suppresses bacteria and their ability to reproduce.

ANTIEMETIC brings a stop to vomiting.

ANTIFUNGAL a substance that destroys or prevents the growth of fungi.

ANTI-INFLAMMATORY a substance that prevents or reduces inflammation.

ANTIMICROBIAL a substance that destroys or suppresses the growth of micro-organisms.

ANTIOXIDANT a substance that prevents oxidation or the reactions caused by exposure to oxygen.

ANTIPARASITIC a substance that will treat parasitic infestations, by killing the parasite.

ANTIPRURITIC reduces itching.

ANTISEPTIC a substance that destroys or prevents the growth of disease producing micro-organisms.

ARTERIOSCLEROSIS hardening and loss of elasticity of the arteries, caused by a build up of fatty deposits in the artery walls.

ASTERACEAE plants belonging to the daisy family.

ASTRINGENT a substance that contracts cell walls and draws them together, drawing out and drying up unwanted or excess discharges and blood.

ATHEROSCLEROSIS hardening of the walls of the arteries due to the build up of fatty materials such as cholesterol.

CANDIDA ALBICANS a fungus present on the skin and in the mucous membranes of the body. It can can get out of balance and form an overgrowth. The symptoms of a Candida overgrowth are extremely wide ranging and can include thrush, fungal infections, chronic fatigue syndrome, anxiety, depression, allergies and many more.

CARDIO-VASCULAR pertaining to the heart and blood vessels and the network which delivers oxygen and nutrients around the body, whilst removing waste products.

CELLULITIS a bacterial infection of the deepest skin and subcutaneous layers, causing chronic inflammation.

COLIC abdominal pain caused by trapped wind in the intestines.

COLITIS inflammation of the large intestine.

COMPOSITAE plants in the daisy family.

DECONGESTANT relieves congestion.

DETOXIFIER a substance that aids in the removal of poisons, reducing their toxic effect.

DIURETIC increases the volume of urine.

DIVERTICULITIS a common digestive disease where small pockets poke out of the side of the large intestine.

DYSPEPSIA indigestion.

EPIDIDYMITIS a painful inflammation of the epididymis, a curved structure at the back of the testicles where the sperm matures and is stored. As a side effect the scrotum may become red and swollen.

EXPECTORANT promotes the expulsion of mucous from the respiratory passages.

FUNGICIDAL a substance that kills fungi.

GASTROENTERITIS acute diarrhea accompanied by inflammation of the gastrointestinal tract caused by an infection.

GASTROINTESTINAL TRACT the tract that runs all the way from the mouth to the anus and processes food from the intake, through the digestion to its expulsion as waste.

GERMICIDAL a substance that kills germs.

IBS Irritable Bowel Syndrome.

IMMUNO-STIMULANT stimulates the immune system.

IMPETIGO a contagious infection of the skin.

LACTATION the production of milk from within the breast.

LAXATIVE induces bowel movements for the relief of constipation.

LUMBAGO pain or discomfort in the lower back (lumbar region).

LYMPHATIC SYSTEM a network of nodes that carry a clear liquid throughout the body which transports immune cells, fatty acids and removes interstitial fluid from the tissues. A healthy lymphatic system helps the body fight infection.

MACULAR a small area of the retina in the eye.

NEURALGIA severe nerve pain.

OXIDIZE to combine with oxygen.

PMS pre-menstrual syndrome.

PMT pre-menstrual tension.

RESPIRATORY TRACT the tract that runs from the nose to the end points in the lungs, the alveoli. It is through this system that one takes in and expels air, thereby breathing.

RHIZOME a horizontally growing branching stem that bears roots and leafy growth.

SCIATICA pain along the sciatic nerve that runs from the lower back down the back of the leg. The pain is caused by compression of, or damage to this nerve.

SHINGLES a viral infection of one of the nerves to the skin causing rashes and blistering. It is related to chickenpox.

TOURETTE'S SYNDROME a neurological disorder characterized by involuntary physical tics or spasms and vocalisations.

VASODILATOR a substance that dilates (expands) the blood vessels.

VASOPROTECTIVE a substance that protects and treats conditions of the blood vessels.

Bibliography

Allen, David E. & Gabrielle Hatfield Medicinal Plants in Folk Tradition; An Ethnobotany of Britain and Ireland Timber Press, 2004

Bown, Deni The Royal Horticultural Society Encyclopedia Of Herbs & Their Uses Dorling Kindersley, 1995

Conway, Peter Tree Medicine; A Comprehensive Guide to the Healing Power of Over 170 Trees Judy Piatkus Limited, 2001

Cunningham, Scott Cunningham's Encyclopedia of Magical Herbs Llewellyn Publications, 1985

Edgson, Vicki & Marber, Ian The Food Doctor; Healing Foods For Mind and Body Collins & Brown Ltd., 1999

Engel, Cindy Wild Health; Lessons in Natural Wellness From the Animal Kingdom Houghton Mifflin Company, 2002

Evert Hopman, Ellen Tree Medicine Tree Magic Phoenix Publishing Inc., 1991

Fern, Ken Plants for a Future; Edible and Useful Plants for a Healthier World Permanent Publications, 1997

Farmer-Knowles, Helen The Garden Healer; Natural Remedies From Flowers, Herbs and Trees Gaia Books Ltd, 1998

Grieve, Mrs M. A. Modern Herbal Jonathon Cape Ltd, 1931 (revised and reprinted 1973)

Harrod Buhner, Stephen Sacred Plant Medicine; Explorations in the Practice of Indigenous Herbalism Raven Press, 2001

Harrod Buhner, Stephen The Fasting Path Avery, 2003

Harrod Buhner, Stephen The Lost Language of Plants; The Ecological Importance of Plant Medicines to Life on Earth Chelsea Green, 2002

Hemphill, John & Rosemary Herbs, Their Cultivation and Usage Blandford, 1983

Hilton, Jonathan Wild Food for Free Octopus Publishing Group Ltd, 2007

Hoffman, David The Complete Illustrated Holistic Herbal Element Books Ltd., 1996

Kircher, Tamara Herbs for the Soul; Emotional Healing with Chinese and Western Herbs and Bach Flower Remedies Thorsons, 2001

Lavelle, Christine & Michael The Organic Garden; A Practical Guide to Natural Gardens, From Planning and Planting to Harvesting and Maintenance Anness Publishing Ltd, 2003

Lipp, Frank J. Herbalism Macmillan, 1996

Mabey, Richard Food for Free Collins, 1972

Mabey, Richard The Complete New Herbal Gaia Books Ltd, 1988, (Penguin, 1991)

Mindell, Earl The New Herb Bible; How to Use Herbs to Revolutionise the Way You Work, Play, Sleep, Feel and Heal Vermillion, 2000

Patenaude, Frederic The Sunfood Cuisine Genesis 129 Publishing, 2001

Paterson, Jacqueline Memory Tree Wisdom; The definitive guidebook to the myth, folklore and healing power of trees. Thorsons, 1996.

Pendell, Dale Pharmako/Poeia; Plant Powers, Poisons, and Herbcraft Mercury House, 1995

Peterson, Nicola Herbal Remedies; A Practical Guide To Herbs and Their Healing Properties Blitz Editions, 1995

Polunin, Miriam & Christopher Robbins The Natural Pharmacy Dorling Kindersley, 1992

Roberts, Margaret Edible and Medicinal Flowers New Africa Books, 2000

Rodway, Marie A. Wiccan Herbal; Healing Secrets of Natural Magic Quantum, 1997

Van Straten, Michael & Griggs, Barbara Superfoods Dorling Kindersley, 1990

Vaughan, J.G. & Judd P. A. The Oxford Book of Health Foods; The Science Behind Herbal Remedies and Nutrition Oxford University Press, 2003

Weise, Vivien Cooking Weeds Prospect Books, 2004

Wolfe, David The Sunfood diet Success System Maul Bros. Publishing, 1999

Wood, Matthew The Book of Herbal Wisdom; Using Plants as Medicines North Atlantic Books, 1997

Wren, R.C. Potter's New Cyclopaedia of Botanical Drugs and Preparations The C W Daniel Company Ltd., 1907 (revised and reprinted 1988)

About the Author

Rachel Corby is a gardener and a healer. She spent many years working on environmental projects around the globe, learning about plants in their natural setting and how they can be used to heal degraded landscapes. This led to her studying both Permaculture and sustainable land use with Patrick Whitefield. She subsequently worked in a herb nursery for several years, where she began to learn the therapeutic benefits of plants relating to human health.

The quest to deepen her relationship with plants took her to local medicinal herbalists and medicine men as far and wide as the Amazon basin to the Highlands of Kenya, where she discovered the healing qualities of plants on not only the physical, but also the emotional and spiritual levels. This has culminated in a working knowledge of folk medicine.

Rachel has most recently completed a 9 month apprenticeship in Sacred Plant Medicine with Stephen Harrod Buhner and, combining this with her previous training in Plant Spirit Medicine, she now teaches, passing on these beautiful and ancient ways of working with plants. She believes that learning to communicate with plants and nature helps bring in a powerful sense of balance and healing, not only for the individual but also the wider environment.

For more information and workshop dates please visit www.gatewaystoeden.com

Index of Plant Names

Achillea millefolium 47
Acorus calamus 157
Aegopodium podagraria 82
Agastache foeniculum 62
Alcea rosea 63
Alchemilla vulgaris 67
Alliaria petiolata 141
Allium cepa 105
Allium sativum 100
Allium ursinum 150
Althaea officinalis 171
Amaranth 84
Amaranthus caudatus 85
Anethum graveolens 29
Angelica 147
Angelica archangelica 147
Anthriscus cerefolium 27
Apium graveolens 93
Apple 85
Aquilegia vulgaris 53
Arctium lappa 133
Armoracia rusticana 140
Arnica 49
Arnica montana 49
Artemesia absinthium 113
Artemesia vulgaris 163
Asparagus 86
Asparagus officinalis 86
Balloon flower 50
Basil 23
Bay 24
Beech 115
Beetroot 87
Bellis perennis 44
Bergamot 51
Beta vulgaris 187
Betula pendula 186
Bilberry 167
Birch 116
Blackberry 131
Black currant 89
Blackthorn 132
Bladder wrack 170

Borage 90
Borago officinalis 90
Brassica oleracea 102
Burdock 133
Calendula officinalis 103
Calluna vulgaris 168
Capsicum annuum 94
Carnation 52
Carrot 91
Catmint 25
Celandine, greater 154
Celery 93
Chaenomeles speciosa 127
Chamaemelum nobile 26
Chamomile 26
Chelidonium majus 154
Chervil 27
Chickweed 81
Chilli pepper 94
Cleavers 134
Clover, red 42
Columbine 53
Comfrey 96
Coriander 28
Coriandrum sativum 28
Corylus avellana 148
Cowslip 161
Crab apple 136
Crataegus oxyacantha 139
Crocus 53
Crocus sativus 53
Cucumber 98
Cucumis sativa 98
Curcubita maxima 107
Daisy 44
Dandelion 44
Daucus carota sativa 91
Dianthus chinensis 52
Dill 29
Echinacea 54
Echinacea purpurea 54
Elder 137
Elecampane 56

The Medicine Garden

Equisetum arvense 155
Eruca vesicaria subsp. Sativa 110
Eryngium maritimum 173
Evening primrose 57
Fagus sylvatica 115
Fennel 30
Feverfew 58
Ficus carica 99
Fig 99
Filipendula ulmaria 156
Foeniculum vulgare 30
Fragaria vesca/ x ananassa 111
Fucus vesiculosus 170
Galium aparine 134
Garlic 100
Gentiana lutea 59
Gentian, yellow 59
Geranium 61
Geranium maculatum 61
Ginger 31
Ginkgo 117
Ginkgo biloba 117
Golden rod 62
Ground elder 82
Hamamelis virginiana 130
Hawthorn 139
Hazel 148
Heartsease 71
Heather 168
Hedera helix 121
Hedge garlic 141
Helianthemum nummularium 72
Helianthus annuus 76
Hippophae rhamnoides 172
Holly 118
Hollyhock 63
Honeysuckle 119
Hops 120
Horseradish 140
Horsetail 155
Houseleek 32
Humulus lupulus 120
Hypericum perforatum 165
Hyssop 64
Giant hyssop 62
Hyssopus officinalis 64

Ilex aquifolium 118
Inula helenium 56
Iris 65
Iris versicolor 65
Ivy 121
Jack in the hedge 141
Jacob's ladder 66
Jasmine 122
Jasminum officinale 122
Juglans regia 129
Kale 102
Lady's mantle 67
Laurus nobilis 24
Lavender 68
Lavendula angustifolia 68
Lemonbalm 33
Levisticum officinale 34
Lime 122
Lonicera periclymenum 119
Lovage 34
Lungwort 149
Mallow 124
Malus sylvestris 136
Malva sylvestris 124
Marigold 103
Marigold, French 70
Marjoram 35
Marshmallow 171
Meadowsweet 156
Melissa officinalis 33
Mentha aquatica 159
Mentha spp. 37
Milk thistle 162
Monarda didyma 51
Morus nigra 124
Mountain ash 128
Mugwort 163
Mulberry 124
Mullein 164
Myrrhis odorata 151
Nasturtium 104
Nasturtium officinale 158
Nepeta cataria 25
Ocimum basilicum 23
Oenothera biennis 57
Onion 105

Oregano 36
Origanum vulgare 35
Pansy 71
Parsley 36
Passiflora incarnata 125
Passion flower 125
Peppermint 37
Periwinkle, greater 72
Petroselinum crispum 36
Pinks 52
Plantago major 45
Plantain 45
Platycodon grandiflorus 50
Plum 126
Polemonium caeruleum 66
Potentilla erecta 168
Primrose 150
Primula veris 161
Primula vulgaris 150
Prunella vulgaris 47
Prunus domestica 126
Prunus spinosa 132
Pulmonaria officinalis 149
Pumpkin 107
Pyrus malus 85
Quince 127
Radish 108
Ramsons 150
Raphanus sativus 108
Raspberry 109
Ribes nigrum 89
Rocket 110
Rock rose 72
Rosa spp. 73
Rose 73
Rosmarinus officinalis 38
Rosemary 38
Rowan 128
Rubus fruticosus 131
Rubus idaeus 109
Rumex crispus 145
Sage 40
St. John's wort 165
Salix alba 159
Salvia officinalis 40
Sambucus nigra 137

Scutellaria lateriflora 75
Sea buckthorn 172
Sea holly 173
Selfheal 47
Sempervivum tectorum 32
Silybum marianum 162
Skullcap 75
Solidago virgaurea 62
Sorbus aucuparia 128
Speedwell 76
Stachys officinalis 152
Stellaria media 81
Stinging nettle 142
Strawberry 111
Sunflower 76
Sweet cicely 151
Sweet flag 157
Symphytum officinale 96
Tagetes patula 70
Tanacetum parthenium 58
Taraxacum officinale 44
Thyme 41
Thymus vulgaris 41
Tilia europaea 122
Tormentil 168
Tropaeolum majus 104
Urtica dioica 142
Vaccinium myrtillus 167
Valerian 78
Valeriana officinalis 78
Verbascum thapsus 164
Veronica officinalis 76
Vinca major 72
Viola odorata 79
Viola tricolor 71
Violet, sweet 79
Walnut 129
Watercress 158
Wild garlic 150
Willow 159
Witch hazel 130
Wood betony 152
Wormwood 113
Yarrow 47
Yellow dock 145
Zingiber officinale 31

The Good Life Press Ltd.
PO Box 536
Preston
PR2 9ZY
01772 652693

The Good Life Press is a family run business specialising in publishing a wide range of titles for the smallholder, 'goodlifer' and farmer. We also publish **Home Farmer,** the monthly magazine for anyone who wants to grab a slice of the good life - whether they live in the country or the city. Other titles of interest:

A Guide to Traditional Pig Keeping by Carol Harris
An Introduction to Keeping Cattle by Peter King
An Introduction to Keeping Sheep by J. Upton/D. Soden
Build It! by Joe Jacobs
Build It!....With Pallets by Joe Jacobs
Building Fences and Gates by Andy Radford
Craft Cider Making by Andrew Lea
First Buy a Field by Rosamund Young
Flowerpot Farming by Jayne Neville
Grow and Cook by Brian Tucker
How to Butcher Livestock and Game by Paul Peacock
Making Country Wines, Ales and Cordials by Brian Tucker
Making Jams and Preserves by Diana Sutton
Precycle! by Paul Peacock
Raising Chickens for Eggs and Meat by Mike Woolnough
Raising Goats - Meat-Dairy-Fibre by Felicity Stockwell
Showing Sheep by Sue Kendrick
Talking Sheepdogs by Derek Scrimgeour
The Bread and Butter Book by Diana Sutton
The Cheese Making Book by Paul Peacock
The Frugal Life by Piper Terrett
The Pocket Guide to Wild Food by Paul Peacock
The Polytunnel Companion by Jayne Neville
The Sausage Book by Paul Peacock
The Secret Life of Cows by Rosamund Young
The Shepherd's Pup (DVD) with Derek Scrimgeour
The Smoking and Curing Book by Paul Peacock
The Urban Farmer's Handbook by Paul Peacock

www.goodlifepress.co.uk
www.homefarmer.co.uk